WE

WEB DESIGN INDEX
2

Compiled by Günter Beer

THE PEPIN PRESS / AGILE RABBIT EDITIONS
AMSTERDAM AND SINGAPORE

With special thanks to Magda Garcia Masana from LocTeam S.L., Barcelona

Compiled and edited by Günter Beer
www.webdesignindex.org
compilation and concept copyright © 2001 Günter Beer

Cover and page design by Pepin van Roojen
Cover image by Paul Davis (www.copyrightdavis.com)
Layout by Kathrin Günter

Introduction by Günter Beer and Pepin van Roojen
Translations by LocTeam, Barcelona (German, Spanish, French and Italian),
and Mitaka, Leeds (Japanese).

ISBN 90 5768 026 2

Agile Rabbit Editions
c/o The Pepin Press BV
P.O. Box 10349
1001 EH Amsterdam
The Netherlands

Tel +31 20 4202021
Fax +31 20 4201152
mail@pepinpress.com
www.pepinpress.com

Printed in Singapore

Web Design Index

In this second edition of the highly successful Web Design Index, another 1,002 outstanding web pages are presented. With each design, the URL is indicated, followed by the names of those involved in the design and programming of the site concerned.
The following codes have been used:

D = design
C = coding
P = production
A = agency
M = designer's mail/contact

The purpose of the Web Design Index is to provide a source of inspiration and reference, and a means of communication for designers and others with an interest in web design. Should you be inspired by designs in this book, please observe that all designs are copyright, and that copying is not permitted. Most designers who made work available for this book can be contacted as indicated, and for easy reference the designers and agencies are listed in the back of the book.

The principal criteria on which the index's selection is based are design quality and innovation, and the page's effectiveness. No attempt has been made to classify the selection, other than arrange and group the designs on principal colour.

The internet's technical possibilities, language of navigation, and users' perception are in a constant state of flux; all of which have a profound effect on web design. So pages designed not that long ago may already look dated. Since we selected them for the index, some pages may have changed, or even disappeared from the net. This being the case, this book and CD-Rom give an accurate and lasting overview of the state of the art in current web design.

In the inside back cover, you will find a CD-ROM containing almost all designs, arranged according to their location in this book. You can view them on your monitor with a minimum of loading time, and access the internet to explore the selected site in full.

Submissions
The Web Design Index is published annually. Should you wish to submit or recommend a design for consideration for the next edition of the Web Design Index, please access the submission form at www.webdesignindex.org.

The Pepin Press/Agile Rabbit Editions
The Pepin Press/Agile Rabbit Editions publishes a wide range of books and CD-ROMs with visual reference material and ready-to-use images for designers, for internet applications as well as high-resolution printed media. For more information visit www.pepinpress.com.

Index de modèles de sites Web

Cette seconde édition de l'Index de modèles de sites Web, dont la première avait obtenu un franc succès, présente 1.002 nouvelles pages Web exceptionnelles. Pour chacune d'elles sont indiqués son adresse URL ainsi que le nom des personnes ayant collaboré à sa conception et sa programmation.
Les codes ci-après ont été employés :

D = conception
C = codage
P = production
A = agence
M = coordonnées/adresse électronique du concepteur

L'Index de modèles de sites Web sert de source d'inspiration, de référence et représente un moyen de communication pour les concepteurs et toute personne intéressée par la conception de pages Web. Si certaines des conceptions de ce recueil vous inspirent, sachez qu'il est formellement interdit de les reproduire car elles sont protégées par des droits d'auteur. La plupart des concepteurs ayant participé à la réalisation de ce livre peuvent être contactés comme indiqué. Pour trouver facilement leurs références, reportez-vous à la liste des concepteurs et agences indiquée au dos du livre.

Les principaux critères de sélection de cet index ont été la qualité des images, le degré d'innovation et les performances de la page. Les conceptions n'ont été classées et regroupées qu'en fonction de leur couleur dominante.

La technologie d'Internet, le langage de navigation et la perception des pages Internet par les utilisateurs sont en perpétuelle évolution. Ces éléments ont un effet considérable sur la conception de pages Web. Ainsi, les pages conçues il y a pas peu peuvent déjà paraître dépassées. Certaines des pages apparaissant dans cet index ont peut-être déjà été modifiées, ou peuvent avoir disparu de la toile. Cela étant dit, ce livre et son CD-ROM donnent un aperçu précis et actuel de ce qui se fait de mieux en conception de pages Web.

À l'intérieur du livre, vous trouverez un CD-ROM contenant la quasi totalité des pages Web, classées selon leur emplacement dans ce livre. Vous pouvez les télécharger en un minimum de temps afin de les visualiser sur votre écran d'ordinateur et accéder à Internet pour explorer le site sélectionné dans son intégralité.

Propositions de sites :
L'Index de modèles de sites Web est publié annuellement. Si vous souhaitez soumettre ou recommander un site Web pour la prochaine édition de l'Index de modèles de sites Web, complétez le formulaire à l'adresse : www.webdesignindex.org

Les éditions Pepin Press/Agile Rabbit
Les éditions Pepin Press/Agile Rabbit publient un vaste éventail de livres et de CD-ROM comportant du matériel de référence visuel et des images prêtes à l'emploi destinées aux concepteurs et aux applications Internet, ainsi que des supports imprimés à haute résolution. Pour en savoir plus, visitez le site : www.pepinpress.com

Web Design Index

In dieser zweiten Ausgabe des höchst erfolgreichen Web Design Index, werden eintausendundzwei aktuelle, herausragend gestaltete Webseiten vorgestellt.

Qualität des Designs, Innovation, Handhabbarkeit und Verständlichkeit der Navigation sowie die Gesamtwirkung einer Seite bestimmten die Auswahl für diesen Index. Die Reihenfolge der Abbildungen spiegelt keine Wertung wieder, sortiert wurde nur nach dem Farbeindruck.

Der Web Design Index will zu Qualität bei der Gestaltung von Websites anregen und Kontakt zu exzellenten Web-Professionals herstellen. Die Gestaltungsideen sind geistiges Eigentum der jeweiligen Designer. Bitte respektieren Sie das, wenn Sie sich inspirieren lassen.

Zu jedem Design sind der URL-Link sowie Namen und Kontaktadresse der Designer angegeben. Die Buchstaben haben folgende Bedeutung:

D = Design
C = Programmierung, Code Erstellung
P = Produktion
A = Agentur
M = Mail oder Website des Designers

Schneller als bei anderen Medien ändert sich die Formen- und Bildsprache des Internets. Aus diesem Grund können Seiten, die vor zwei Jahren gestaltet wurden, heute bereits altmodisch oder altbacken erscheinen. Auch kann es sein, dass nach Fertigstellung des vorliegenden Indexes manche Seiten geändert worden oder sogar ganz aus dem Internet verschwunden sein werden. So behält diese auf CD-ROM konservierte Momentaufnahme des aktuellen Webdesigns bleibenden Wert.

Im inneren Rücktitel finden Sie ein CD-ROM die fast die fast sämtliche im vorliegenden Buch vorgestellten Sites in der Reihenfolge ihrer Präsentation enthält. So können Sie so bequem offline das jeweilige vorgestellte Design auf ihrem Bildschirm sehen.

Vorschlagen einer Website:
Der Web Design Index wird jährlich herausgegeben. Wenn Sie für die nächste Ausgabe eine Site vorschlagen wollen, wenden Sie sich bitte an unsere Website: www.webdesignindex.org. Dort finden Sie ein Formular.

Die Pepin Press/Agile Rabbit Editions
The Pepin Press/Agile Rabbit Editions verlegt eine breite Palette an Büchern und CD-ROMs mit Bildreferenzmaterial und gebrauchsfertigen Bildern für Designer, Internetanwendungen sowie hochauflösende Druckmedien. Nähere Informationen erhalten Sie unter: www.pepin-press.com.

L´Indice del Disegno Web

In questa seconda edizione del L´Indice del Disegno Web vengono
presentate altre 1.002 straordinarie pagine web. Con ogni modello
viene indicata l'URL, seguita dai nomi di coloro che hanno partecipato
alla creazione e alla programmazione del sito in questione.
Sono stati usati i seguenti codici:

D = disegno
C = codificazione
P = produzione
A = agenzia
M = mail/contatto dell'autore

Lo scopo del L´Indice del Disegno Web è quello di offrire una fonte di
ispira-zione e di riferimento, nonché un mezzo di comunicazione per
autori di pagine web ed altre persone interessate alla creazione di siti
web. Se doveste trarre ispirazione dai modelli di questo libro, tenete
presente che sono tutti copyright e che ne è proibita la riproduzione.
La maggior parte degli autori che hanno messo a disposizione il loro
lavoro per questo libro si può contattare come indicato –per comodità
gli autori e le agenzie sono elencate sul retro del libro.

I principali criteri su cui si basa la selezione dell'indice sono la qualità
del design e l'innovazione, nonché l'impatto della pagina. Le pagine
selezionate sono state classificate raggruppando i modelli unicamente
in base al colore dominante.

Le possibilità tecniche di internet, il linguaggio di navigazione e la
percezione degli utenti sono in costante trasformazione, e tutto ciò
incide considerevolmente sulla creazione di pagine web. Ecco perché
pagine create non molto tempo fa possono apparire obsolete. Da
quando le abbiamo selezionate per l'indice, alcune pagine possono
essere cambiate, o addirittura scomparse dalla rete. In questo caso,
il libro o il CD Rom offrono una panoramica accurata e durevole delle
ultime novità nella creazione di pagine web attuale.

All'interno della penultima di copertina troverete un CD-Rom che contiene quasi tutti i modelli, organizzati in base alla loro collocazione
nel libro. Potete visualizzarli sul monitor in pochi istanti ed accedere
ad Internet per esplorare il sito scelto in tutte le sue parti.

Proposte
Il L´Indice del Disegno Web viene pubblicato annualmente. Se desi-
derate presentare o raccomandare il design di una pagina da prendere
in consi-derazione per la prossima edizione del Web Design Index,
accedete al modulo di presentazione all'indirizzo
www.webdesignindex.org.

La Pepin Press/Agile Rabbit Editions
La Pepin Press/Agile Rabbit Editions pubblica un'ampia gamma di libri
e CD-ROM con materiale di riferimento visuale ed immagini pronte per
disegnatori, applicazioni Internet e mezzi stampati ad alta risoluzione.
Per maggiori informazioni visitate il sito www.pepinpress.com

Índice de diseño de páginas web

En esta segunda edición del exitoso Índice de diseño de páginas web se presentan otras 1.002 magníficas páginas web. Junto a cada una de ellas se indica el URL, seguido de los nombres de quienes han participado en el diseño y la programación del sitio en cuestión.
En este libro se han utilizado los siguientes códigos:

D = diseño
C = codificación
P = producción
A = agencia
M = correo electrónico del diseñador

El objetivo del Índice de diseños de páginas web es proporcionar una fuente de inspiración y de referencia, y un medio de comunicación a los diseñadores y a aquellas otras personas interesadas en el diseño de páginas web. Si le inspira alguno de los diseños que aparecen en este libro, por favor, tenga en cuenta que todos ellos tienen derechos de autor y que, por lo tanto, está prohibida su copia. Si lo desea, puede ponerse en contacto, tal como le indicamos, con la mayoría de los diseñadores que han participado en la elaboración de esta obra. Para mayor comodidad, al final del libro aparece una lista con el nombre de los diseñadores y las agencias.

Los principales criterios de selección en los que se basa este índice son la calidad y la innovación del diseño y la eficacia de la página web. Para clasificar las páginas seleccionadas, los diseños se han ordenado y agrupado teniendo en cuenta únicamente el color principal de los mismos.

Las posibilidades técnicas de Internet, el lenguaje de la navegación y la percepción de los usuarios cambian continuamente, y todo ello queda reflejado en el diseño de páginas web. De este modo, algunas páginas web diseñadas no hace mucho tiempo pueden parecer anticuadas. Desde que realizamos la selección para incluirlas en el índice, es posible que algunas páginas hayan cambiado o incluso desaparecido de la red. En cualquier caso, este libro y CD-Rom ofrecen una visión de conjunto precisa y permanente del arte en el diseño actual de páginas web.

En el interior de la contracubierta encontrará un CD-ROM que contiene casi todos los diseños, ordenados según aparecen en este libro. Si lo desea, puede verlos en su monitor (el tiempo de descarga es mínimo) o acceder a Internet para explorar en su totalidad el sitio web seleccionado.

Sugerencias
El Índice de diseños de páginas web se publica cada año. Si desea sugerir o recomendar un diseño para que se tenga en cuenta para la próxima edición del Índice de diseños de páginas web, por favor, rellene el formulario de sugerencias que aparece en la dirección www.webdesignindex.org.

The Pepin Press/Agile Rabbit Editions
The Pepin Press/Agile Rabbit Editions publica una gran variedad de libros y CD-ROMs con material de referencia visual e imágenes destinados a diseñadores, aplicaciones de Internet y medios de impresión de alta resolución. Para más información visite www.pepinpress.com.

ウェブ設計インデックス

ウェブ設計インデックスは非常に好評を博し、その第 2 版には、更に 1,002 の素晴らしいウェブページを掲載しています。各設計と共に、まずホームページ、次にそのホームページの設計者とプログラマーの名前を表示しています。その際、下記のコードを使用しています。

D: 設計
C: コード
P: 生産
A: 担当代理店
M: 設計者のメールアドレス/連絡先

設計者、およびウェブ設計に興味のある方々の意思疎通の手段として、示唆と参照の源をご提供することが、このウェブ設計インデックスの目的です。本書に掲載している設計からインスピレーションを受けた場合には、すべての設計には著作権があり、コピーは許可されていませんので、その旨お気をつけください。この本に掲載しているほとんどの設計者に連絡を取ることができます。また、設計者や設計代理店も本書の後ろに挙げていますので、簡単に参照になれます。

このインデックスへの採用基準は、設計の品質と革新性、およびページの効果です。主な色合いでグループ化した以外には、採用したウェブページの分類は実施していません。

インターネット技術の可能性、操作言語、ユーザーの認識が、常に流入してきます。これらはすべてウェブの設計に大きな影響があります。そのため、最近作成したページも、時代遅れに見えることがあります。このインデックスに採用した後に、変更されたウェブページ、またはインターネットから消えたウェブページもあるかもしれませんが、本書と CD-ROM では、現在のウェブ設計の正確で最新の概要をお伝えしています。

裏表紙の内側に、ほぼすべての設計が場所順に入っている CD-ROM があります。最小の読み込み時間で画面に表示でき、インターネットへのアクセスにより選択サイトをすべて探索できます。

出版
ウェブ設計インデックスは、毎年発行しています。次回のウェブ設計インデックスに掲載する設計、または掲載を推奨する設計がある場合、www.webdesignindex.org にアクセスをお願い申し上げます。

The Pepin Press/Agile Rabbit Editions
The Pepin Press/Agile Rabbit Editions は、幅広い書物と CD-ROM を発行しています。これらには、設計者やインターネットの用途に、すぐに使用できる画像や視覚的な参照資料、高解像度の印刷データが記載されています。詳細は、www.pepinpress.com へお越しください。

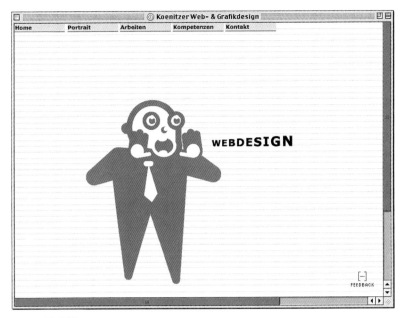

WWW.KOENITZER.CH
C: ANDREA KÖNITZER, P: ANDREA KÖNITZER
M: ANDREA@KOENITZER.CH

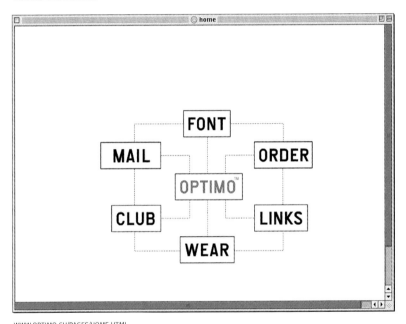

WWW.OPTIMO.CH/PAGES/HOME.HTML
D: GILLES GAVILLET, DAVID RUST
M: GILLES@OPTIMO.CH

WWW.SM.RIM.OR.JP/%7ETONA-PON/INDEX2.HTML
D: USAGI GUMI
M: TONAI@LITTLEFLAG.COM

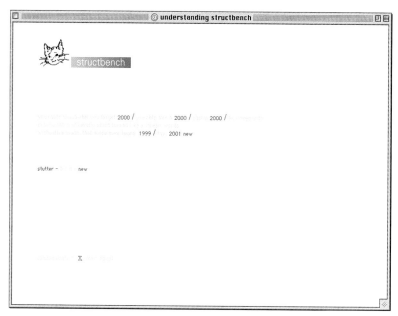

WWW.STRUCTBENCH.COM
D: FLORIAN WEBER, **C:** FLORIAN WEBER
M: CSSHSH@STRUCTBENCH.COM

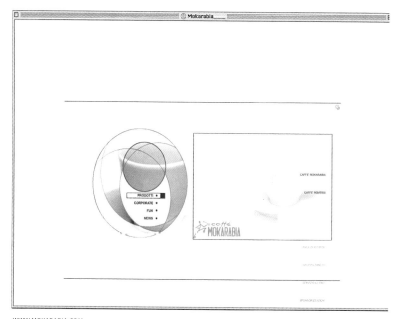

WWW.MOKARABIA.COM
D: ALESSANDRO ORLANDI, ALESSANDRA TOSO

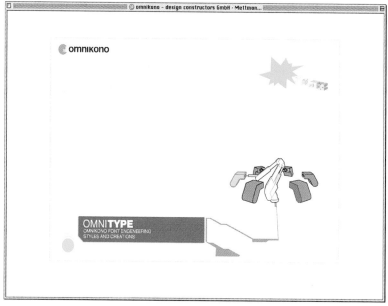

WWW.OMNIKONO.COM
D: MARCEL STAUDT & CLAAS LUDWIG, **C:** MARCEL STAUDT & CLAAS LUDWIG
A: OMNIKONO - DESIGN CONSTRUCTORS, **M:** KONTAKT@OMNIKONO.COM

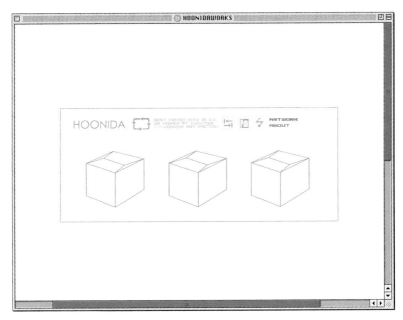

WWW.HOONIDA.COM
A: HOONIDA, **M:** BOX@HOONIDA.COM

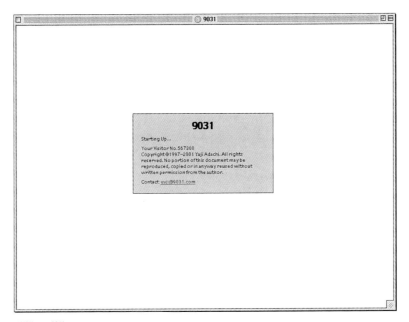

WWW.9031.COM
D: YUJI ADACHI
M: YUJI@9031.COM

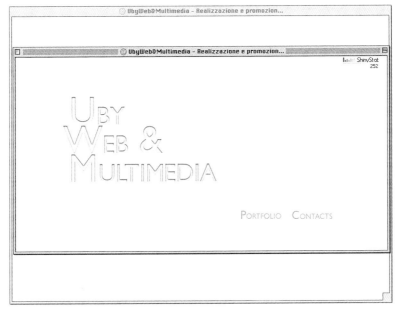

WWW.UBYWEB.COM
M: PONZIOU@ALMA.IT

13

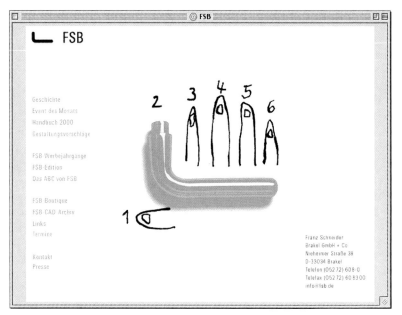

WWW.FSB.DE/INDEX_FULL.HTML
D: CHRISTIAN RIEPE, C: KNUT UHLENBROCK / SIGNALGRAU.
M: CHRISTIAN.RIEPE@FSB.DE

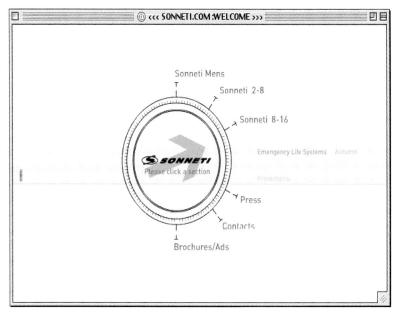

WWW.DIGITLONDON.COM
D: SIMON SANKARAYYA
A: DIGIT, M: DELYTH@DIGITLONDON.COM

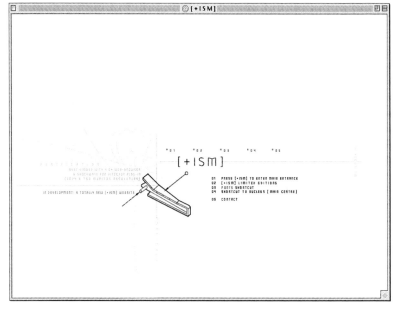

WWW.PLUSISM.COM
M: A90037TM@PLUSISM.COM

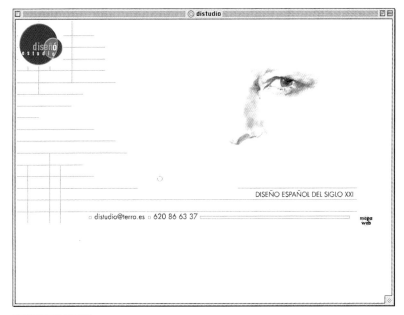

WWW.DISTUDIO.ZZN.COM
D: LAURA RINCÓN CRESPO, BEATRIZ Y BLANCA FERNÁNDEZ CAMARZANA
M: DISTUDIO@TERRA.ES

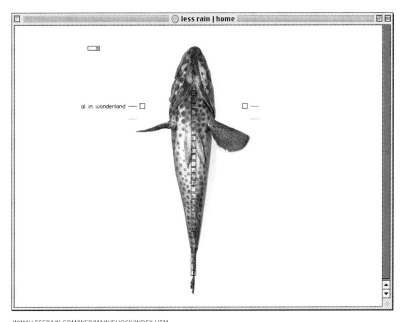

WWW.LESSRAIN.COM/WEB/MAIN/SHOCK/INDEX.HTM
M: RECEPTION@LESSRAIN.COM

WWW.BACHMANNUNDPARTNER.CH
D: OLIVER ZAHORKA, C: OLIVER ZAHORKA, P: BACHMANN UND PARTNER
M: URS@OUT.TO

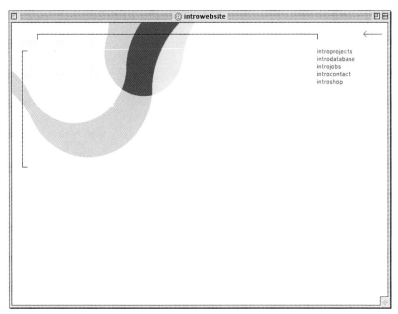

WWW.INTROWEBSITE.COM
D: MAT COOK
A: INTRO, **M**: GEORGEL@INTRO-UK.COM

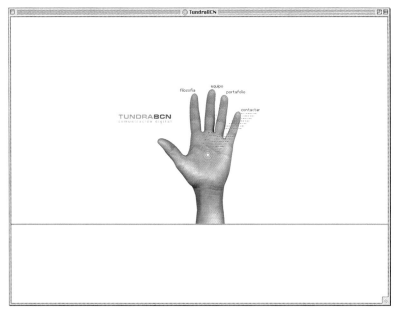

WWW.TUNDRABCN.COM
D: SANTI SALLÉS, **C**: SANTI SALLÉS
A: TUNDRABCN, **M**: INFO@TUNDRABCN.COM

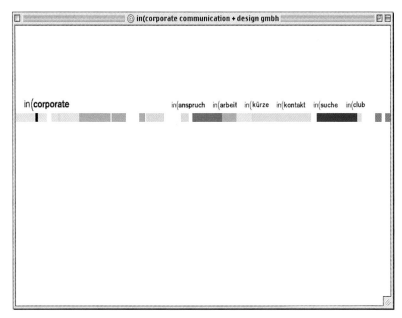

WWW.INCORPORATE.DE
M: HEINEN@INCORPORATE.DE

WWW.DIESEL.COM
A: DIESEL CREATIVE TEAM & EHSREALTIME, M: RICHARD_HOLLEY@DIESEL.COM

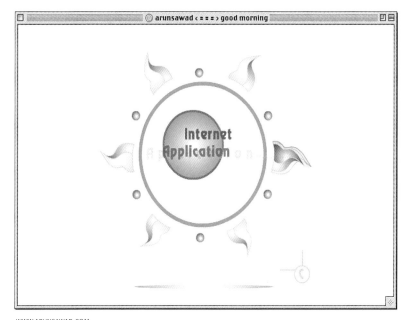

WWW.ARUNSAWAD.COM
D: ARTTY, C: ISARA S., P: KITTINAN A.
A: ARUNSAWAD DOT COM CO.,LTD., M: KITTINAN@ARUNSAWAD.COM

WWW.JOCHENPHOTO.COM
D: CHRISTIAN KAHL, RALF BRESSER
M: CHRISTIAN_KAHL@GMX.DE, RBRESSER@MAC.COM

WWW.BIGMAGAZINE.COM/BIGTEST/BIGHOME.HTML
A: GRAFIKONSTRUCT, WWW.GRAFIKONSTRUCT.COM.BR, M: INFO@GRAFIKONSTRUCT.COM.BR

WWW.10PM.ORG/DEAR
A: 10PM, M: MOOG@10PM.ORG

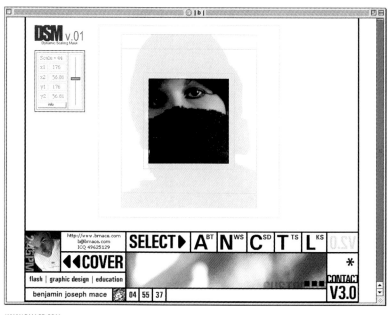

WWW.BMACE.COM
D: BJ MACE
M: B@BMACE.COM

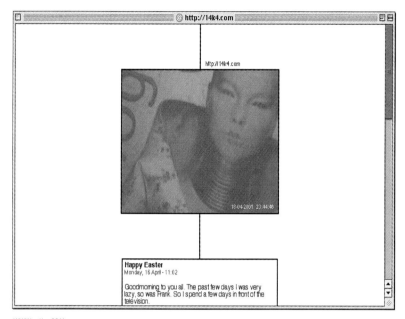

WWW.14K4..COM
D: FRANK HARTMAN
M: FRANK@VIDEOGAMER.NL

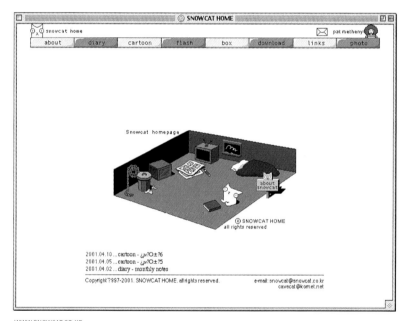

WWW.SNOWCAT.CO.KR
D: YOONJOO KWON
M: SNOWCAT@SNOWCAT.CO.KR

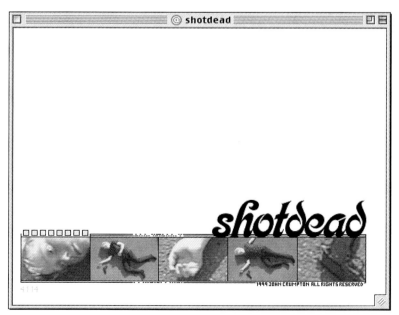

WWW.SHOTDEAD.CO.UK/VER2.HTML
D: JOHN CRUMPTON
M: JC@SHOTDEAD.COM

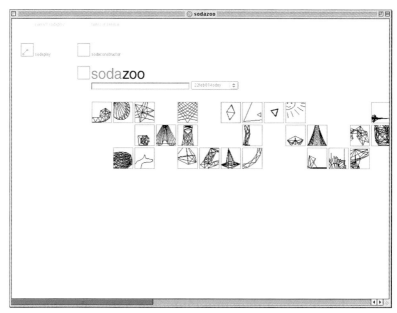

WWW.SODAPLAY.COM/ZOO/INDEX.HTM
D: ED BURTON
M: INFO@SODA.CO.UK

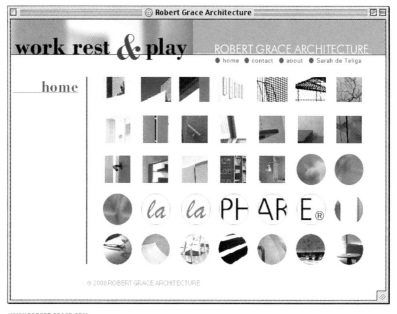

WWW.ROBERT-GRACE.COM
A: SPILL INDUSTRIES, M: CONTACT@SPILL.NET

WWW.MAGANDA.ORG/MAIN.HTML
D: CHRISTINE CASTRO
M: CHRISTINE@MAGANDA.ORG

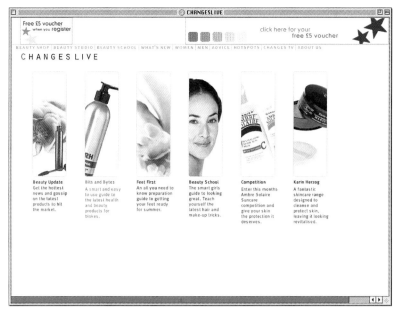

WWW.CHANGESLIVE.COM/INDEX.ASP
A: ZONEGROUP LTD, M: INFO@ZONEGROUP.COM

WWW.HOMEPAGE.MAC.COM/NACRE/STUDIO/INDEX.HTML
D: KENJI ABE
A: NACRE STUDIO, M: NACRE@MAC.COM

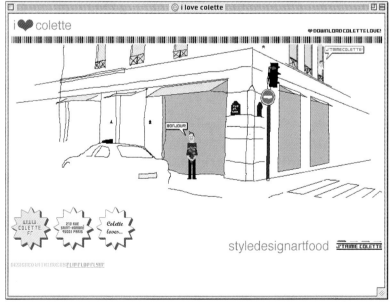

WWW.ILOVECOLETTE.COM/INDEX2.HTML
M: INFO@COLETTE.TM.FR

WWW.SABRINAPARAVICINI.IT
C: ALESSIA MONTELEONE, P: SABRINA PARAVICINI
M: INFORMAZIONI@INEDITOMULTIMEDIA.IT

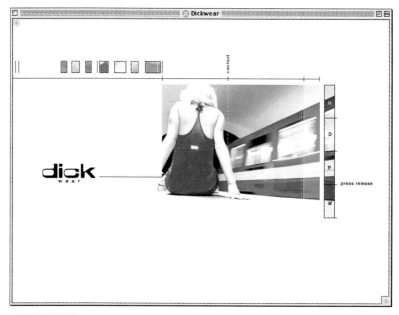

WWW.DICKWEAR.COM
A: BLASFEM INTERACTIF, M: INFO@DICKWEAR.COM

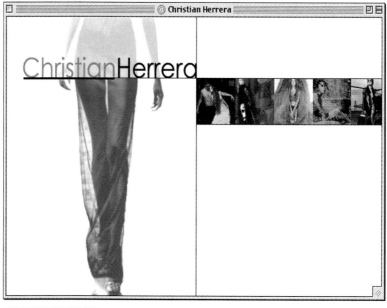

WWW.CHRISTIANHERRERA.COM
A: EABARCELONA, M: INFO@CHRISTIANHERRERA.COM

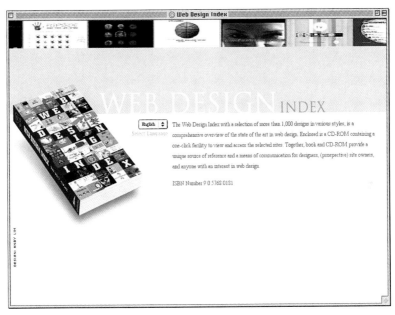

WWW.WEBDESIGNINDEX.ORG
D: ANDY LIM, C: ANDY LIM, P: PACO LALUCA
M: MAIL.BCN@BAMBOO-PRODUCTIONS.COM

WWW.ALBISBRUNN.CH
D: OLIVER ZAHORKA, C: OLIVER ZAHORKA, P: STIFTUNG ALBISBRUNN
A: OUT MEDIA DESIGN GMBH, M: URS@OUT.TO

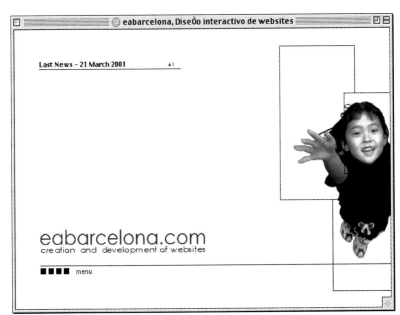

WWW.EABARCELONA.COM
D: ARTURO MARIMON GUISAN
A: EABARCELONA , M: INFO@EABARCELONA.COM

WWW.ARCHINED.NL/MVRDV/MVRDV.HTML
D: FRED INKLAAR (AIRPLANT)
M: OFFICE@MVRDV.NL

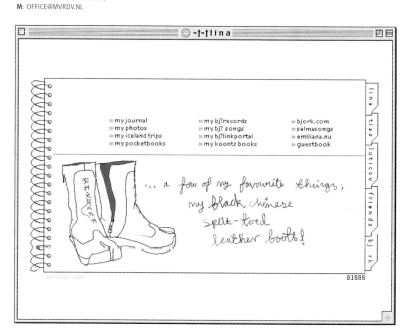

WWW.EMILIANA.NU/LINA
A: LUNARGIRL, M: LINA@MMEDIA.IS

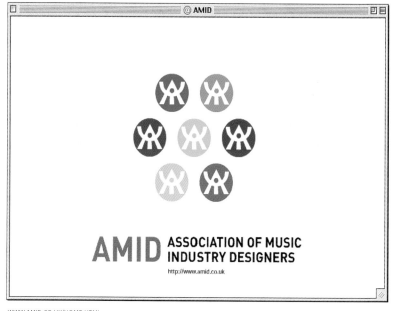

WWW.AMID.CO.UK/HOME.HTML
D: PAUL WEST, C: GREG FINDON
A: FORM®, M: FORM@DIRCON.CO.UK

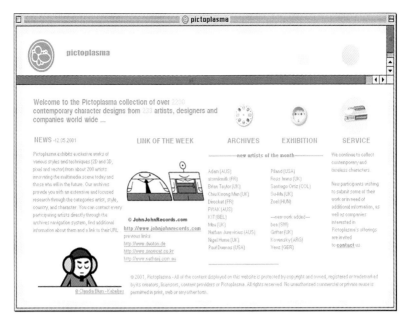

WWW.PICTOPLASMA.COM
A: PICTOPLASMA, **M:** PETER@PICTOPLASMA.COM

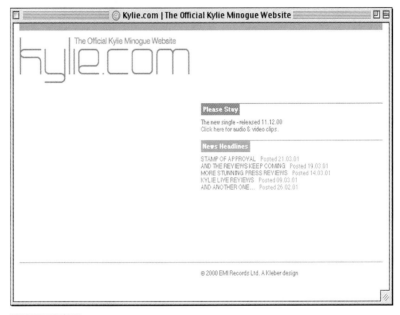

WWW.KYLIE.COM/KYLIE
D: KLEBER
M: CAROLINE@KLEBER.NET

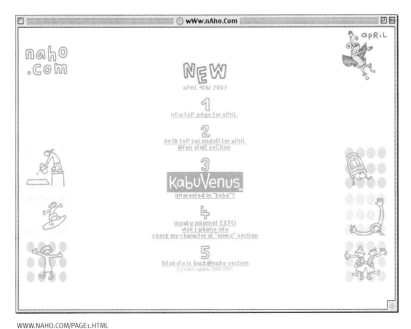

WWW.NAHO.COM/PAGE1.HTML
D: NAHO OGAWA
M: MAIL@NAHO.COM

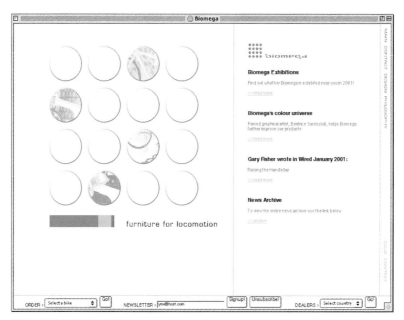

WWW.BIOMEGA.NET/HTML/DEFAULT.ASP
A: WWW.HOME-SWEET-HOME.DK, M: CHRISTOFFER@BIOMEGA.DK

WWW.GUGGENHEIM-BILBAO.ES
A: ARISTA INTERACTIVA

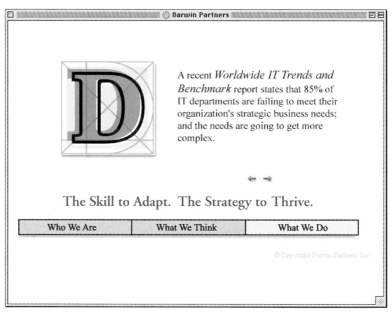

WWW.DARWINPARTNERS.COM
D: EFREN, C: GARRY HARSTED, P: KATE PINTO
A: BX.COM, M: EFREN@BX.COM

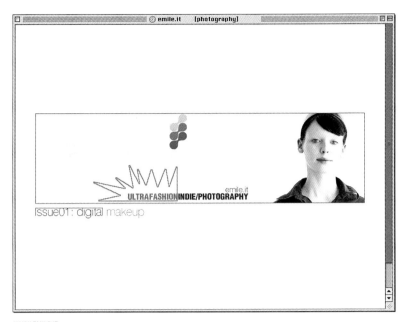

WWW.EMILE.IT
D: EMILE
M: EMILE@EMILE.IT

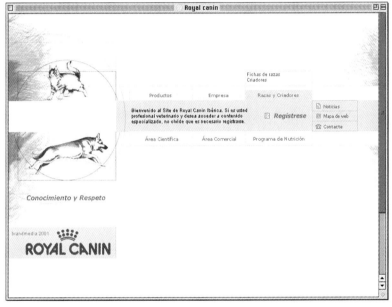

WWW.ROYALCANIN.ES
A: EQUIPO BRANDMEDIA, **M:** INFO@BRANDMEDIA.COM

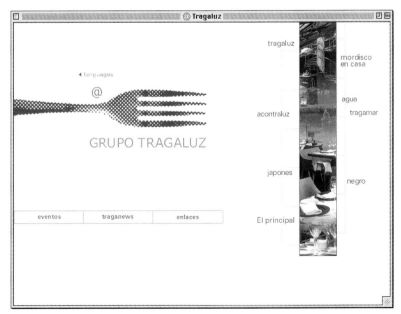

WWW.GRUPOTRAGALUZ.COM
D: SANTI SALLÉS, **C:** SANTI SALLÉS
A: TUNDRABCN

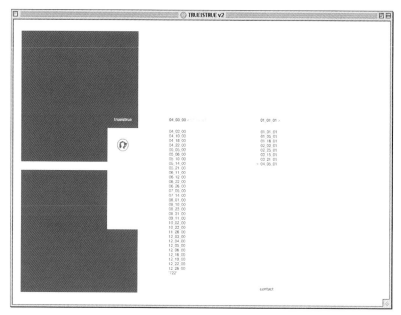

WWW.TRUEISTRUE.COM
D: MICHAEL CINA
M: INFO@TRUEISTRUE.COM

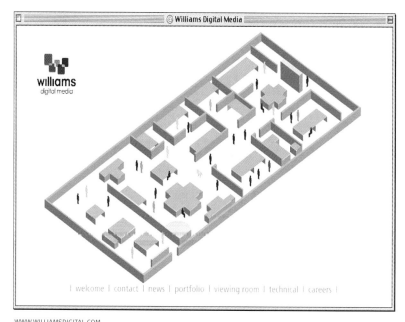

WWW.WILLIAMSDIGITAL.COM
D: ARIELLE BREIT, **C:** JASON STANLEY, **P:** MATHEW MARCH SMITH
A: WILLIAMS DIGITAL MEDIA, **M:** ABREIT@HOTMAIL.COM

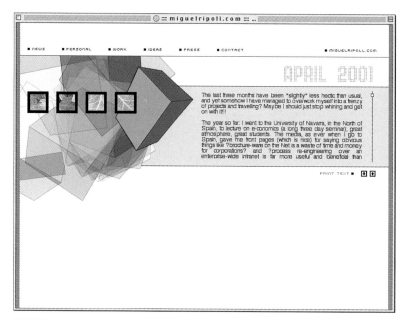

WWW.MIGUELRIPOLL.COM
D: MIGUEL RIPOLL, **C:** MIGUEL RIPOLL
A: MIGUEL RIPOLL, **M:** TITO@KIU.ES

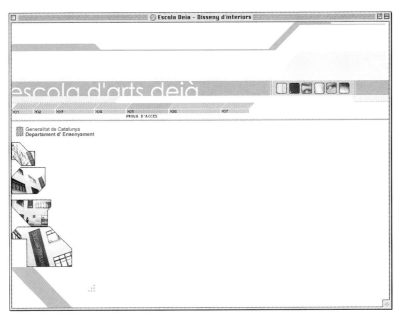

WWW.DEIADISSENY.COM
A: EABARCELONA, M: INFO@EABARCELONA.COM

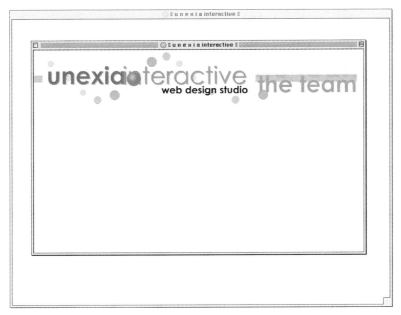

WWW.UNEXIA.COM
D: RENE TARDIF, C: LUC BESNER, P: ERIC BERGERON
A: UNEXIA INTERACTIVE

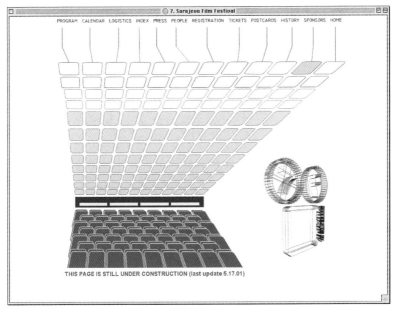

WWW.SFF.BA
D: MIREL, C: DEJAN, P: OBALA ART CENTAR
A: BOOM PRODUCTION, M: COMUNIC@HOTMAIL.COM

WWW.AIHH.COM
D: LAWRENCE MOUAWAD
M: LAWRENCE.MOUAWAD@AIHH.COM

WWW.KATHERINE-DUNN.COM
D: DEB KOCH
A: RED CANOE INC., M: KATHERINE@KATHERINE-DUNN.COM

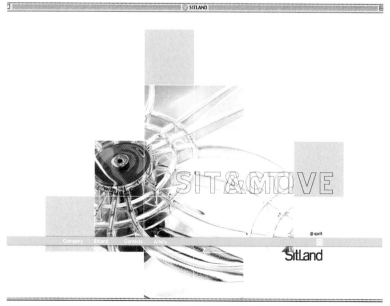

WWW.SITLAND.COM
D: MIRCO PASQUALINI, C: MIRCO PASQUALINI, P: OOTWORLD
A: SITLAND, M: MIRCO.PASQUALINI@OOTWORLD.COM

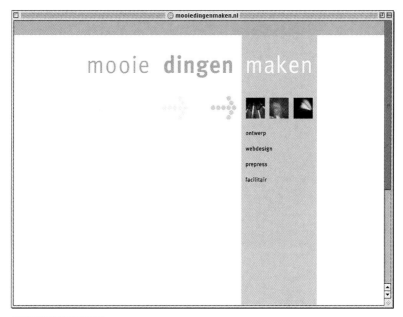

WWW.MOOIEDINGENMAKEN.NL
D: FRANK HARTMAN
M: FRANK@MOOIEDINGENMAKEN.NL

WWW.PLANTERS.IT
D: GAIA DE PAOLI
A: WWW.PINXIT.IT, **M:** GDEPAOLI@PINXIT.IT

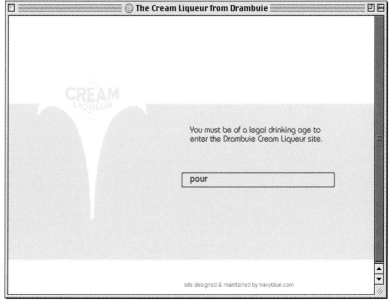

WWW.DRAMBUIECREAM.COM/FLASH.HTML
A: NAVYBLUE NEW MEDIA, **M:** NEWMEDIA@NAVYBLUE.COM

WWW.TOWATEI.COM
D: TOWA TEI & TYCOON GRAPHICS
M: OI@TOWATEI.COM

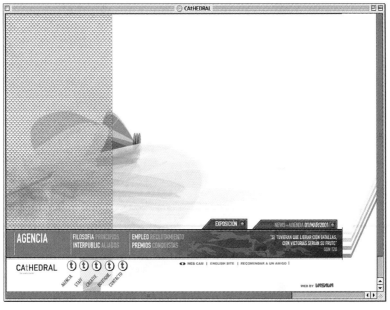

WWW.CATHEDRALCC.COM
A: VASAVA ARTWORKS, **M:** VASAVA@VASAVA.ES

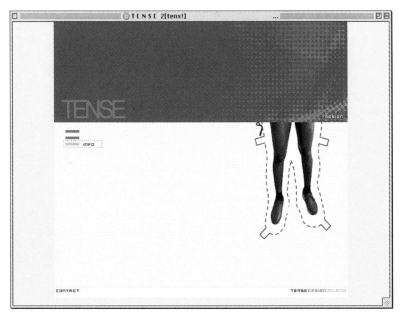

WWW.TENSE.IT
D: FRANCESCO BERTELLI
M: INFO@TENSE.IT

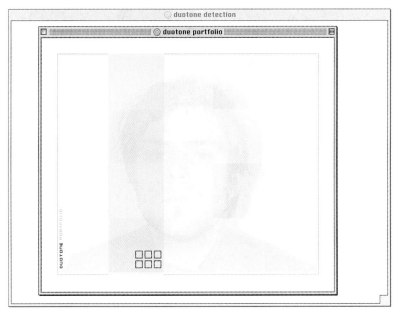

WWW.DUOTONE-PORTFOLIO.COM
D: STEVE KOPP
M: SKOPP@BUSINESSOBJECTS.COM

WWW.APT13.COM
D: PHILLIP DWYER

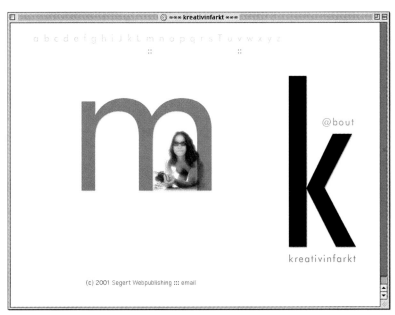

WWW.KREATIVINFARKT.DE
D: RALPH SEGERT, **C:** RALPH SEGERT
A: SEGERT WEBPUBLISHING, **M:** SW@KREATIVINFARKT

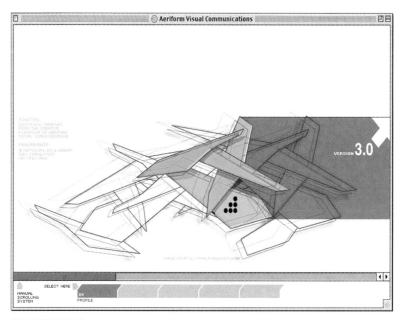

WWW.AERIFORM.CO.UK
D: SEAN RODWELL, C: ANGELA CARTER
A: AERIFORM, M: ROD@AERIFORM.CO.UK

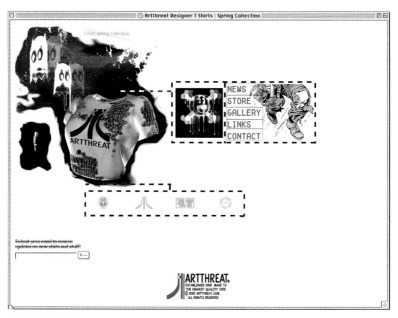

WWW.ARTTHREAT.COM
A: ARTTHREAT, M: X@ARTTHREAT.COM

WWW.LINKCLUB.OR.JP/~MO-MO
D: KENZO HIRAMATSU
M: KENZO@VAGAAIR.COM

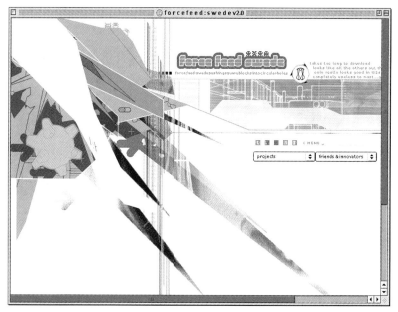

WWW.FORCEFEEDSWEDE.COM
D: OZ DEAN
M: OZ@FORCEFEEDSWEDE.COM

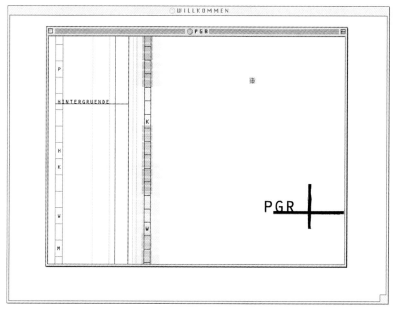

WWW.KIRCHELEBT.DE
D: CHRISTIAN BRACKMANN, C: CHRISTIAN BRACKMANN, P: BJS WERBEAGENTUR
A: BJS WERBEAGENTUR, M: CHRIS@OZ-ZONE.DE

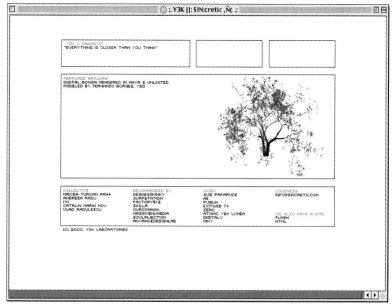

WWW.SINCRETIC.COM
D: TURCAN ARH MIRCEA
M: ARH@SINCRETIC.COM

WWW.BAYS.COM
A: DESIGNKITCHEN, INC., **M:** SCOTTY@DESIGNKITCHEN.COM

WWW.CAT-Y.COM/MAINFRAME.HTM
D: YUMIKO HAYAKAWA
M: CATJA@CAT-Y.COM

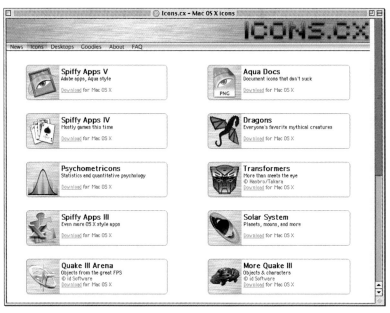

WWW.ICONS.CX/ICONS
D: RICK ROE
M: ICONS@ICONS.CX)

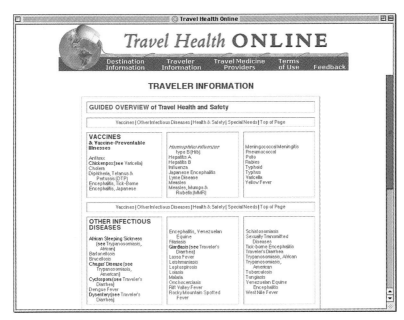

WWW.TRIPPREP.COM/TRAVINFO_FRAME.ASP
A: SHORELAND, INC., M: TRIPPREP@SHORELAND.COM

WWW.FASHIONDIG.COM
D: BARRY BRYANT
A: OBJECT CULTURE, M: DESIGN@OBJECTCULTURE.COM

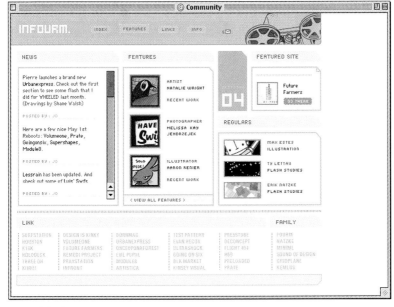

WWW.INFOURM.COM
D: ERIC NATZKE
M: ERIK@NATZKE.COM

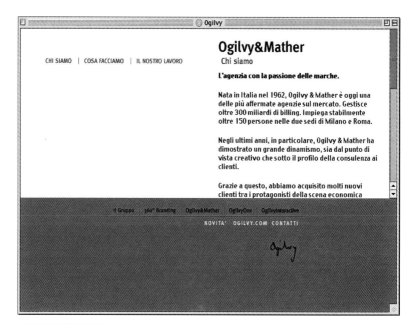

WWW.OGILVY.IT/FR_OEM.HTML
D: GUERINO DELFINO
M: DELFINO@HYPHEN.IT

WWW2.ODN.NE.JP/~CCM74860/DESIGN/TOP.HTM
M: CCM74860@SYD.ODN.NE.JP

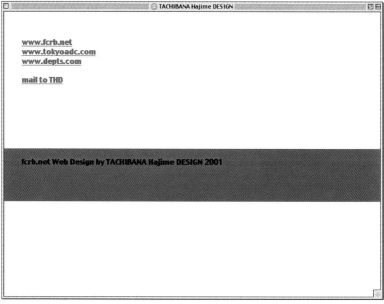

WWW.TACHIBANAHAJIMEDESIGN.COM
A: TACHIBANA HAJIME DESIGN, M: H@TACHIBANAHAJIMEDESIGN.COM

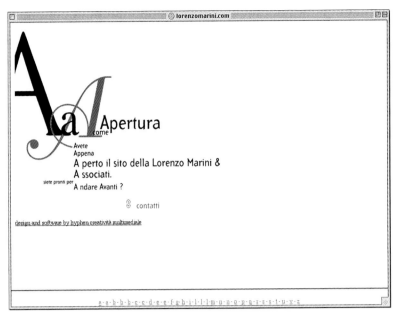

WWW.LORENZOMARINI.COM
D: GUERINO DELFINO
M: DELFINO@HYPHEN.IT

WWW.TKOUSA.COM/MAIN.HTML
D: JAMES WALKER, JOSHUA FINTO, C: COLLECTED WORK

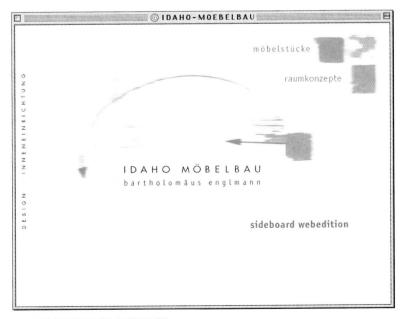

WWW.IDAHO-MOEBELBAU.DE/GO4MAC/HOME.HTML
A: CUBUS|MEDIA, M: CUBUS@CUBUSMEDIA.COM

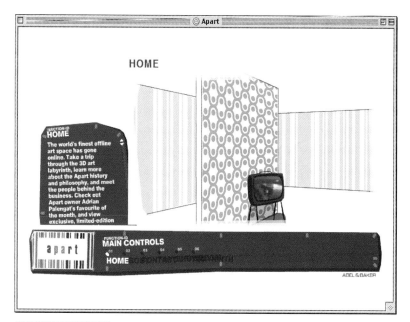

WWW.AP-ART.CO.UK/HOME.ASP
D: CHRISTEL LARSSON
M: INFO@ABELBAKER.COM

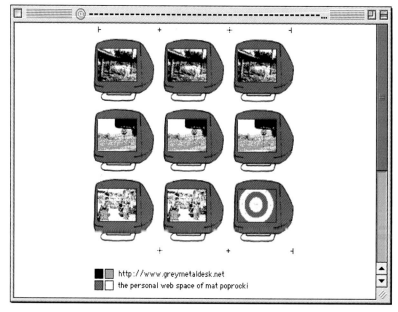

WWW.GREYMETALDESK.NET
D: MAT POPROCKI
M: MAT@INFERIORDESIGN.COM

WWW.PLOT20TWO.COM/001/001.HTML
M: BREAKTHESILENCE@PLOT20TWO.COM

WWW.CUBADUST.COM
D: STRANDBERG JONAS
A: DYNATOP, M: HAGA@HOME.SE

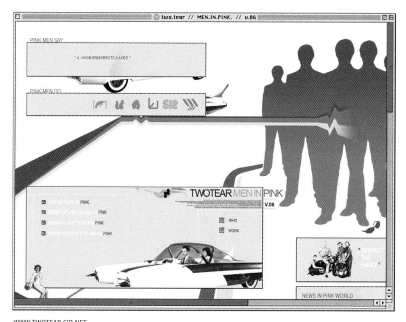

WWW.TWOTEAR.CJB.NET
D: LEE MCKENZIE
M: CHILLED.OUT@NTLWORLD.COM

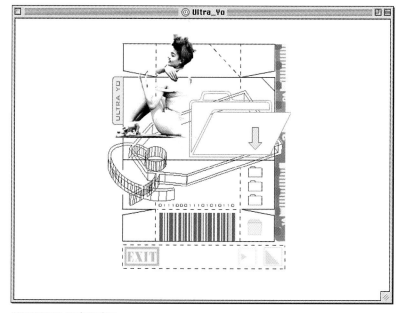

WWW.ANGELFIRE.COM/SUPER/YOo
D: PAULA, C: PAULA
M: PAULA@ON-THE-ROAD.CO.UK

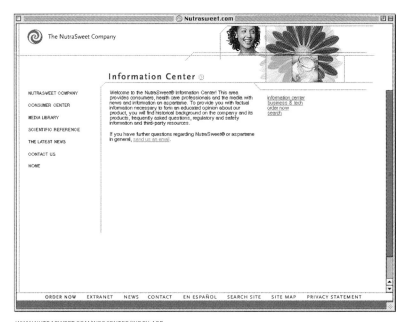

WWW.NUTRASWEET.COM/INFOCENTER/INDEX.ASP
A: DESIGNKITCHEN, INC., **M:** SCOTTY@DESIGNKITCHEN.COM

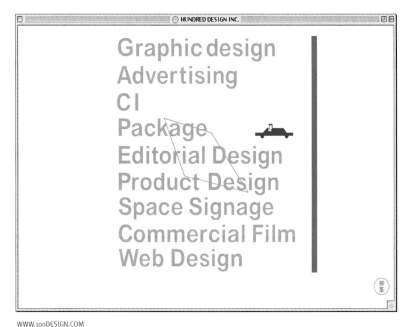

WWW.100DESIGN.COM
D: KEIZO MATSUI
A: HUNDRED DESIGN INC., **M:** STUDIO@100DESIGN.COM

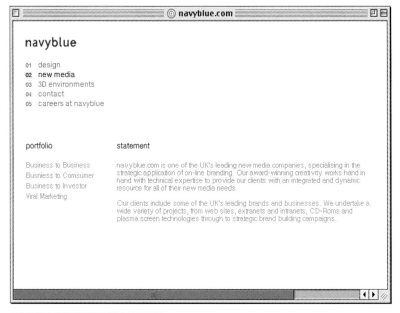

WWW.NAVYBLUE.COM/NEWMEDIA/NM_STATE.HTML
A: NAVYBLUE NEW MEDIA, **M:** NEWMEDIA@NAVYBLUE.COM

WWW.AUDI.DE/INDEX_DE.HTML
A: METADESIGN, M: MAIL@METADESIGN.DE

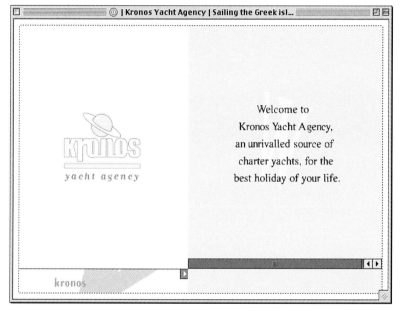

WWW.KRONOSYACHT.GR
C: LEFTERIS THEODOSSIADIS, P: LEFTERIS THEODOSSIADIS
M: SPEIRA@INAME.COM

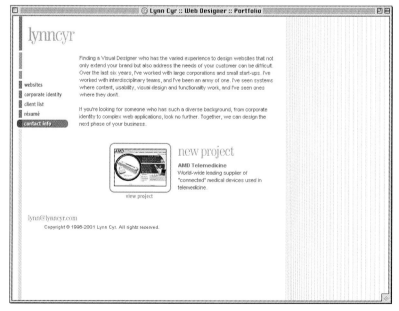

WWW.LYNNCYR.COM
D: LYNN CYR, C: LYNN CYR
M: LYNN@LYNNCYR.COM

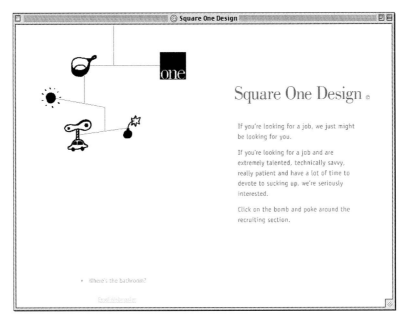

WWW.SQUAREONEDESIGN.COM/LOTECH.HTML
D: BRANDON GOHSMAN
A: SQUARE ONE DESIGN, **M:** BRANDON@SQUAREONEDESIGN.COM

WWW.ENK3.COM
D: DAVID NAVARRO GÓMEZ, **C:** DAVID NAVARRO GÓMEZ
A: ENK3 COMUNICACIÓN, **M:** NAVARRO@ENK3.COM

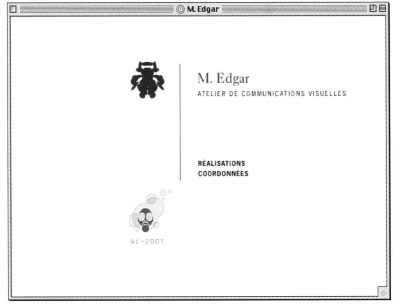

WWW.MR-EDGAR.COM
D: MR. EDGAR
M: CONTACT@MR-EDGAR.COM

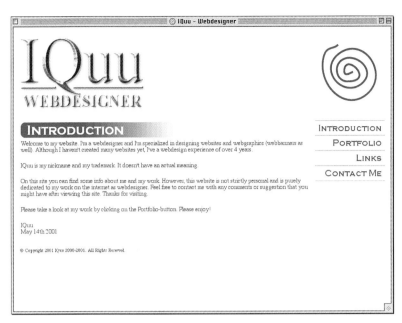

WWW.IQUU.CJB.NET
D: WUI SANG TANG
M: IQUU@USA.NET

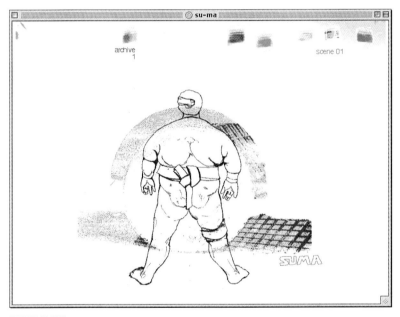

WWW.SU-MA.COM
D: SIARON
M: SIARON@SU-MA.COM

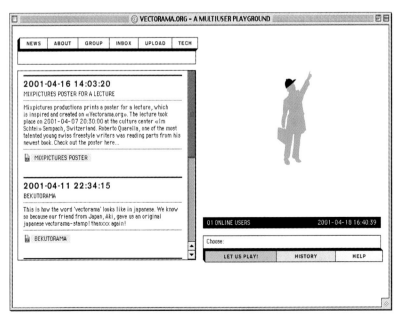

WWW.VECTORAMA.ORG
D: JUERG LEHNI, URS LEHNI, RAFI KOCH
M: INFO@VECTORAMA.ORG

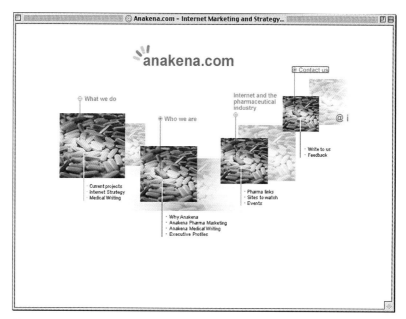

WWW.ANAKENA.COM
D: SANTI SALLÉS, **C:** SANTI SALLÉS
A: TUNDRABCN, **M:** INFO@TUNDRABCN.COM

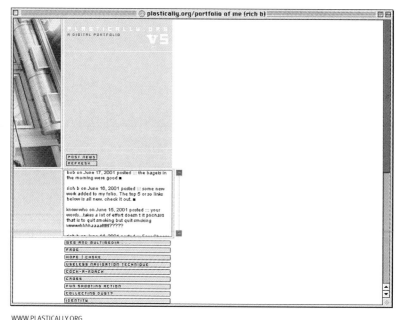

WWW.PLASTICALLY.ORG
D: RICH BARAN, **C:** RICH BARAN
M: RICH@PLASTICALLY.ORG

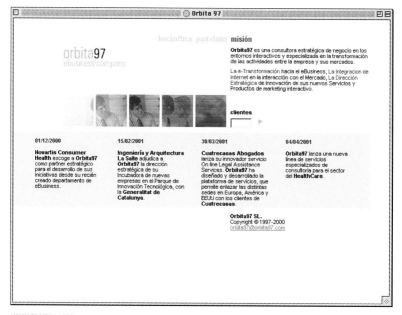

WWW.ORBITA97.COM
D: SANTI SALLÉS, **C:** SANTI SALLÉS
A: TUNDRABCN, **M:** INFO@TUNDRABCN.COM

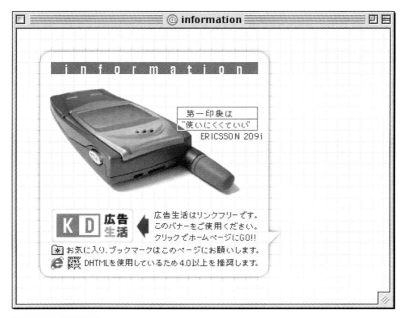

WWW.KURODA-DESIGN.COM
A: KURODA-DESIGN, **M:** INFO@KURODA-DESIGN.COM›

TANDEMCREATIVO.TRIPOD.COM
C: DIEGO MENDIGUREN, **P:** DIEGO MENDIGUREN
M: MENDIART@HOTMAIL.COM

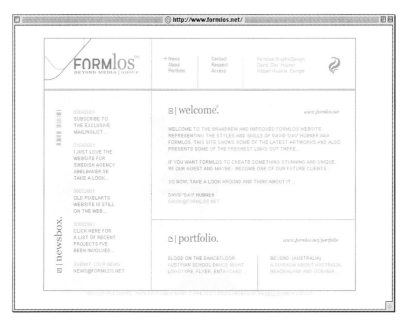

WWW.PIXELARTS.NU
C: HANS DERFUGZ RABER
M: DAVID@THECLICKLABS.COM

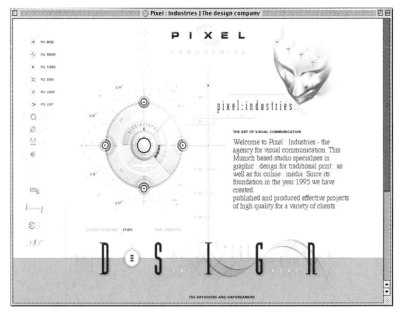

WWW4.PIXEL-INDUSTRIES.COM
D: MARC KLEIN
M: GENERATOR@PIXEL-INDUSTRIES.COM

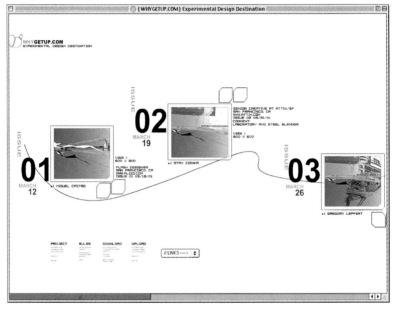

WWW.WHYGETUP.COM
D: MIGUEL CASTRO
A: PLIZO.COM, **M:** DESIGN@WHYGETUP.COM

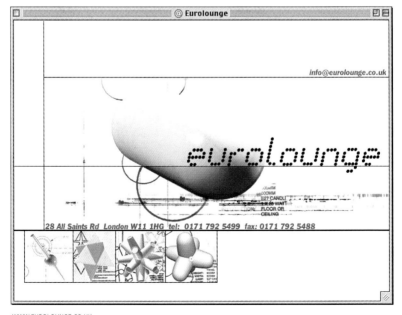

WWW.EUROLOUNGE.CO.UK
A: WAX, **M:** JAMES.GHANI@WAX.CO.UK

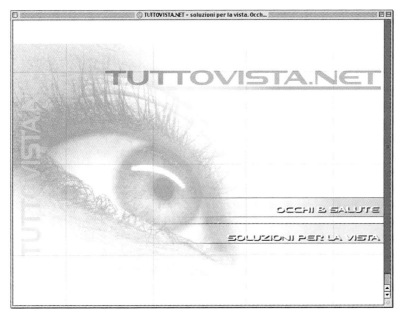

WWW.TUTTOVISTA.NET/
D: MICHELE GUGLIELMIN

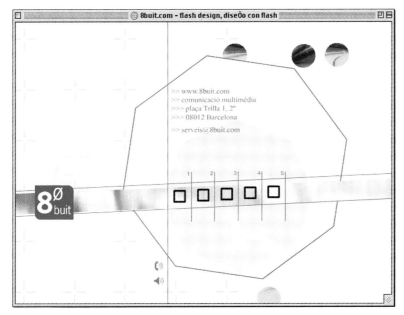

WWW.8BUIT.COM/8BUIT.HTM
D: ORIOL ARMEGOU
A: TOORMIX, M: INFO@TOORMIX.COM

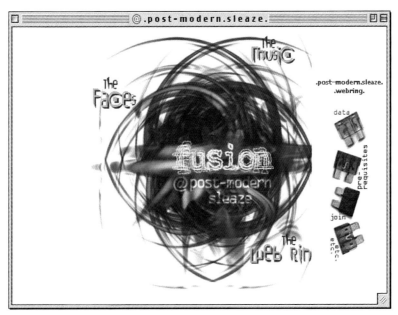

WWW.SUBURBANCHAOS.COM/SLEAZE/WEBRING
D: DAWN M. CROSS
M: DAWN@SUBURBANCHAOS.COM

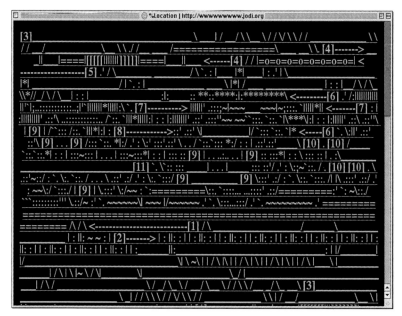

WWWWWWWW.JODI.ORG
M: 7061@JODI.ORG

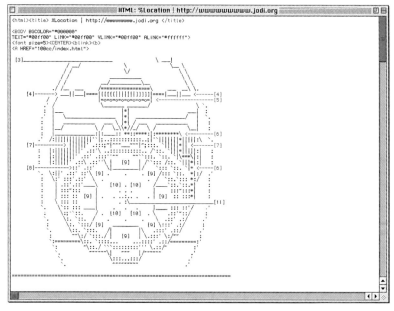

WWWWWWWW.JODI.ORG
M: 7061@JODI.ORG

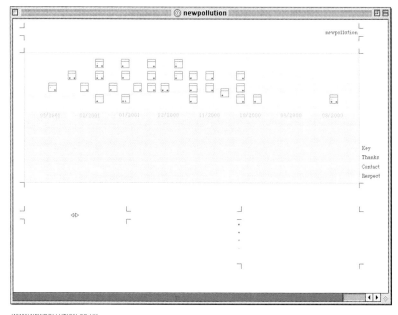

WWW.NEWPOLLUTION.CO.UK
D: JONNY, C: JONNY
M: J@NEWPOLLUTION.CO.UK

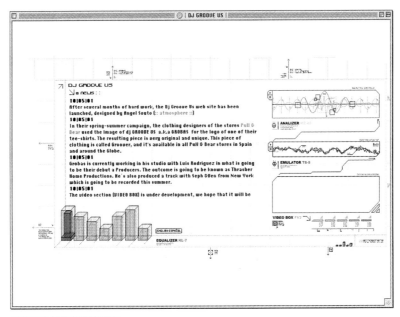

WWW.DJGROOVEUS.COM/CONT.HTM
A: THREEOH, M: ANGEL@THREEOH.COM

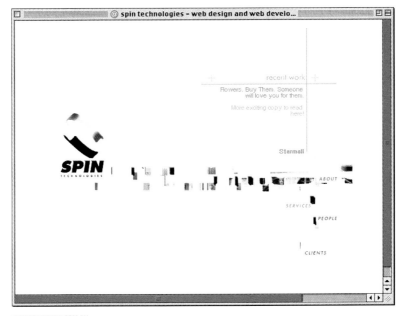

WWW.SPINTECH.COM.AU
C: SPIN TECHNOLOGIES
A: THE GLOBE, M: SIMON@THE-GLOBE.COM.AU

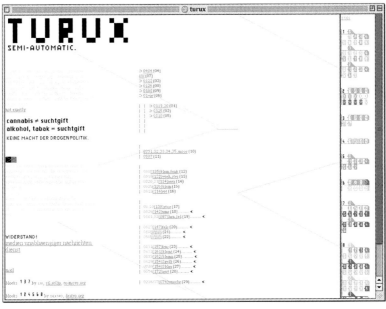

WWW.TURUX.ORG
D: DEXTRO, LIA
M: DEXTRO@DEXTRO.ORG, LIA@SILVERSERVER.CO.AT

195.222.219.39/FLASH/TXT_FS.HTML
A: ELEPHANT SEVEN, M: TEXTERSCHMIEDE@T-ONLINE.DE

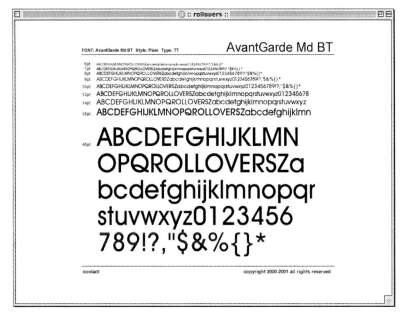

WWW.ROLLOVERS.F2S.COM
D: YOEL
M: ROLLOVERS@SOFTHOME.NET

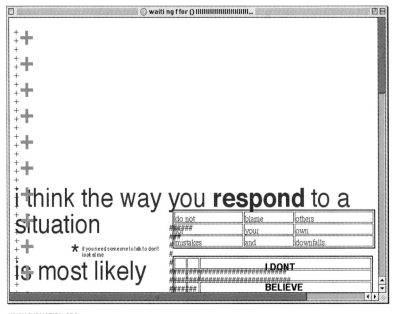

WWW.CHEMOTION.ORG
M: DOMNIK@CHEMOTION.ORG

WWW.CUATROGRADOS.COM
D: CUATROGRADOS, C: CUATROGRADOS
A: CUATROGRADOS, M: CUATRO@CUATROGRADOS.COM

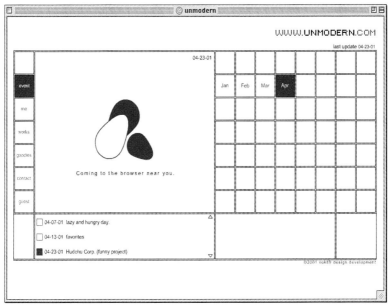

WWW.UNMODERN.COM
D: SARANONT L.
M: SARANONT@FUNCSION.COM

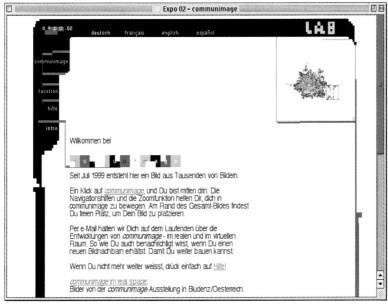

WWW.COMMUNIMAGE.CH
D: CALC, C: CALC, P: CALC & JOHANNES GEES
A: CALC, M: OMI@LAS.ES

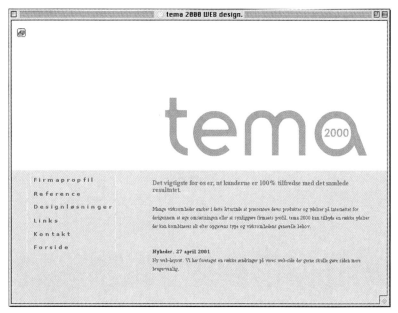

WWW.TEMA2000.DK
D: PETER BREMER, **C:** PETER BREMER
A: TEMA2000.DK, **M:** TEMA2000@MAIL.DK

WWW.SUPERLOOPER.DE
D: SVEN STÜBER
M: INF@SUPERLOOPER.DE

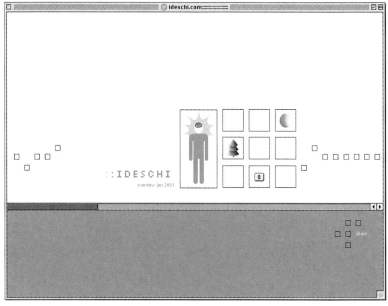

WWW.IDESCHI.COM
D: NINA DAVID
M: ICH@NINADAVID.DE

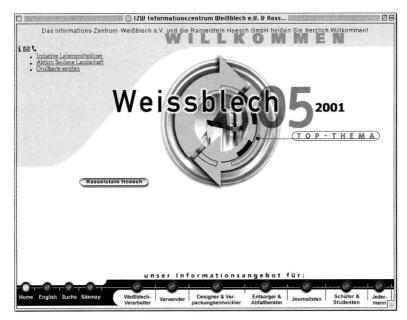

WWW.IZW.DE
D: KATRIN BRACKMANN, C: RALF FRIEDRICHS, P: INFORMATIONSZENTRUM WEISSBLECH
A: ONLINE RELATIONS, M: CHRIS@OZ-ZONE.DE

WWW.ELELEC.COM
D: EDUARDO DE FELIPE, C: EDUARDO DE FELIPE
M: EDUARDO@ELELEC.COM

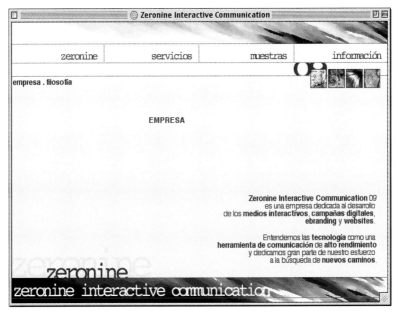

WWW.ZER09INE.COM
C: RAFAEL PAVÓN, MIGUEL COBIÁN
M: RPAVON@ZER09INE.COM

WWW.GIANNAMELIANI.IT
D: GIANNA MELIANI
M: INFO@GIANNAMELIANI.IT

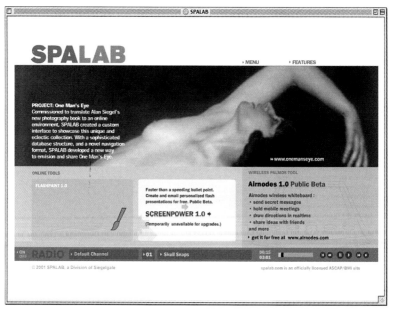

WWW.SPALAB.COM
D: JURGEN ALTZEIBLER, C: ARI JACOBS, P: TODD HOLLOBECK
M: DIANA@SPALAB.COM

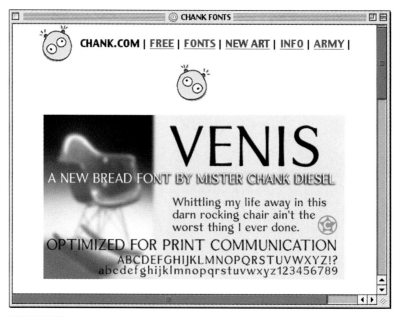

WWW.CHANK.COM
D: CHANK DIESEL / DAVID BUCK
M: INFO@CHANK.COM

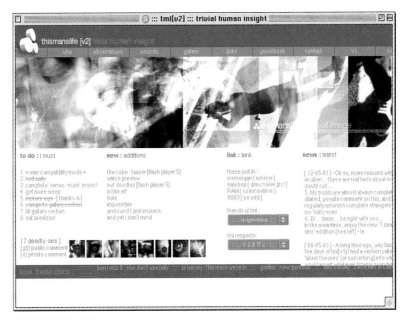

WWW.THISMANSLIFE.CO.UK
D: MELLERS JAMES, C: MELLERS JAMES
A: MELLERS JAMES, M: JAMES@THISMANSLIFE.CO.UK

WWW.PORTFOLJ.COM
D: JOHAN THORNGREN
M: JOHAN@PORTFOLJ.COM

WWW.LMDK.COM
A: LMDK, M: LMDK@LMDK.COM

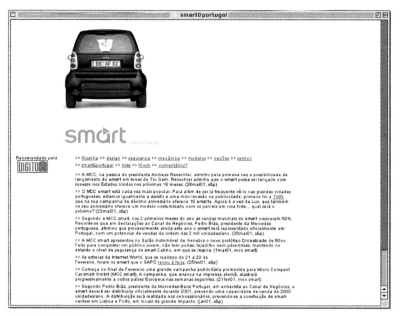

WWW.SMARTPORTUGAL.COM
D: FILIPE MIGUEL TAVARES
A: MASMADERA.NET, M: FMT@FMTAVARES.NET

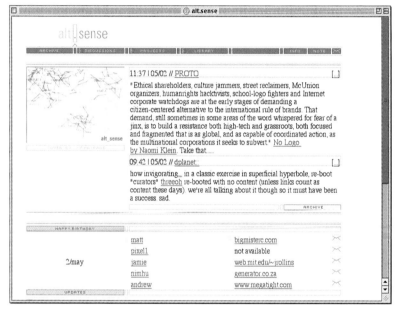

WWW.ALTSENSE.NET
D: FRANÇOIS NAUDÉ
M: ALT.SENSE@ALTSENSE.NET

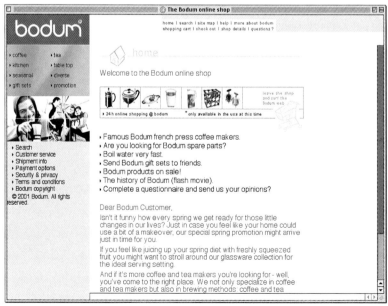

WWW.BODUM.COM/SHOP/HOME.ASP
D: THOMAS CASANOVA
M: TCASANOVA@BODUM.CH

WWW.DENKK.COM
D: JASON CHONG, C: NIKOLAI ZAUBER, P: NET INTEGRATORS
M: RONALDMOL@DENKK.COM

WWW.ADBUSTERS.ORG/HOME
D: JEFF HARRIS
M: JEFF@ADBUSTERS.ORG

WWW.SIXTHLIGHT.COM
D: MICHAEL IRIZARRY, C: LESSER DEMARCHENA, P: MICHAEL IRIZARRY
A: SIXTHLIGHT STUDIOS CORP., M: FLASHWAVE2K@HOTMAIL.COM

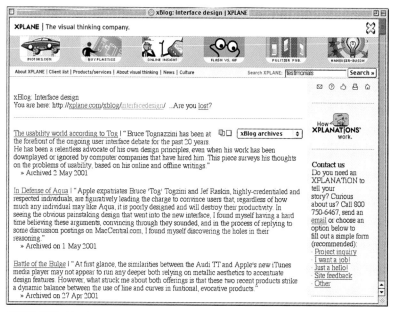

WWW.XPLANE.COM/XBLOG/INTERFACEDESIGN
D: BILL KEAGGY / JEFF LASH
M: HERMAN@XPLANE.COM

WWW.ROTODESIGN.COM/DESIGN/DESIGN.HTML
D: PAT BRODERICK
A: ROTODESIGN, M: PAT@ROTODESIGN.COM

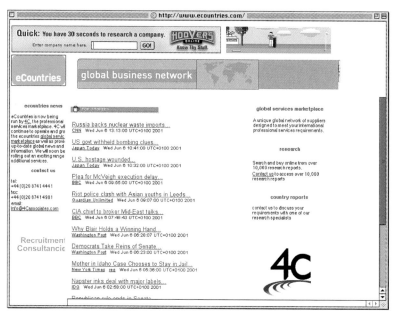

WWW.ECOUNTRIES.COM
D: OVEN DIGITAL, C: OVEN DIGITAL
A: OVEN DIGITAL LONDON, M: TOKE@OVEN.COM

WWW.DAMBACH.DE
D: MICHAEL MAUCH, C: MICHAEL BURGSTAHLER, P: MICHAEL BURGSTAHLER
A: TWO TRIBES INFORMATIONSGESTALTUNG GMBH, M: INFO@TWOTRIBES.DE

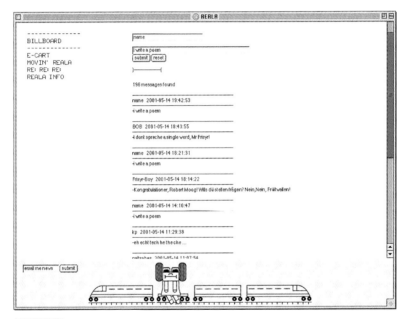

WWW.REALA.SE
D: REALA, C: FILIP
M: SAMUEL@REALA.SE

WWW.MHLN.COM
A: 415 INC. COPYRIGHT © THE MCGRAW-HILL COMPANIES, INC. M: INFO@415.COM

WWW.SARASCHWARTZ.COM/MAIN.HTML
D: SARA SCHWARTZ
M: STYLINSARA@AOL.COM

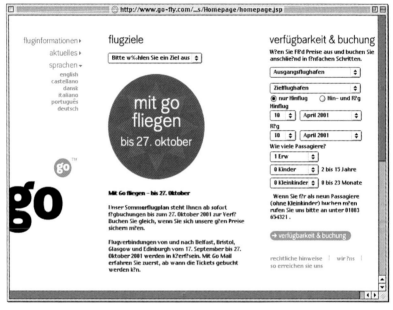

WWW.GO-FLY.COM
A: OYSTER PARTNERS, **M:** INFO@OYSTER.COM

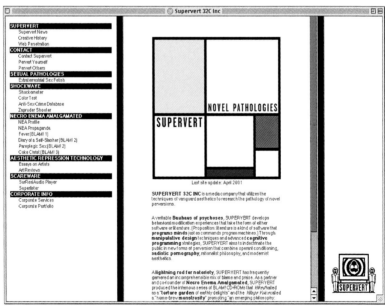

WWW.SUPERVERT.COM
A: SUPERVERT 32C INC., **M:** INFO@SUPERVERT.COM

WWW.WINNEY.COM/NEWS1.HTML
D: OLIVIER KUNTZEL / FLORENCE DEYGAS
M: WINNEY@WINNEY.COM

WWW.PLUS49.COM
D: LUTZ FISCHMANN, C: LUTZ FISCHMANN, P: PLUS 49 MEDIENSERVICE GMBH
A: SPROXY NEW MEDIA, M: POST@SPROXY.COM

WWW.STUDIOWD.COM.BR
D: SIMAS CARNEIRO JR., C: SIMAS CARNEIRO JR.
M: SIMASJR@STUDIOWD.COM.BR

WWW.MTGEZINE.COM
D: WUI SANG TANG
M: IQUU@USA.NET

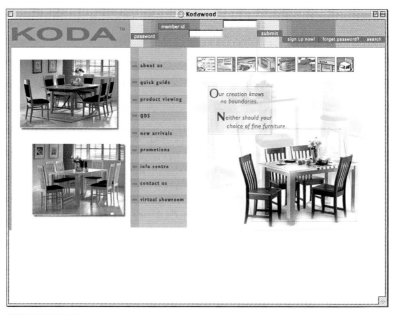

WWW.KODAONLINE.COM
D: BAY SIOW WE, C: SIE LAYTIN, P: DON TAN
M: JOE@DCSSOLUTIONS.NET

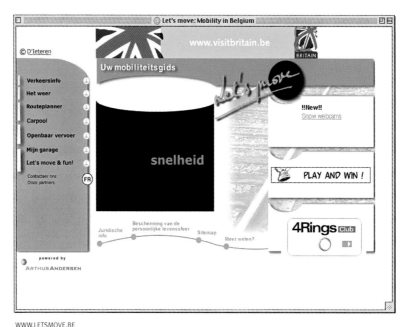

WWW.LETSMOVE.BE
D: HERMAN VAN DURME
M: HERMAN.VAN.DURME@BE.ARTHURANDERSEN.COM

WWW.GANZ.GOROD.RU
D: ALEXEY SHVABAUER
M: GANZZZ@MAIL.RU

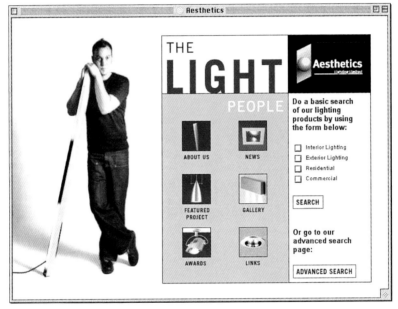

WWW.AESTHETICS.CO.NZ
D: BRONWEN THOMSON, C: TONY MCCRAE, P: BRONWEN THOMSON
A: COMPOSITE DESIGN, M: BRON@COMPOSITE.CO.NZ

WWW.CHICACHICA.COM
D: ANTONIO BALLESTEROS, C: NHT-NORWICK, P: EDICIONES MAIRI
A: NHT-NORWICK, M: ABALLESTEROS@NHT-NORWICK.NET

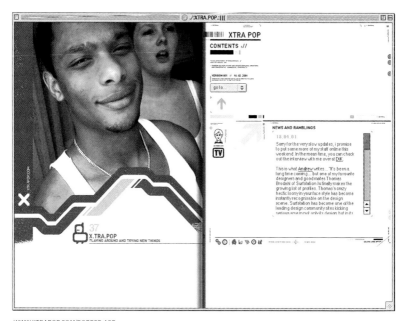

WWW.XTRAPOP.COM/POPPER.ASP
D: THOMAS BRODAHL
A: SURF DESIGN, **M:** SURF@SURF.LU

WWW.DETTERBECKWIDER.ORG/DEFAULT.HTM
D: EGO MEDIA
M: INFO@EGOMEDIA.COM

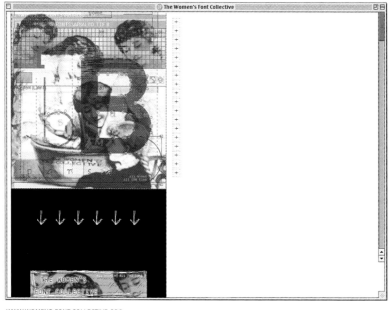

WWW.WOMENS-FONT-COLLECTIVE.ORG
A: THENETSTAR, **M:** JO@THENETSTAR.ORG

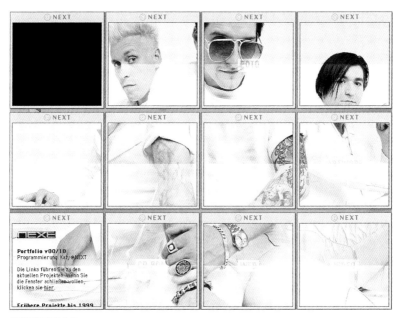

WWW.NEXT-BERLIN.DE
D: KATHARINA MATTHIES
M: KATZY@T-ONLINE.DE

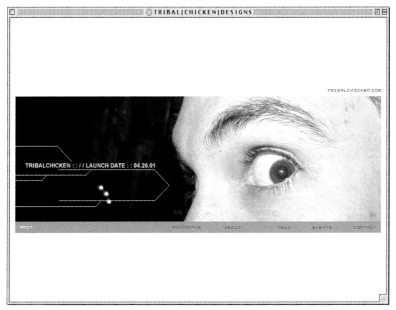

WWW.TRIBALCHICKEN.COM
D: MARK LANFORD, C: MARK LANFORD
A: TRIBAL CHICKEN DESIGNS, M: MARK@TRIBALCHICKEN.COM

WWW.NETDIVER.NET
D: CAROLE GUEVIN
A: SOULMEDIA STUDIO, M: CAROLE@SOULMEDIA.COM

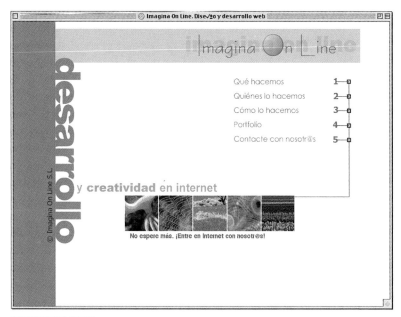

WWW.IMAGINAONLINE.COM
D: MAR SAN ALBERTO/ IRENE BENAIGES
M: IRENE@IMAGINAONLINE.COM

WWW.URBANATURAL.FR.ST
D: TWEN, C: TWEN
M: TWEN@SPRAY.FR

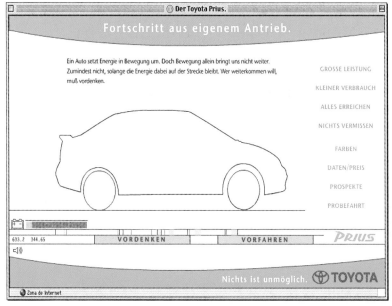

WWW.TOYOTA-PRIUS.DE
D: DINO FRANKE, C: MORE INTERACTIVE, P: MORE INTERACTIVE
M: DINO.FRANKE@MOREINTERACTIVE.DE

WWW.THESMARTEROFFICE.COM.AU
D: MICHAEL SIGNAL
A: ARTICHOKE WEB DESIGN, M: SALES@ARTICHOKEDESIGN.COM.AU

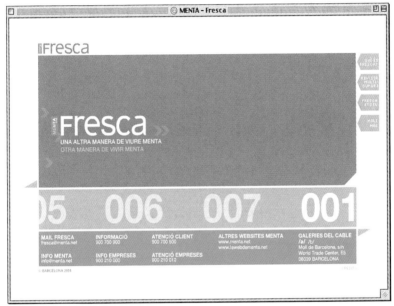

WWW.MENTAFRESCA.NET
D: ORIOL ARMEGOU
A: TOORMIX, M: INFO@TOORMIX.COM

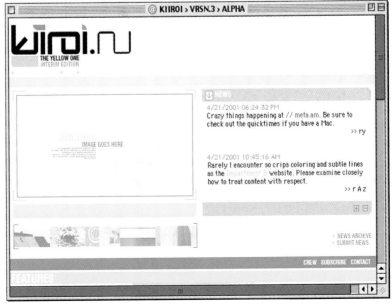

WWW.KIIROI.NU
D: RY WHARTON, CHRISTIAN ZANDER
M: INFO@KIIROI.NU

WWW.UNCLAIMEDCARGO.COM
M: INFO@UNCLAIMEDBAGGAGE.COM

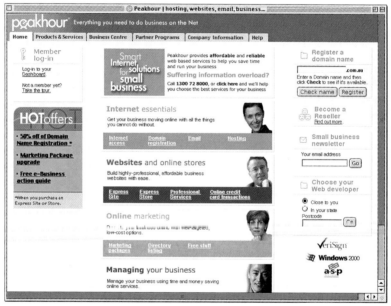

WWW.PEAKHOUR.COM.AU/HOME/DEFAULT.ASP
D: MICHAEL SIGNAL
A: ARTICHOKE WEB DESIGN, M: SALES@ARTICHOKEDESIGN.COM.AU

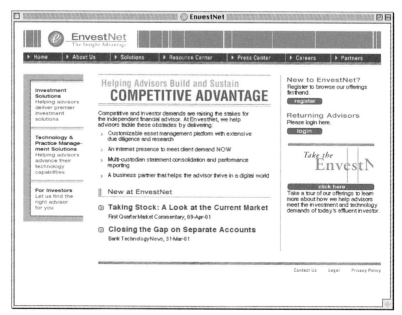

WWW.ENVESTNET.COM
A: DESIGNKITCHEN, INC., M: SCOTTY@DESIGNKITCHEN.COM

WWW.FRIEZE.COM
D: BEATRICE COLLIER
M: ANNA@FRIEZE.CO.UK

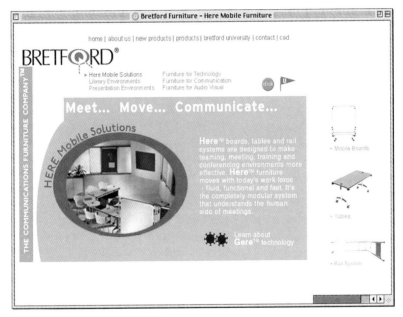

WWW.BRETFORD.COM/NEW_PRODUCTS/HERE.HTM
M: CPEDDICORD@BRETFORD.COM

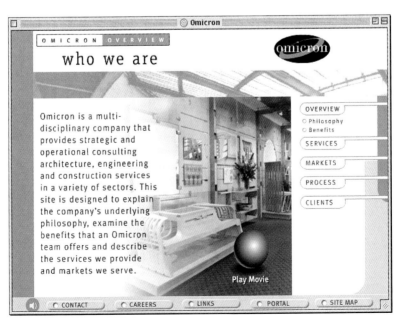

WWW.OMICRONCONSULTING.COM
A: AXIS INTERACTIVE DESIGN INC., M: DESIGN@AXIS-MEDIA.COM

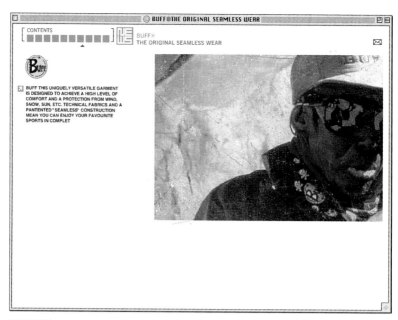

WWW.BUFF.ES
A: VASAVA ARTWORKS, M: VASAVA@VASAVA.ES

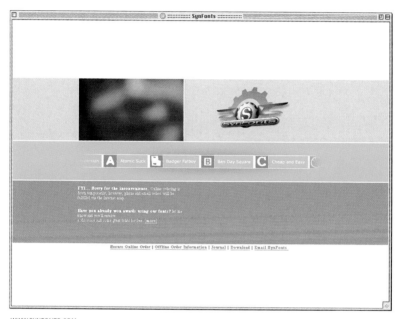

WWW.SYNFONTS.COM
D: DON SYNSTELIEN, C: DON SYNSTELIEN
A: SYNSTELIEN DESIGN, M: DON@SYNSTELIEN.COM

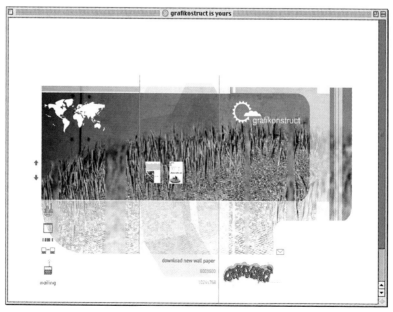

WWW.GRAFIKONSTRUCT.COM.BR/GRFKFLASH.HTML
A: GRAFIKONSTRUCT M: INFO@GRAFIKONSTRUCT.COM.BR

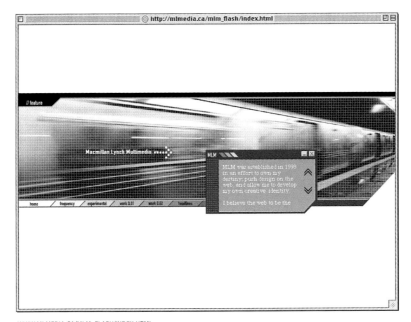

WWW.MLMEDIA.CA/MLM_FLASH/INDEX.HTML
D: KERRY (MACMILLAN) LYNCH
A: MACMILLAN LYNCH MULTIMEDIA, M: NFO@MLMEDIA.CA

WWW.XURURU.ORG/INDEX2.HTML
A: THUDERHOUSE BRAZIL, M: MAXIMO23@YAHOO.COM

WWW.DESIGNKITCHEN.COM/NEWDKISITE01_11.HTML
A: DESIGNKITCHEN, INC., M: SCOTTY@DESIGNKITCHEN.COM

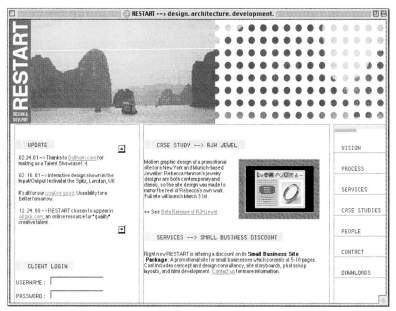

WWW.RESTARTSTUDIO.COM
D: MARGARET PENNEY
A: RESTART , M: INFO@RESTARTSTUDIO.COM

WWW.REFLEXCS.COM.AU
C: SPIN TECHNOLOGIES
A: THE GLOBE, M: SIMON@THE-GLOBE.COM.AU

WWW.MBH-ONLINE.DE/SERVICE
A: CUBUS|MEDIA, M: CUBUS@CUBUSMEDIA.COM

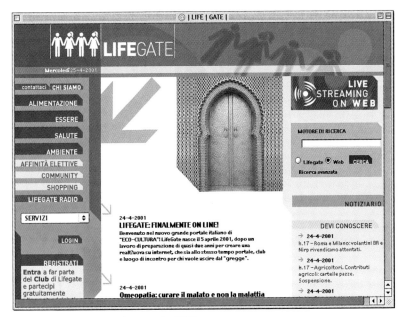

WWW.LIFEGATE.IT/LG/AMMSETT.NSF/PRINCIPALE?OPENFORM
D: GUERINO DELFINO
M: DELFINO@HYPHEN.IT

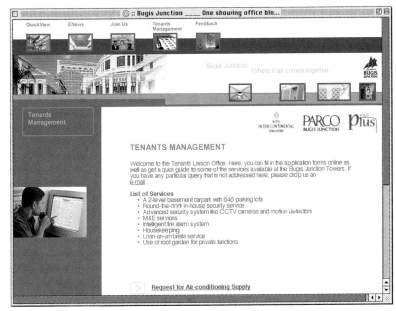

WWW.BUGISJUNCTION.COM.SG/TENANT_MANAGEMENT.ASP
A: STARTECH MULTIMEDIA PTE LTD., M: EUGENE@STARTECHMM.COM

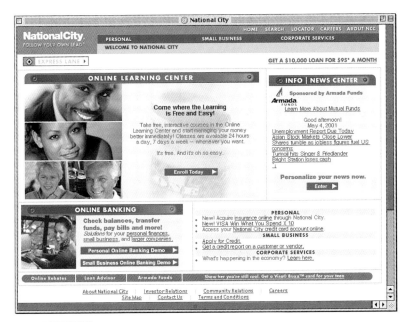

WWW.NATIONALCITY.COM
D: HOWARD CLEVELAND
M: HOWARDC@DIGITAL-DAY.COM

WWW.THEBARK.COM
D: DEBORAH KOCH, C: DEBORAH KOCH
M: DEB@REDCANOE.COM

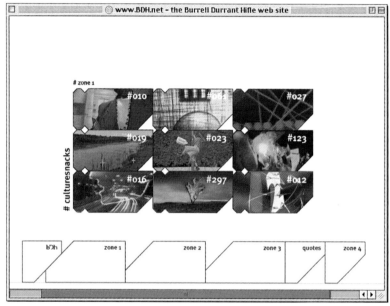

WWW.BDH.NET/HTML/ZONE1/ZONE1INDEX/ZONE1INDEX.HTM
D: TIM WEST
M: PIC@BDH.NET

WWW.ZIEGENFEUTER.DE
D: DIETER ZIEGENFEUTER, C: MICHAEL ALBERS, P: DIETER ZIEGENFEUTER
M: DIETER@ZIEGENFEUTER.DE

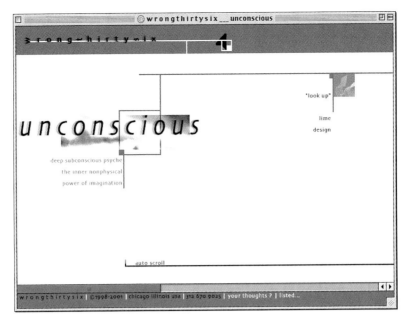

WWW.W36.COM
A: WRONGTHIRTYSIX, M: WRONG@W36.COM

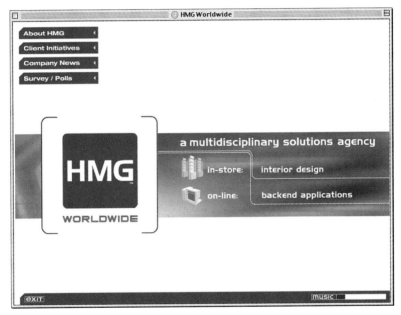

WWW.HMGWORLDWIDE.COM/FLASH/MAIN.HTM
D: EGO MEDIA
M: INFO@EGOMEDIA.COM

WWW.INVERGORDONDISTILLERS.CO.UK/HTML/FRMMASTER.HTM
A: BLACK ID, M: BLACK@BLACKID.COM

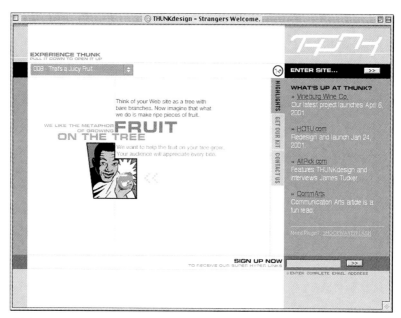

WWW.THUNKDESIGN.COM
D: JAMES TUCKER
M: JAMES@THUNKDESIGN.COM

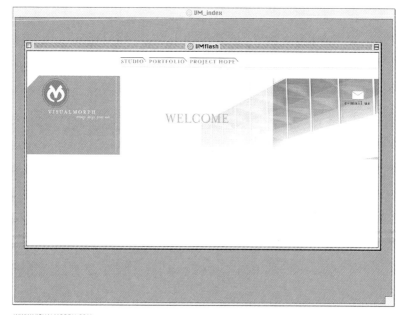

WWW.VISUALMORPH.COM
D: ROB GRANT

WWW.THREEOH.COM/ATMOSPHERE
D: ANGEL SOUTO
M: ANGEL@THREEOH.COM

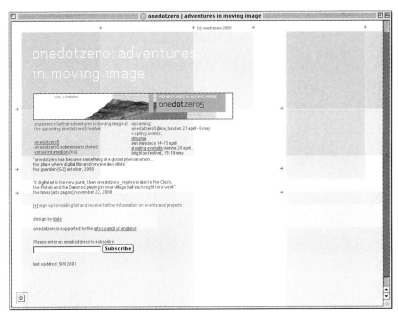

WWW.ONEDOTZERO.COM
A: STATE DESIGN, M: PHILIP@STATEDESIGN.COM

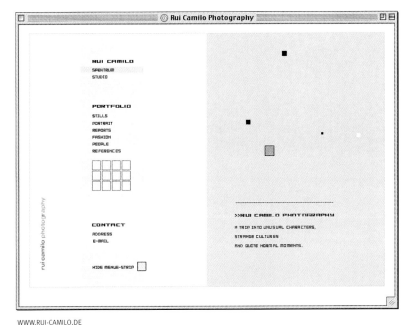

WWW.RUI-CAMILO.DE
A: SCHOLZ & VOLKMER, M: MAIL@RUI-CAMILO.DE

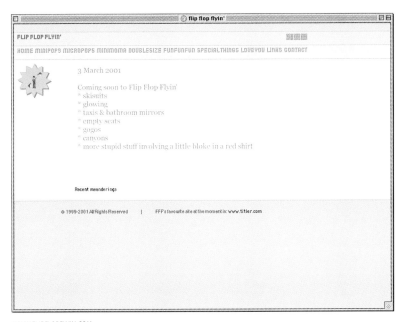

WWW.FLIPFLOPFLYIN.COM
A: FLIP FLOP FLYIN, M: CRAIG@FLIPFLOPFLYIN.COM

WWW.PROLOGO.AT
D: MARKUS HÜBNER, **C:** MARKUS HÜBNER
A: WORLD-DIRECT.COM, **M:** OFFICE@WORLD-DIRECT.COM

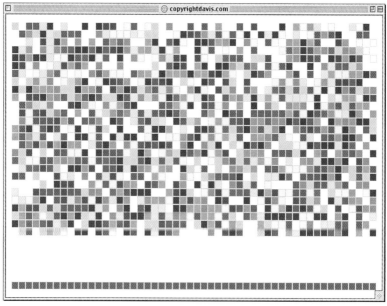

WWW.COPYRIGHTDAVIS.COM/INDEX_2.HTML
D: PAUL DAVIS
M: DAVIS@COPYRIGHTDAVIS.COM

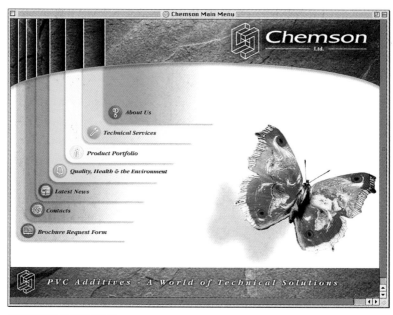

WWW.CHEMSON.CO.UK/INDEX.HTML
D: CHRIS JONES, **C:** CHRIS JONES
A: CLOCKWORK DESIGN, **M:** CHRIS@CLOCKWORK-DESIGN.CO.UK

WWW.DESIGNMUSEUM.ORG/FLASH/INDEX.HTML
D: FRED FLADE
A: DEEPEND, WWW.DEEPGROUP.COM, DESIGN MUSEUM, SPONSORED BY FORD MOTOR COMPANY

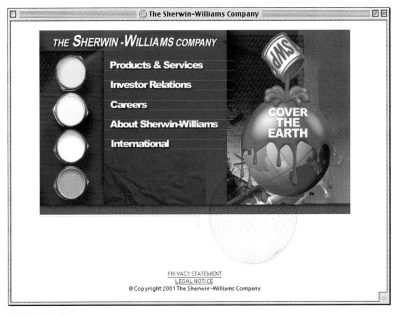

WWW.SHERWIN.COM
D: HOWARD CLEVELAND
M: HOWARDC@DIGITAL-DAY.COM

WWW.EVOLUTIVE.NET
A: VASAVA, M: VASAVA@VASAVA.ES

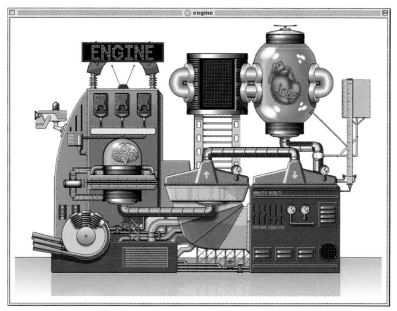

WWW.ENGINE-DESIGN.CO.UK
D: MATT KEY, **C:** MATT KEY
A: ENGINE, **M:** MATT@ENGINE-DESIGN.CO.UK

WWW.DESTROYROCKCITY.COM/AUGUSToo/GO.HTML
D: LEE MISENHEIMER
M: LEE@DESTROYROCKCITY.COM

WWW.PEHMUSTE.COM
D: ALEKSI KEMPPAINEN, **C:** ALEKSI KEMPPAINEN
A: PEHMUSTE, **M:** SUPERSTAR@PEHMUSTE.COM

WWW.MUSICANOCORACAO.PT
D: GIL CORREIA, **C:** GIL CORREIA
M: DESIGN@NETAMORPHOSE.PT

WWW.ARTICHOKEDESIGN.COM.AU
D: MICHAEL SIGNAL
A: ARTICHOKE WEB DESIGN, **M:** MIKE@ARTICHOKEDESIGN.COM.AU

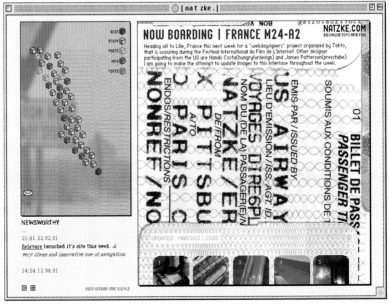

WWW.NATZKE.COM
D: ERIK NATZKE
M: ERIK@NATZKE.COM

WWW.DAMICODESIGN.IT
D: FABIO TINELLI, C: FABIO TINELLI
A: INTERNET2U, M: INFO@INTERNET2U.IT

WWW.ACRSYSTEMS.COM/QRY/DEFAULT.HTM
A: AXIS INTERACTIVE DESIGN INC., M: DESIGN@AXIS-MEDIA.COM

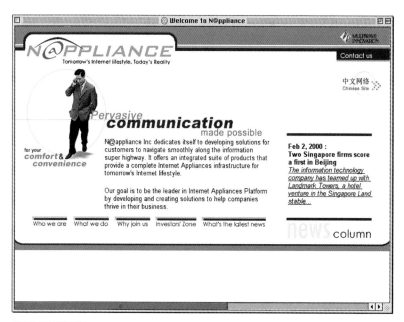

WWW.N-APPLIANCE.COM
D: KALINDA LOW, C: FOO YANLING, P: JOE CHUA
M: JOE@DCSSOLUTIONS.NET

WWW.KOELNER-HOLZHAUS.DE
C: DIETMAR SCHMIDT, P: UNIKOM./KINGMEDIA
A: KINGMEDIA, M: SCHMIDT@UNIT-MEDIENHAUS.DE

WWW.DIMENSIONIDUE.IT
D: FABIO TINELLI, C: FABIO TINELLI
A: FABIO TINELLI, M: INFO@INTERNET2U.IT

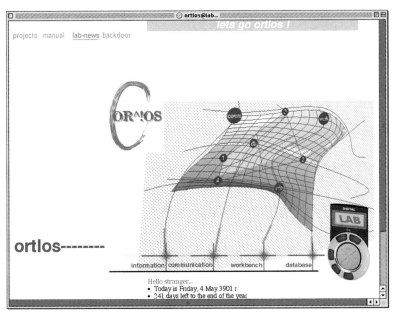

WWW.ORTLOS.COM
D: IVAN REDI
A: ORTLOS ARCHITECTS, M: OFFICE@ORTLOS.COM

WWW.SURFSTATION.LU
D: THOMAS BRODAHL , C: THOMAS BRODAHL
A: SURFSTATION

WWW1.VC-NET.NE.JP/°SIDE77/INDEX.HTML
D: SACHIKO TANABE
M: SIDE77@VC-NET.NE.JP

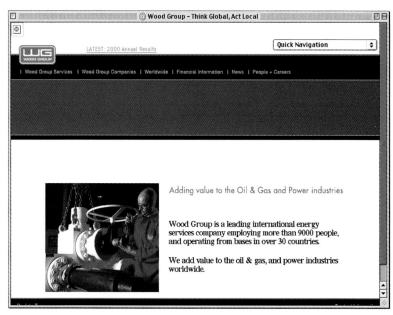

WWW.WOODGROUP.CO.UK
A: NAVYBLUE NEW MEDIA, M: NEWMEDIA@NAVYBLUE.COM.

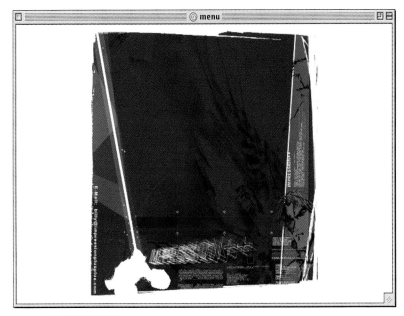

WWW.IMPRESSIONPLUSPLUS.COM
D: BILLY KWAN
M: BILLY@IMPRESSIONPLUSPLUS.COM

WWW.LINCHPINDESIGN.COM
D: PHIL RAMPULLA, **C:** PHIL RAMPULLA
M: PHIL@LINCHPINDESIGN.COM

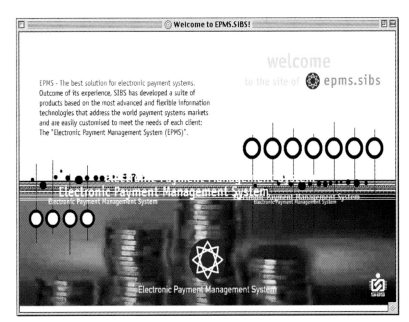

WWW.EPMS.SIBS.PT
D: GIL CORREIA, **C:** GIL CORREIA
M: DESIGN@NETAMORPHOSE.PT

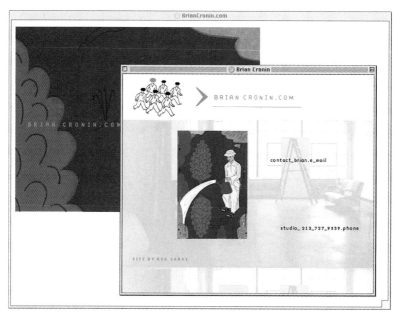

WWW.BRIANCRONIN.COM
D: DEBORAH KOCH, C: DEBORAH KOCH
A: RED CANOE

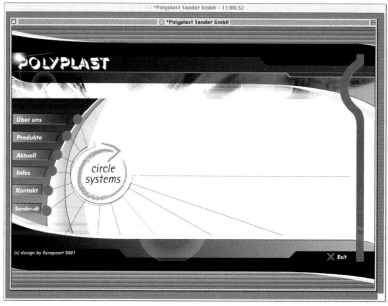

WWW.POLYPLAST.DE
C: JOSE IBAÑEZ SORIA, P: EUROPEART WEB SERVICES S.L.
A: EUROPEART WEB SERVICES S.L., M: JOSE@EUROPEART.COM

WWW.FASHIONLIVE.COM
D: JOHN GILLIGAN
M: GILLIGAN@WORLDMEDIA.FR

WWW.GELPAS.IT
D: CARLO SCIARRA, C: FABIO TINELLI, P: FABIO TINELLI
A: INTERNET2U, M: INFO@INTERNET2U.IT

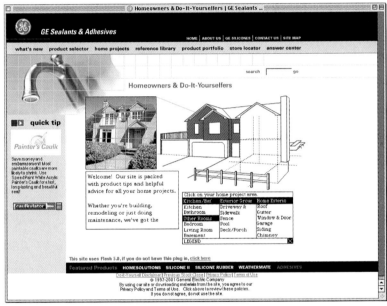

WWW.GESEALANTS.COM/SEALANTS/DIY/DEFAULT.SHTML
D: HOWARD CLEVELAND
M: HOWARDC@DIGITAL-DAY.COM

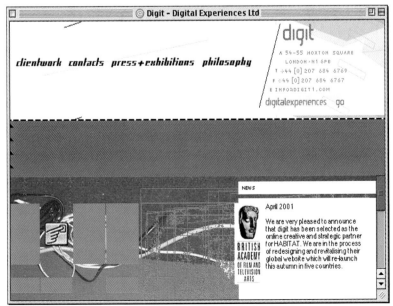

WWW.DIGITLONDON.COM
D: BRAD SMITH
A: DIGIT, M: DELYTH@DIGITLONDON.COM

WWW.TRANSEDEN.COM
D: BRAD SMITH
A: DIGIT, M: DELYTH@DIGITLONDON.COM

WWW.ISHRAG.NET
D: AVINASH GITE, C: AVINASH GITE
A: INDIA DOMAIN, M: TUBY_20@YAHOO.COM

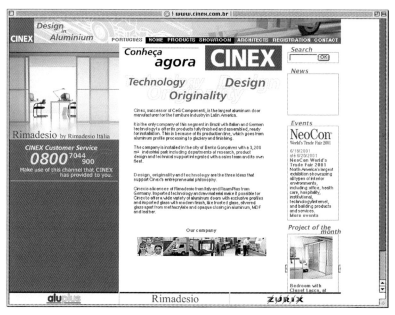

WWW.CINEX.COM.BR
D: TATIANA BRUGALLI, C: GLADIMIR DUTRA, P: FABIANO DE ANDRADE
A: ALDEIA DESIGN, M: FABIANO@ALDEIADESIGN.COM.BR

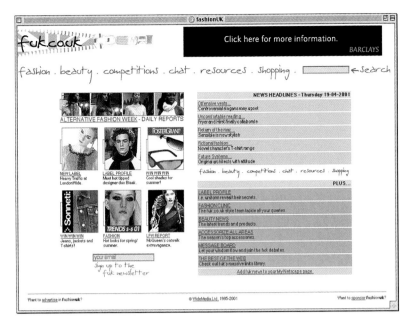

WWW.FUK.CO.UK
D: BRAD SIDEY
A: WIDEMEDIA, M: FUK@WIDEMEDIA.COM

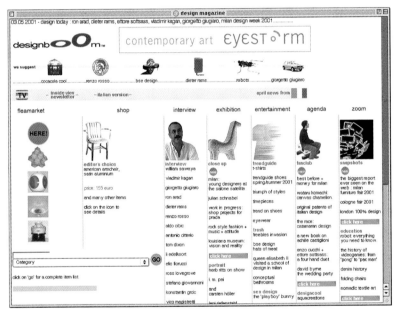

WWW.DESIGNBOOM.COM
D: BIRGIT LOHMANN, MASSIMO MINI
M: MAIL@DESIGNBOOM.COM

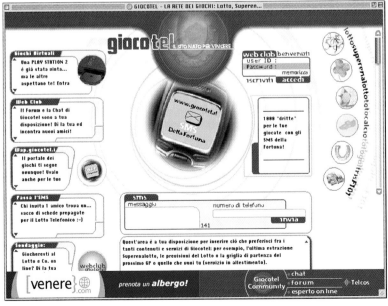

WWW.GIOCOTEL.IT
C: LUIGI GAETA, P: MARCO TRIPI
A: EURO RSCG, M: M.SCARI@TISCALINET.IT

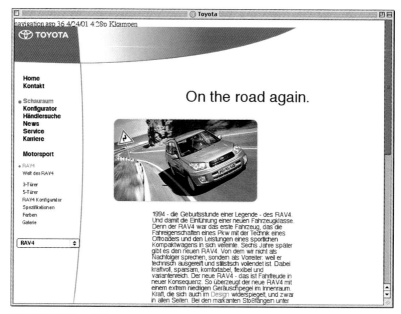

WWW.TOYOTA.DE/G/G01_11.HTML
D: DINO FRANKE, C: JÖRG MÜLLER, P: MORE INTERACTIVE
M: DINO.FRANKE@MOREINTERACTIVE.DE

WWW.CSAM.COM/INDEX_FLASH_CONTENT.HTML
A: 415 INC.,COPYRIGHT © THE MCGRAW-HILL COMPANIES, M: INFO@415.COM

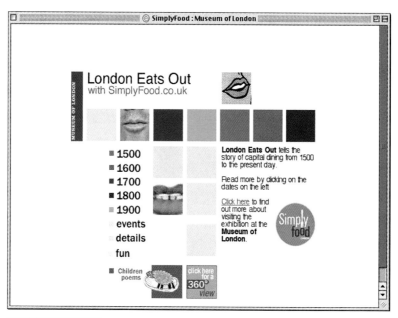

WWW.LONDONEATSOUT.CO.UK
D: EMERALD MOSLEY & SARAH MORISSET
M: GOLDTOP@GOLDTOP.ORG

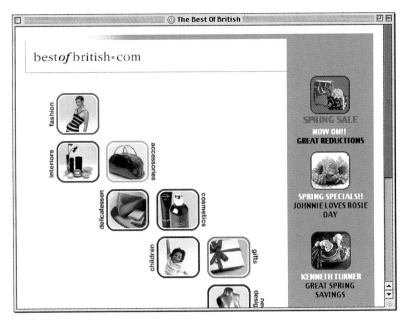

WWW.WHITTARD.COM
D: ANNA PENNEY

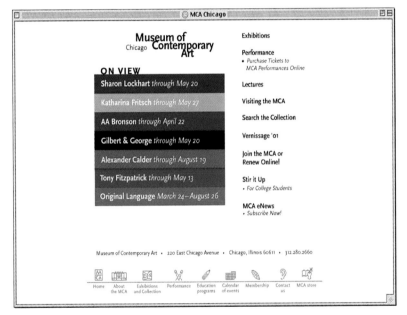

WWW.MCACHICAGO.ORG
D: MUSEUM OF CONTEMPORARY ART
M: TNEUHOFF@MCACHICAGO.ORG

WWW.LONDONWIDE.CO.UK
A: WIDEMEDIA, M: CONTACT@WIDEMEDIA.COM

WWW.CREATIVEBASE.COM
D: JAMES GOGGINS
A: PRACTISE, M: INFO@CREATIVEBASE.COM

WWW.BARCELONART.COM
M: INFO@BARCELONART.COM

WWW.GRAF-DESIGN.DE
D: JOHANNES GRAF, C: MICHAEL HERBERTS, P: JOHANNES GRAF
M: JOHANNES@GRAF-DESIGN.DE

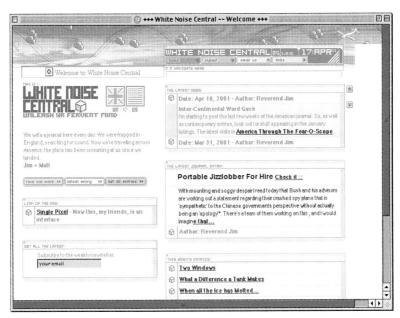

WWW.WHITENOISECENTRAL.ORG
A: 3FORM / WWW.3FORM.CO.UK

WWW.FUNDACIOBARCELONAOLIMPICA.ES
D: SANTI SALLÉS, C: SANTI SALLÉS
A: TUNDRABCN, M: INFO@TUNDRABCN.COM

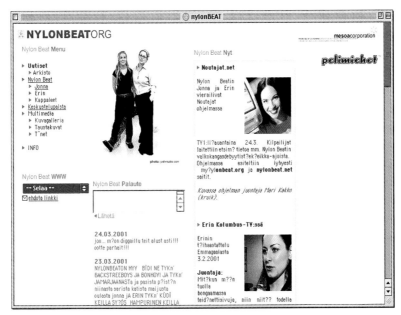

WWW.NYLONBEAT.ORG
D: BENNY BLANCO
M: BENNY.BLANCO@MESOA.COM

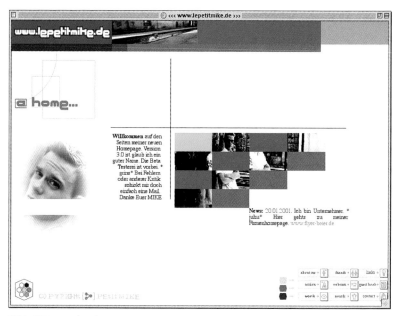

WWW.LEPETITMIKE.DE/MIKE/HOME.HTML
A: WWW.FLYER-BEIER.DE, M: MIKE@LEPETITMIKE.DE

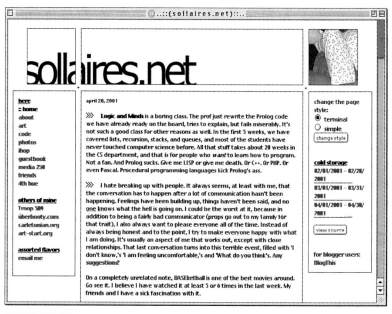

WWW.SOLLAIRES.NET
C: DAVID HENDLER, P: DAVID HENDLER
M: ME@SOLLAIRES.NET

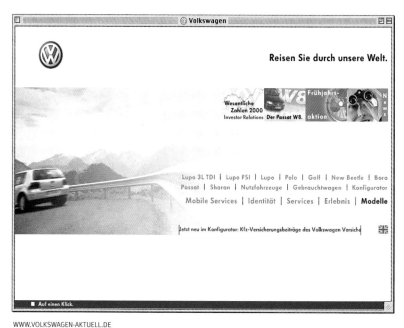

WWW.VOLKSWAGEN-AKTUELL.DE
D: HELGE WINDISCH, C: JOERG WASCHAT, P: BBDO-INTERACTIVE
A: FLANEUR DESIGN, M: INFO@FLANEUR.DE

WWW.BUCHKATALOG.DE
D: ANDREA BRÄUNING
M: BRÄUNING@BEAUFORT8.DE

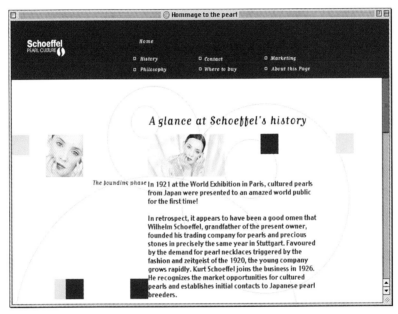

WWW.SCHOEFFEL-PEARL.COM/SHOCK_E/INDEX_SCHOEFFEL.HTML
D: LARS EBERLE
A: LESS RAIN, M: LARS@LESSRAIN.COM

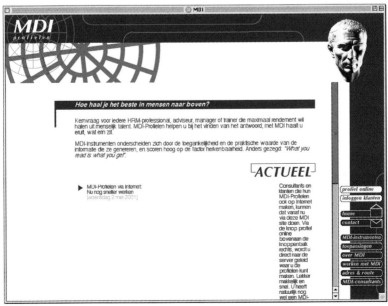

INFO@WHIZZWEB.NL
D: ARNOUD VAN DELDEN, C: ARNOUD VAN DELDEN
A: WWW.MDI.NL

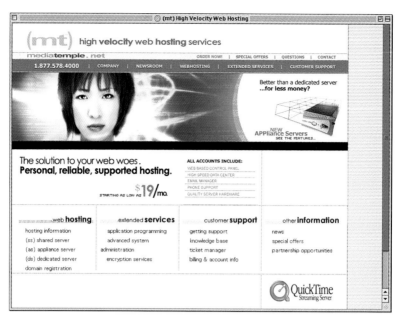

WWW.MEDIATEMPLE.NET
D: GREG HUNTOON
M: GREG@MEDIATEMPLE.COM

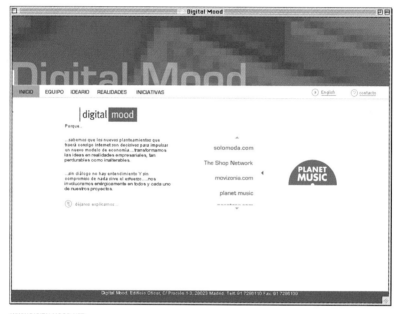

WWW.DIGITALMOOD.NET
A: EQUIPO BRANDMEDIA, M: INFO@BRANDMEDIA.COM

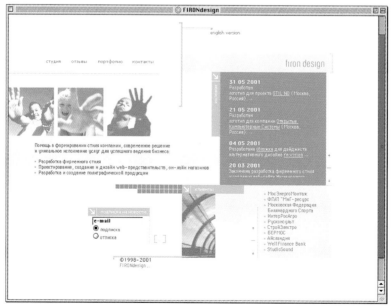

WWW.FIRON.COM
D: VALERY FIRON, C: ROMAN GRIGOROVICH, P: VALERY FIRON
A: FIRONDESIGN, M: INFO@FIRON.COM

WWW.DISENADORMEJIA.CAFEPROGRESSIVE.COM/CERROS/CERRO.HTML
D: IVAN MEJIA FABELA
M: IMEJIA32@PRODIGY.NET.MX

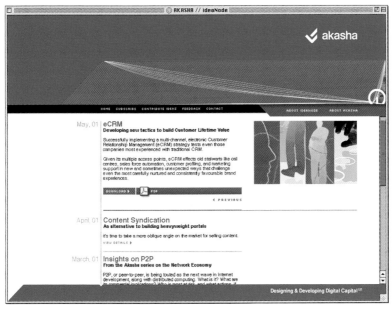

WWW.AKASHA-MEDIA.COM/IDEANODE
D: JOHAN ENGELBRECHT, **C:** YOUSEF LAMLUM, **P:** ANTHONY SHAFTO
A: AKASHA MEDIA, **M:** ANTHONY@AKASHA-MEDIA.COM

WWW.TRIEXONLINE.COM.BR
D: DEIVID, **C:** DEIVID, **P:** TRIEX-ONLINE
A: TRIEX-ONLINE, **M:** DEIVID@TRIEXONLINE.COM.BR

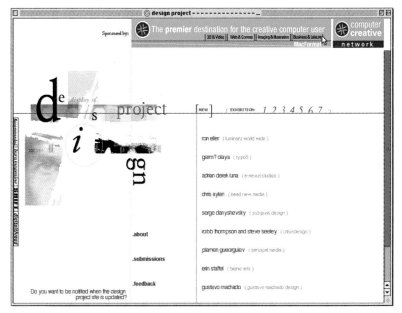

WWW.DESIGN-AGENCY.COM/PROJECT/MAIN.HTML
D: ANDREY KOVALENKO
M: ANDREY@DESIGN-AGENCY.COM

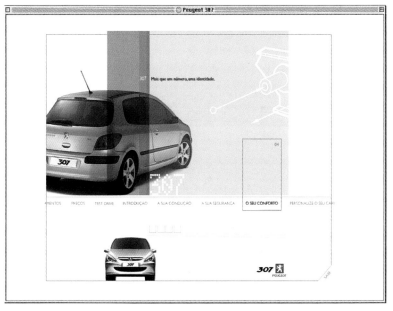

WWW.PEUGEOT.PT/307
D: VIANA RAQUEL, C: PEDRO GASPAR
M: RAKEL-V@HOTMAIL.COM

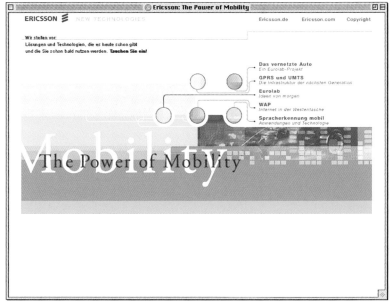

WWW.ERICSSON.DE/MICROSITE
D: KATRIN BRACKMANN, C: BERND BRAUN, P: ERICSSON
A: ONLINE RELATIONS, M: KA@OZ-ZONE.DE

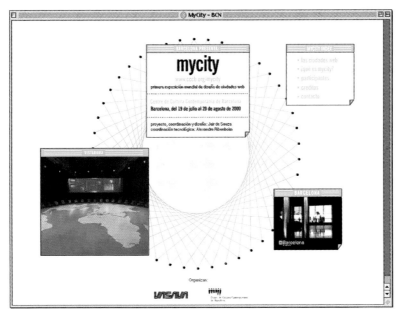

WWW.VASAVA.ES/MYCITY/RE
D: JÖRG RICHTER
A: VASAVA ARTWORKS , **M:** JOERG.VASAVA@MENTA.NET

WWW.ESFEROBITE.COM/HTML/AUDIOVISUAL.HTM
D: JUAN LESTA, BELÉN MONTERO
M: INFO@ESFEROBITE.COM

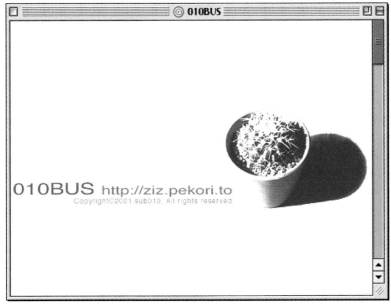

WWW.ZIZ.PEKORI.TO
D: ZIZ PEKORI
M: ZIZ@PEKORI.TO

CUSTOMCRITICAL.FEDEX.COM/
D: HOWARD CLEVELAND
M: HOWARDC@DIGITAL-DAY.COM

XPERIMENTZ.COM
D: HYE JIN, YANG, C: KWON GOO, JUNG, P: KWON GOO, JUNG
A: VISUAL XPERIMENTZ, M: VISUALI@DREAMWIZ.COM

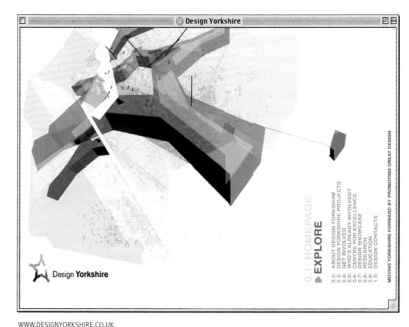

WWW.DESIGNYORKSHIRE.CO.UK
A: ATTIK.COM, M: TRACEYT@ATTIK.COM

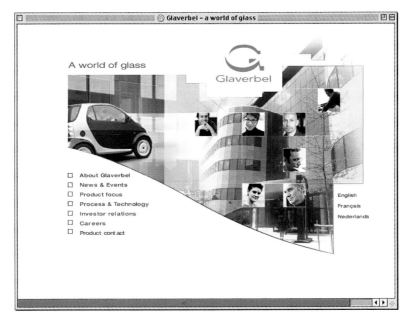

WWW.GLAVERBEL.COM
D: NICOLAS JANDRAIN
A: WWW.EMAKINA.COM, **M:** CORPORATE.COM@GLAVERBEL.COM

WWW.GESTALTUNGSFRAGEN.DE
D: DANIEL GODDEMEYER, **C:** KLAUS VOLTMER, **P:** SANDRO LÜTGENS
A: FORK UNSTABLE MEDIA, **M:** SVENJA@FORK.DE

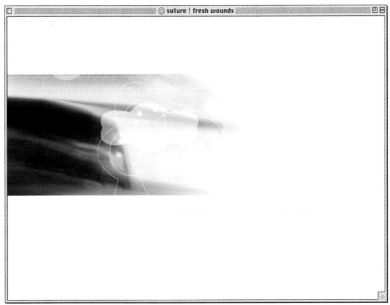

WWW.SUTURE.COM
D: JEREMY ABBETT, **C:** JEREMY ABBETT
A: TRUTHDAREDOUBLEDARE, **M:** JEREMY@TRUTHDAREDOUBLEDARE.COM

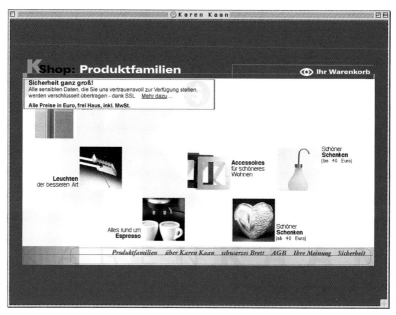

WWW.KARENKAAN.DE
D: CHRISTIAN BRACKMANN, C: CHRISTIAN BRACKMANN, P: UDO NACKE
A: OZ KOMMUNIKATIONSDESIGN, M: CHRIS@OZ-ZONE.DE

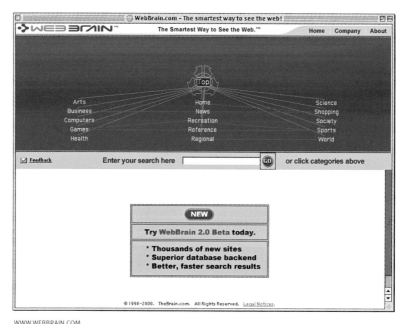

WWW.WEBBRAIN.COM
A: THEBRAIN, M: INFO@THEBRAIN.COM

WWW.ELECTRONICSTYLE.COM/PROD.HTML
M: INFO@ABARA.DE

WWW.NORBERTBAYER.DE
D: NORBERT BAYER
M: NB@NORBERTBAYER.DE

WWW.WEBCLIMBING.COM
M: INFO@WEBCLIMBING.COM

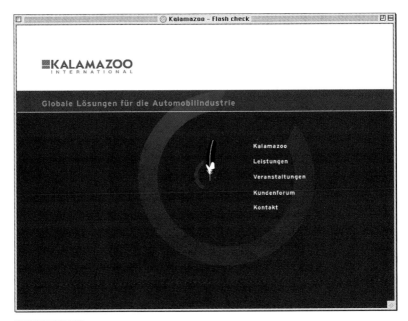

WWW.KALAMAZOO.DE
D: ANDREA BRÄUNING
M: BRÄUNING@BEAUFORT8.DE

WWW.CIVILIUM.NET
D: FILIPE MIGUEL TAVARES
A: MASMADERA.NET, M: FMT@FMTAVARES.NET

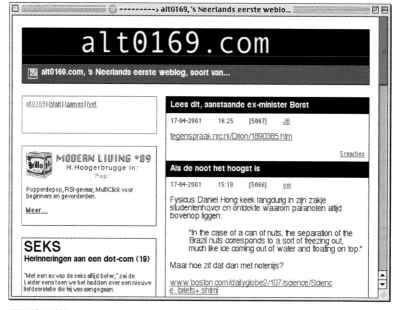

WWW.ALTo169.COM
D: JEROEN BOSCH
M: JBOSCH@ALTo169.COM

WWW.BEST-OF-ITALY.COM
D: WALTER SCHRAMM
M: INFO@BEST-OF-ITALY.COM

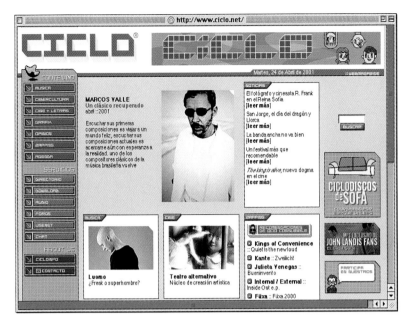

WWW.CICLO.NET
D: DANIEL TORRES
M: CICLO@CICLO.NET

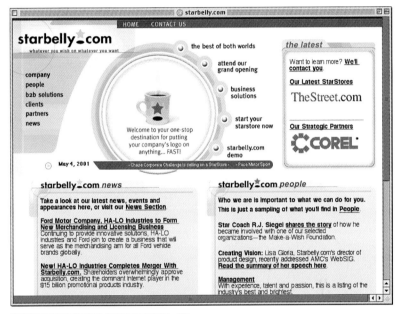

WWW.SHOP.STARBELLYORDER.COM/WELCOME/MAINoo.JSP
A: DESIGNKITCHEN, INC., M: SCOTTY@DESIGNKITCHEN.COM

WWW.SANDER.DE
D: ROLAND PECHER, C: ANSGAR KNIPSCHILD, P: KINGMEDIA/PECHER & SOIRON
A: KINGMEDIA/PECHER & SOIRON, M: SCHMIDT@UNIT-MEDIENHAUS.DE

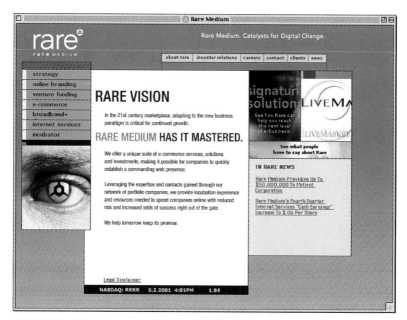

WWW.RAREMEDIUM.COM
D: STEVEN BIRGFELD
M: INFO@RAREMEDIUM.COM

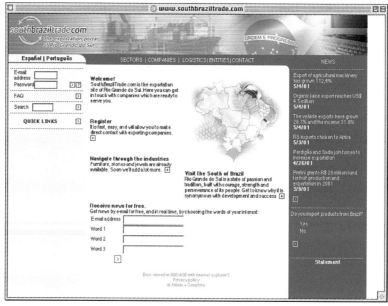

WWW.SOUTHBRAZILTRADE.COM
D: TATIANA BRUGALLI, **C:** GLADIMIR DUTRA, **P:** FABIANO DE ANDRADE
A: ALDEIA DESIGN, **M:** FABIANO@ALDEIADESIGN.COM.BR

WWW.CRITI.COM
D: JUAN MARTÍN CUCURULO, **C:** AGUSTÍN GÓMEZ VEGA, **P:** DIEGO FERRARO
M: ESTUDIO@INTERAR.COM.AR

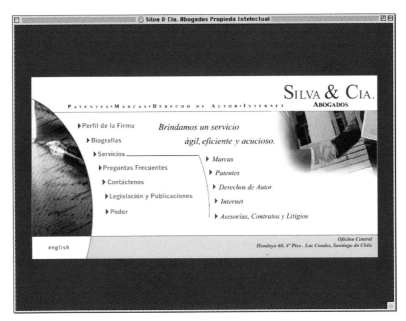

WWW.SILVA.CL
A: SILVA & CIA., ABOGADOS, M: SEBFCO@HOTMAIL.COM

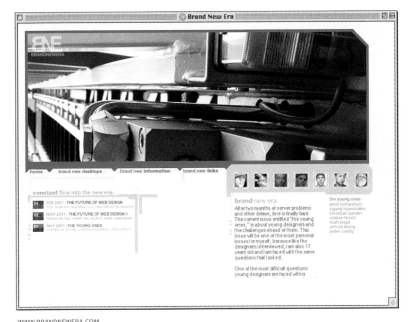

WWW.BRANDNEWERA.COM
D: GREG DURRELL, C: GREG DURRELL
M: GREG@BRANDNEWERA.COM

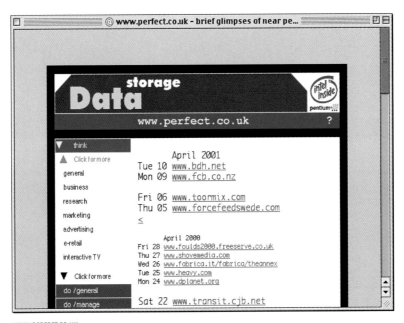

WWW.PERFECT.CO.UK
D: ROBIN GRANT
M: ROBIN@PERFECT.CO.UK

109

WWW.DEKORASYONMERKEZI.COM
A: ODAK.NET, M: KORAY@ODAK.NET

WWW.IHAVEMOVED.COM/
D: MIKE SLOCOMBE
M: MIKE@URBAN75.COM

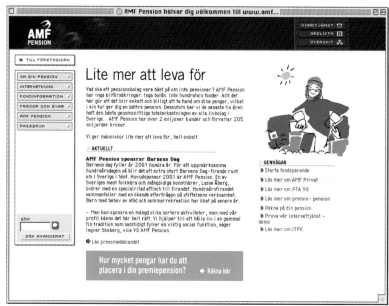

WWW.AMFPENSION.SE/WEB/WEBEDITOR.NSF
D: CHRISTEL LARSSON
M: INFO@ABELBAKER.COM

WWW.FIRSTINDEPENDENT.COM.SG/PRODUCTS_SERVICES.ASP
A: STARTECH MULTIMEDIA PTE LTD., M: EUGENE@STARTECHMM.COM

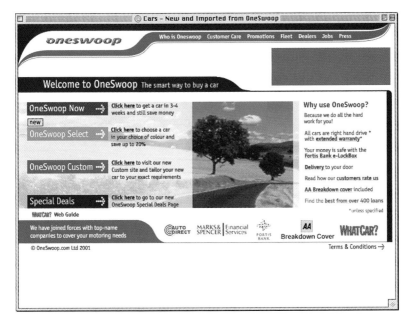

WWW.ONESWOOP.COM
A: DIGIT, M: DELYTH@DIGITLONDON.COM

WWW.PIVOTINTERIORS.COM
D: MICHAEL REED, C: JOE BAZ, P: DAN WARFIELD
A: TANGO STUDIOS, M: WARFIELD@TANGOSTUDIOS.COM

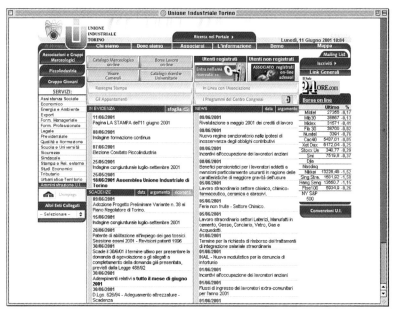

WWW.UI.TORINO.IT
D: CRISTINA BORGARELLI
A: NETHOUSE SRL, M: RELAZIONI.ESTERNE@NETHOUSE.IT

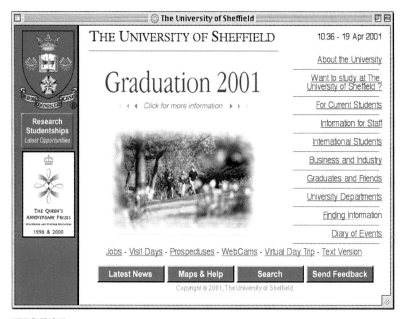

WWW.SHEF.AC.UK
D: NEIL CAMPBELL
M: N.CAMPBELL@SHEFFIELD.AC.UK

WWW.GETACARD.COM
D: SARA SHIMAN
M: SHAWNLOWRY@MINDSPRING.COM

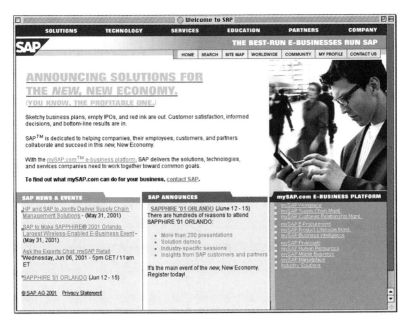

WWW.SAP.COM
A: SAP GLOBAL MARKETING

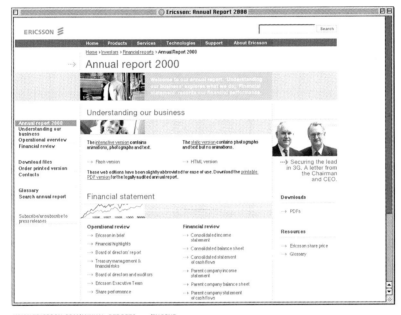

WWW.ERICSSON.COM/ANNUAL_REPORT/2000/ENG/IND
A: SAS, WWW.SASDESIGN.CO.UK, M: HROBERTS@SASDESIGN.CO.UK

WWW.GAW-ASSOCIATES.COM
A: ODAK.NET, M: KORAY@ODAK.NET

WWW.FEDNAV.COM/FLASH/A2.HTML
D: MR. EDGAR
M: CONTACT@MR-EDGAR.COM

WWW.GLOBETROTTER.DE/DE/INDEX_D.PHP3
D: JÜRGEN WEISS
M: INFO@INTERWEAVE-MEDIA.SE

WWW.BIANCHINICAPPONI.IT
D: FRANCESCA MORBIDELLI, C: FRANCESCA MORBIDELLI
A: FRANCESCA MORBIDELLI, M: FRENS@LIBERO.IT

WWW.REALDESIGN.NL
A: REALDESIGN, M: BCRINS@REALDESIGN.NL

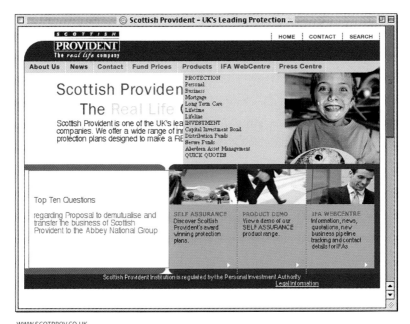

WWW.SCOTPROV.CO.UK
A: BLACK ID, M: BLACK@BLACKID.COM

195.126.141.35/SONYD8/CHECK.HTML
D: DINO FRANKE, C: JÖRG MÜLLER, P: MORE INTERACTIVE
A: DINO.FRANKE@MOREINTERACTIVE.DE

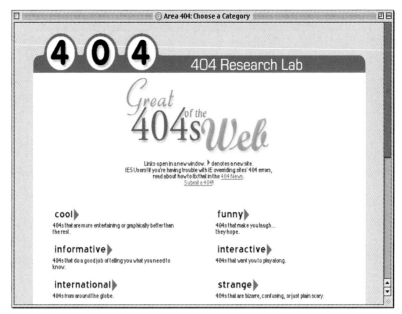

WWW.PLINKO.NET/404/AREA404.ASP
D: JENNI RIPLEY
M: J@PLINKO.NET

WWW.ELLUS.COM.BR/NEWELLUS/FLASHHOME.HTML
A: WWW.GRAFIKONSTRUCT.COM.BR, M: INFO@GRAFIKONSTRUCT.COM.B

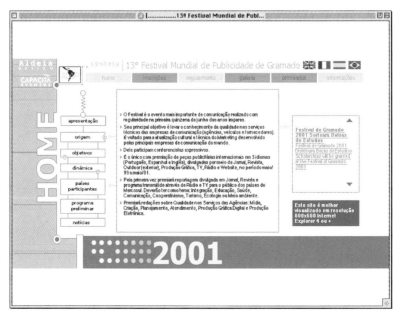

WWW.FESTIVALGRAMADO.COM
D: TATIANA BRUGALLI, C. GLADIMIR DUTRA, P: FABIANO DE ANDRADE
A: ALDEIA DESIGN, M: FABIANO@ALDEIADESIGN.COM.BR

WWW.FLAMETREE.CO.UK
D: NICK CRISTEA
A: DIGIT, M: DELYTH@DIGITLONDON.COM

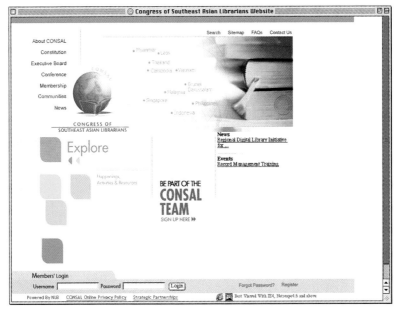

WWW.CONSAL.ORG.SG
D: IVAN M P TAN
M: IVAN.TAN@ARETAE.COM

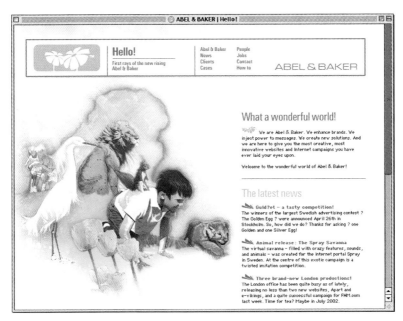

WWW.ABELBAKER.COM
D: CHRISTEL LARSSON
M: INFO@ABELBAKER.COM

WWW.HOMES.MILLER.CO.UK
A: NAVYBLUE NEW MEDIA, M: NEWMEDIA@NAVYBLUE.COM

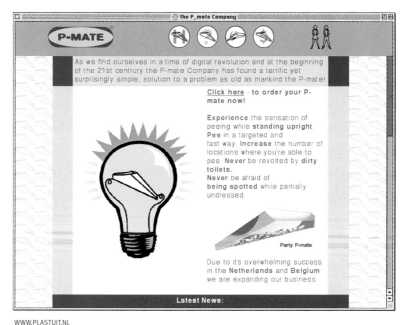

WWW.PLASTUIT.NL
D: HARTMAN
M: M.HARTMAN@WITHARTMAN.COM

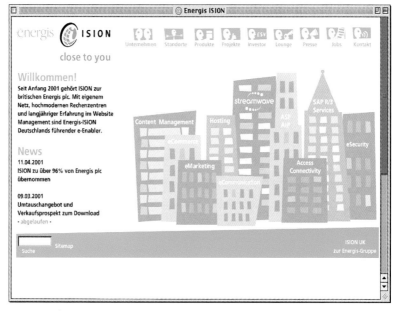

WWW.ISION.NET/GRAU-ORANGE
D: HAUKE HILLE, C: HAUKE HILLE
M: HAUKE.HILLE@ISION.NET

118

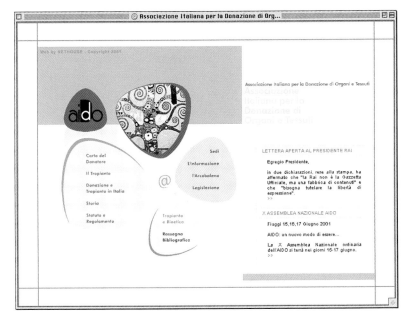

WWW.AIDO.IT
D: CRISTINA BORGARELLI
A: NETHOUSE SRL, M: RELAZIONI.ESTERNE@NETHOUSE.IT

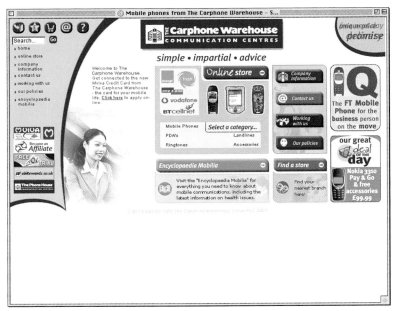

WWW.CARPHONEWAREHOUSE.COM
D: SIMON WHITEHEAD
A: ISE NET SOLUTIONS, M: WHITEHEADS@CPW.CO.UK

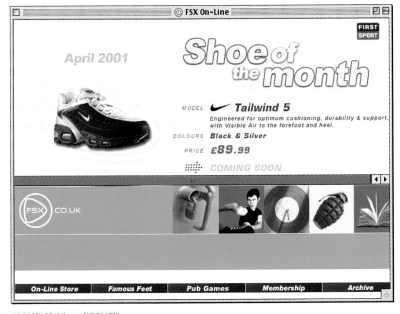

WWW.FSX.CO.UK/04_01/INDEX.HTML
A: WAX, M: JAMES.GHANI@WAX.CO.UK

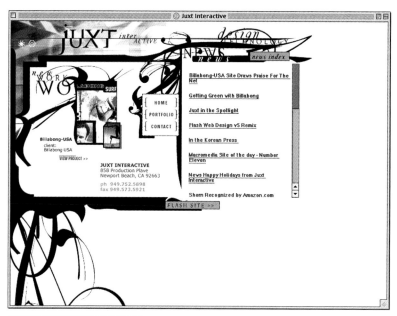

JUXTINTERACTIVE.COM/HTMLSITE/INDEX.HTML
D: TODD PURGASON
A: JUXTINTERACTIVE, M: WWW.JUXTINTERACTIVE.COM

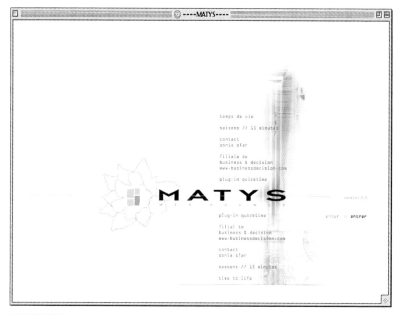

WWW.MATYS.COM
A: MATYS

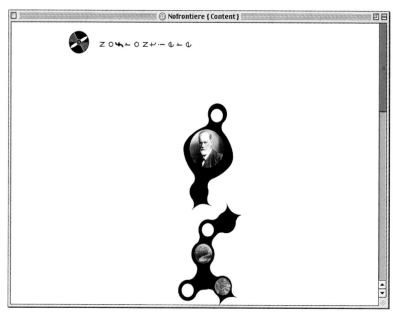

WWW.NOFRONTIERE.COM/RELEASE2_0/
D: ELKE ZIEGLER
A: NOFRONTIERE DESIGN AG , M: ASK@NOFRONTIERE.COM

WWW.BLUE-YELLOW.COM/IMO
A: BLUE & YELLOW CREATIVE, M: INFO@BLUE-YELLOW.COM

WWW.INTERNETINSPIRATIONS.COM
D: LUCAS, C: LUCAS A LICZNERSKI, P: JAMIE JOHNSON
A: INTERNET INSPIRATIONS, M: LUCAS@INTERNETINSPIRATIONS.COM

WWW.VISIBLYSHAKEN.COM
D: DUNCAN
M: CRAZYMG@HOTMAIL.COM

WWW.AWEDIGI.COM/OPTIC/ADODV2/INDEX.HTM
D: ERIC CUNNINGHAM
M: ERIC@AWEDIGI.COM

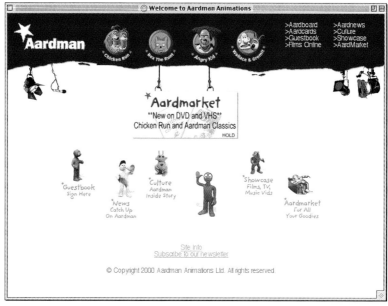

WWW.AARDMAN.COM/
A: WWW.TELEPATHY.CO.UK, M: WEB.PRODUCER@AARDMAN.COM

WWW.SEBCHEVREL.COM/WORK/INDEX.HTML
D: SEB CHEVREL
M: SEB@SEBCHEVREL.COM

WWW.VANDERZANDE.COM
D: ERWIN VAN DER ZANDE
M: INFO@VANDERZANDE.COM

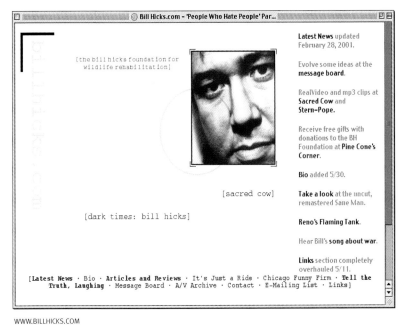

WWW.BILLHICKS.COM
D: SIMON COYLE
M: KBOOTH@AUSTIN.RR.COM

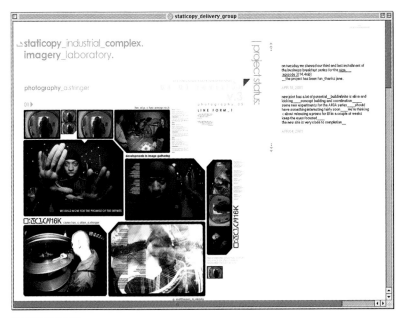

WWW.STATICOPY.COM
D: ANDRÉ STRINGER, CASSIDY GEARHART
M: VOIDONE@STATICOPY.COM

WWW.WARWICKA.CO.UK
A: WARWICKA*, **M:** A@WARWICKA.CO.UK

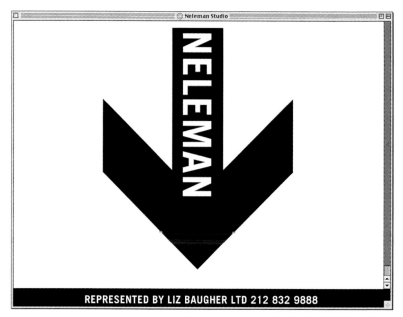

WWW.NELEMAN.COM
D: KEITH SEWARD
M: HANS@NELEMAN.COM

WWW.INTROVERSION.COM
D: PATRICK KALYANAPU
M: PATRICK@INTROVERSION.COM

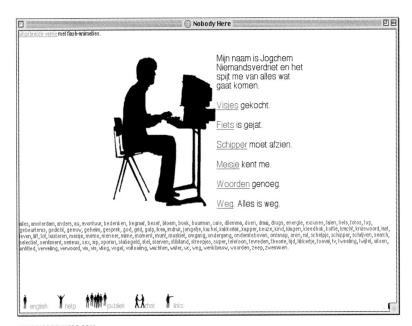

WWW.NOBODYHERE.COM
D: NOBODY HERE
M: NOBODY@NOBODYHERE.COM

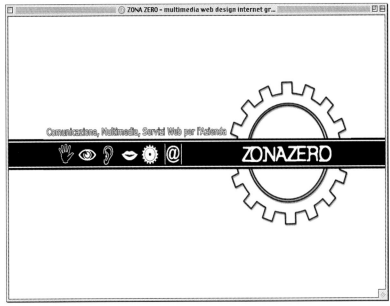

WWW.ZONAZERO.IT
C: MATTEO GRAMIGNI, P: FRANCESCO BAROCCHI
M: STEVE@ZONAZERO.IT

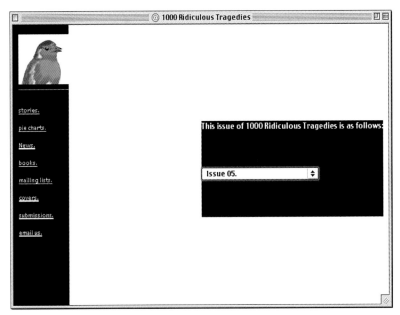

WWW.ONE38.ORG/1000/SETUP.HTML
D: ERYK SALVAGGIO
M: ONE38@ONE38.ORG

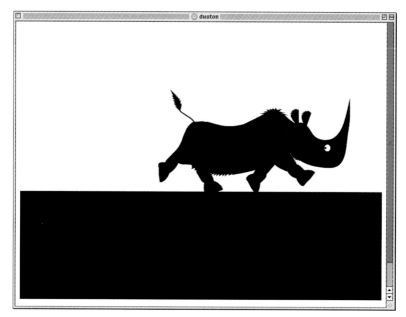

WWW.DUOTON.DE
D: RAIMOND FORKERT
M: RAIMOND@DUOTON.DE

WWW.FUNKBONE.NU
D: KENGO SUGIOKA
M: RADIO@FUNKBONE.NU

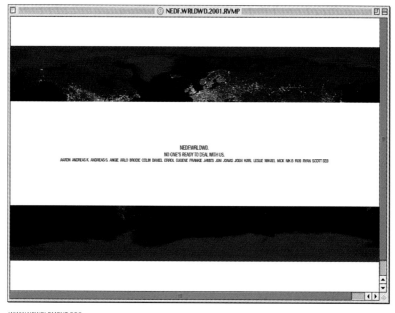

WWW.NEWELEMENT.ORG
D: FRANK MILLER, **C:** FRANK MILLER
M: FMILLER@OWLNET.RICE.EDU

WWW.NOBDESIGN.COM
D: YUJI, MORI, C: YUJI, MORI
M: DA@NOBDESIGN.COM

WWW.URBAN75.CO
D: MIKE SLOCOMBE
M: MIKE@URBAN75.COM

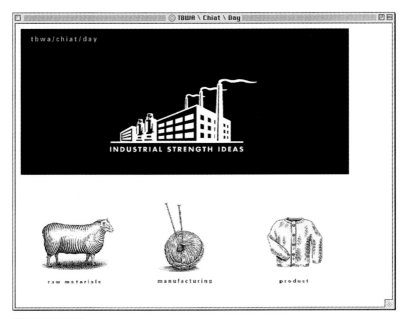

WWW.TBWACHIAT.COM
D: DOUG JAEGER, C: ADRIAN LAFOND

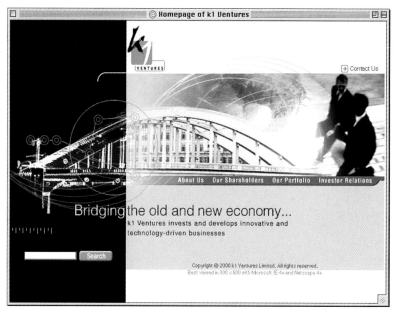

WWW.K1VENTURES.COM
D: IVAN M. P. TAN
A: ARETAE LTD, **M:** IVAN.TAN@ARETAE.COM

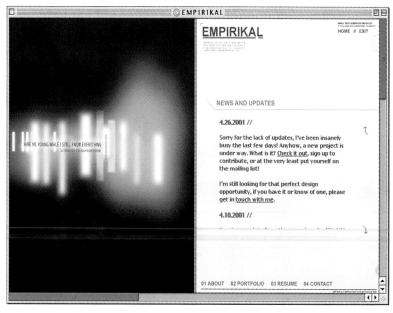

WWW.EMPIRIKAL.COM
D: GABE RUBIN
M: GABE@EMPIRIKAL.COM

WWW.MYM-MODA.COM
D: JULIO LOAYZA, **C:** FRANCOIS CASTRO, **P:** MARCOS BELLO
A: DIGITAL DAWN, **M:** WEBMASTER@DAWNWEB.COM

WWW.INGEN.ORG
D: RICH CROFT
M: GEEK-BOY@DORK.COM

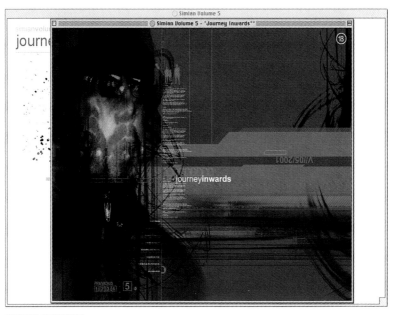

WWW.IKDA.CO.UK/SIMIAN
C: ROSS MAWDSLEY, P: ROSS MAWDSLEY
M: INFO@IKDA.CO.UK

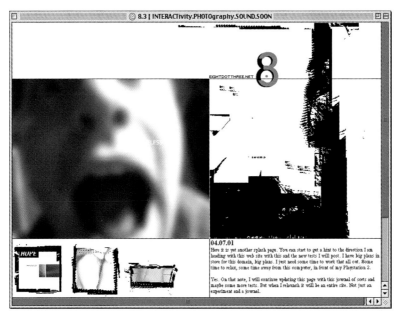

WWW.EIGHTDOTTHREE.NET
D: RYAN SPRAKE, C: RYAN SPRAKE
A: 8IGHT.3HREE, M: RYAN@EIGHTDOTTHREE.NET

151.196.214.41/FRAME_ST.HTML
A: CUBUSíMEDIA, M: CUBUS@CUBUSMEDIA.COM

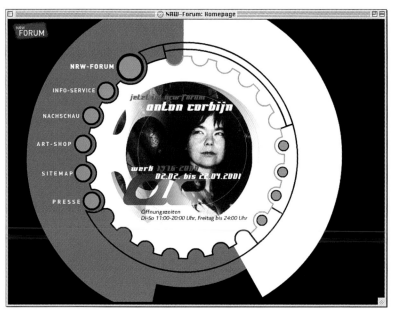

WWW.NRW-FORUM.DE
D: KATRIN BRACKMANN, C: MATTHIAS KOSLOWSKI, P: WERNER LIPPERT
A: ONLINE RELATIONS, M: KA@OZ-ZONE.DE

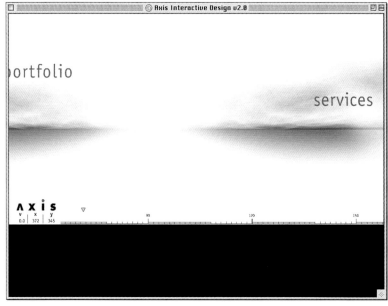

WWW.AXIS-MEDIA.COMí
A: AXIS INTERACTIVE DESIGN INC., M: DESIGN@AXIS-MEDIA.COM

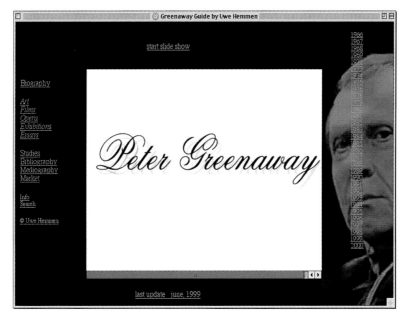

WWW.GREENAWAY.DE
D: UWE HEMMEN, C: UWE HEMMEN
M: HEMMEN@WORLDS4.COM

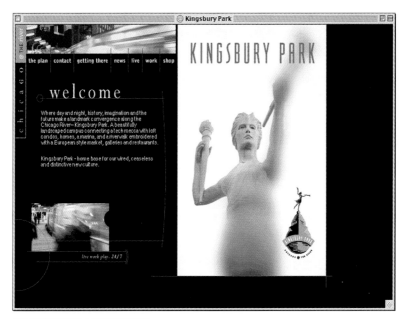

WWW.KINGSBURYPARK.COM/WELCOME.HTML
A: DESIGNKITCHEN, INC., M: SCOTTY@DESIGNKITCHEN.COM

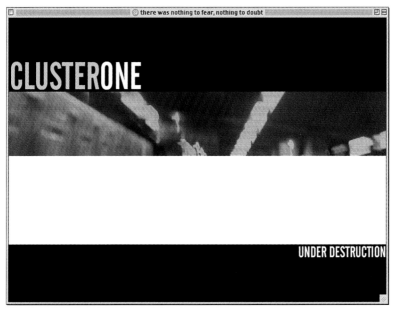

WWW.ILLUSIONMW.COM
C: ADRIANO SANTI, P: ADRIANO SANTI
M: ADSANTI@NETFLASH.COM.BR

WWW.ELOGIC.COM.SG
P: ALFRED QUEK
A: OPENTIDE, M: SKIN@PACIFIC.NET.SG

WWW.EXCELERATETECH.NET
D: AVINASH GITE, C: AVINASH GITE
A: INDIA DOMAIN, M: TUBY_20@YAHOO.COM

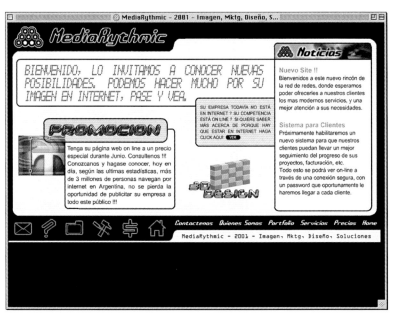

WWW.MEDIARYTHMIC.COM
D: ANTON CHALBAUD, C: ANTON CHALBAUD, P: MEDIARYTHMIC
A: MEDIARYTHMIC

WWW.TV.CARLTON.COM/BRITAINATWAR/MAIN.HTML
A: ATTIK.COM, M: TRACEYT@ATTIK.COM

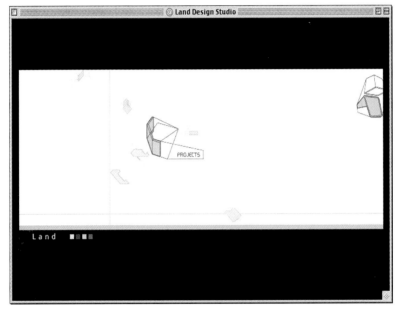

WWW.LANDDESIGNSTUDIO.CO.UK
D: SIMON SANKARAYYA
A: DIGIT, M: DELYTH@DIGITLONDON.COM

WWW.DRAMBUIE.COM/HOME.HTML
A: NAVYBLUE NEW MEDIA, M: NEWMEDIA@NAVYBLUE.COM

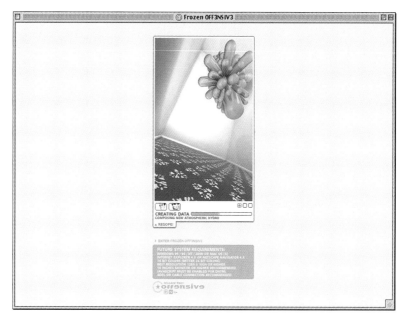

WWW.NEENEENEE.DE/PIXEL
D: ANDRE STUBBE
M: JGORMAN@GMX.NET

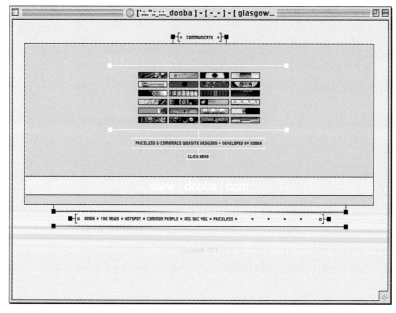

WWW.DOOBA.COM
A: DOOBA , **M:** OT@DOOBA.COM

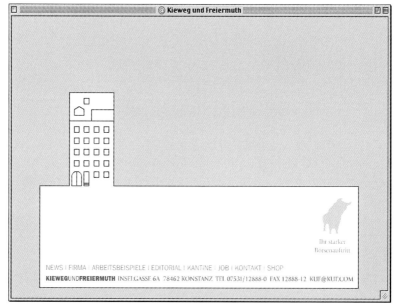

WWW.KUF.COM/KUF_WEB/KUFINDEX.HTML
D: TOBIAS SEYDEL, **C:** TOBIAS SEYDEL, **P:** KIEWEG UND FREIERMUTH
M: TSEYDEL@KUF.COM

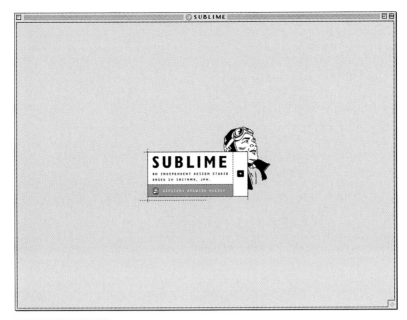

WWW.SUBLIMEGRAPHICS.COM
D: KEITA MATSUBARA
M: INFO@SUBLIMEGRAPHICS.COM

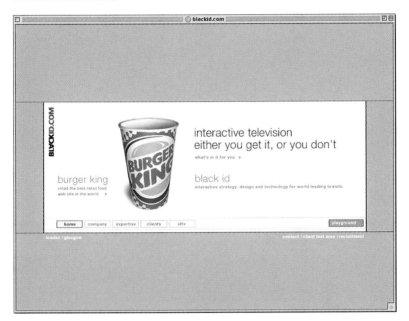

WWW.BLACKID.COM
A: BLACK ID, **M:** BLACK@BLACKID.COM

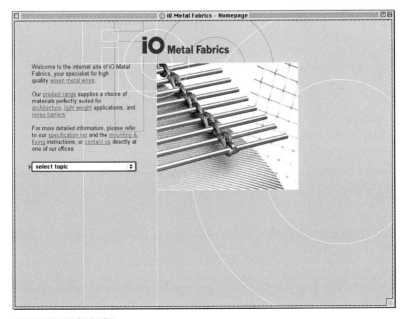

WWW.IO-METAL.COM/INDEX.HTML
D: CHRISTOPH MÜLLER, **C:** GERD BRÜNIG
A: VORSICHT

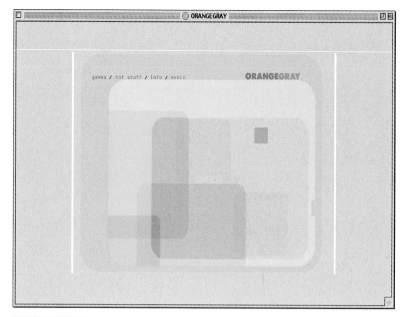

WWW.ORANGEGRAY.COM
D: F.BEIER, C: F.BEIER
M: INFO@ORANGEGRAY.COM

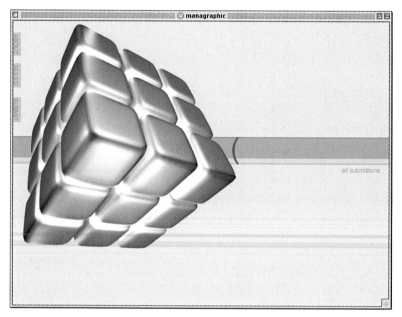

WWW.MANAGRAPHIC.COM
D: MAT POPROCKI, C: STEPHEN POPROCKI, P: MAT POPROCKI
M: WEBMASTER@INFERIORDESGIN.COM

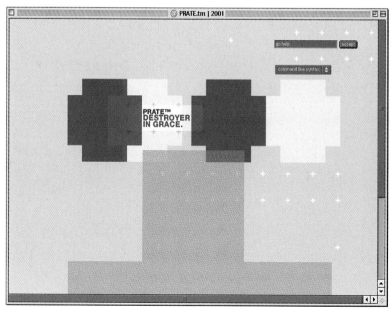

WWW.PRATE.COM
D: JEMMA GURA, C: JEMMA GURA,
M: LENTIL@PRATE.COM

136

WWW.ADD.JP.ORG
D: ATSUSHI AOKI
A: ADD, M: AOKI@ADD.JP.ORG

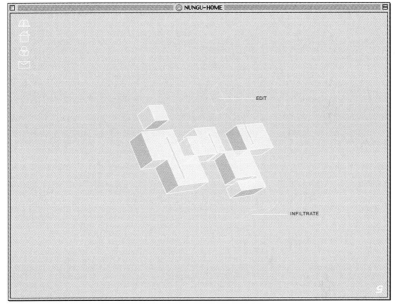

WWW.NUNGU.COM
D: KURNAL RAWAT, C: SHRINIVAS KINI, P: BEATRICE GIBSON
A: GRANDMOTHER INDIA, M: TEJASMANGESHKAR@YAHOO.COM

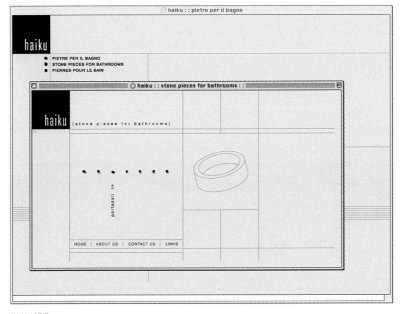

WWW.LBT.IT
D: BALLESTRACCI ROBERTO, C: CALLEGARI MARCO, P: LBT
M: ARCOHAAB@HOTMAIL.COM

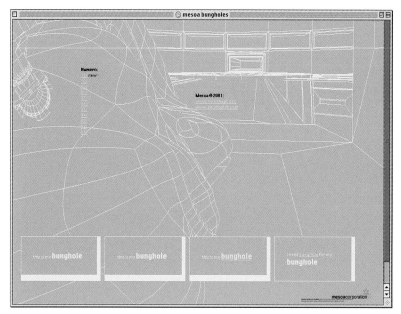

WWW.MESOA.COM
D: BENNY BLANCO
M: JUKKA@MESOA.COM

WWW.FORK.DE
D: OEL@DEPART.AT
A: FORK UNSTABLE MEDIA, **M**: INFO@FORK.DE

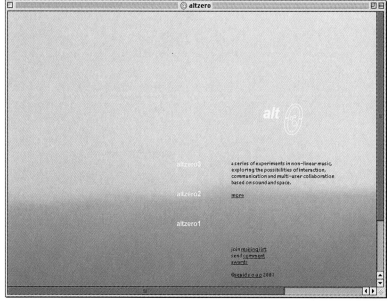

WWW.ALTZERO.COM
A: SQUID S O U P, **M**: ANT@SQUIDSOUP.COM

WWW.ALTERPATH.COM/HOME.HTML
D: ANYA MEDVEDEVA
M: WORKWISE@ALTERPATH.COM

WWW.ANCIENTARTZ.COM
D: CHADWICK SHAO
A: ANCIENTARTZ, **M:** CHADWICK@ANCIENTARTZ.COM

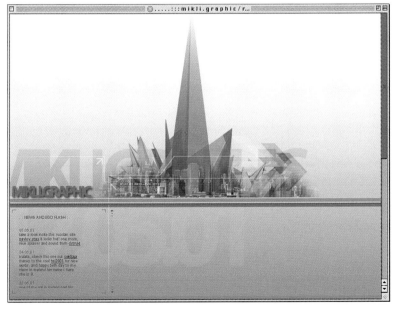

WWW.MIKLI.NET
D: MUMMI, **C:** MUMMI
A: MIKLI.GRAPHIC, **M:** MIKLI@KAGSAA.DK

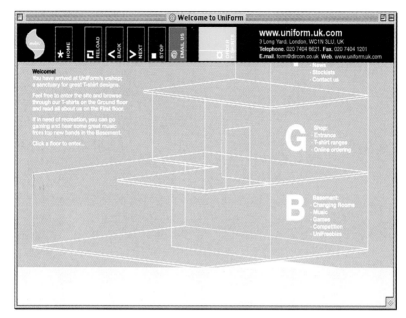

WWW.UNIFORM.UK.COM
D: PAULA BENSON
A: FORM®, M: FORM@DIRCON.CO.UK

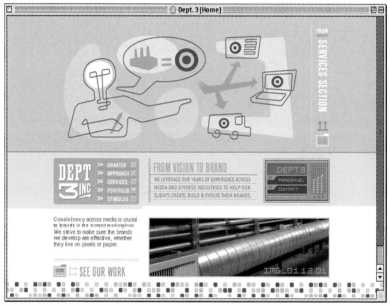

WWW.DEPT3.COM
D: MATTHEW CARLSON, C: NATE KOECHLEY, P: GUTHRIE DOLIN
M: GU3@DEPT3.COM

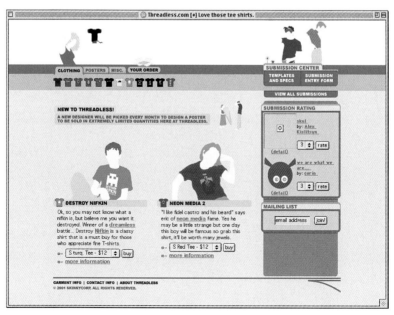

WWW.THREADLESS.COM
D: JAKE NICKELL
M: WAR@THREADLESS.COM

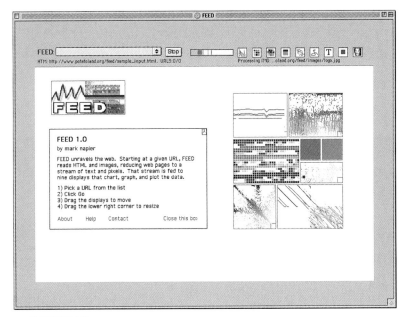

WWW.POTATOLAND.ORG
P: COMISSED BY SAN FRANCISCO MUSEUM OF MODERN ART, PRESENTED BY INTEL
M: NAPIER@INTERPORT.NET

WWW.AMIGOINGDOWN.COM
D: KIP PARKER
M: INFORMATION@AMIGOINGDOWN.COM

WWW.LOTTORNA.SE
A: WWW.HALLABALOO.SE, M: INFO@HALLABALOO.SE

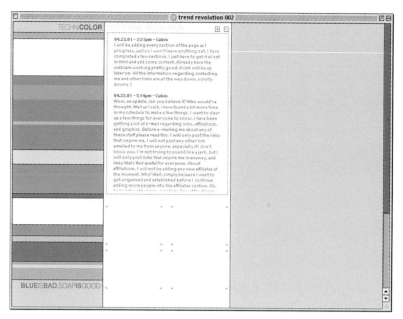

WWW.CUBICGFX.COM/INDEX2.HTML
D: MIGUEL A. ARIAS
M: CUBIC@CUBICGFX.COM

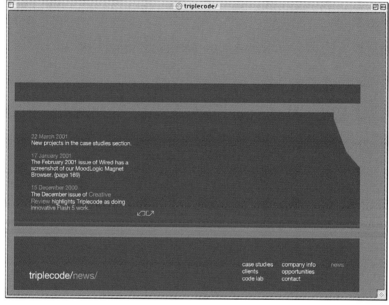

WWW.TRIPLECODE.COM/WEB_02/MAIN.HTML
A: TRIPLECODE, M: DYOUNG@TRIPLECODE.COM

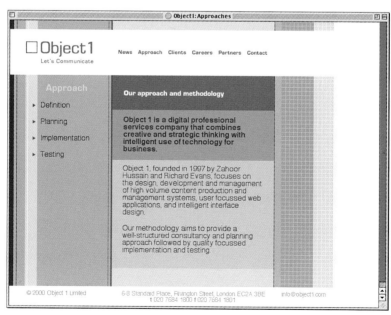

WWW.OBJECT1.COM/APPROACHES
D: TOM EVANS
M: INFO@OBJECT1.COM

WWW.EYEGLASSES.COM/INDEX.PAGE
D: JAMES HILFORD
M: COMMENTS@EYEGLASSES.COM

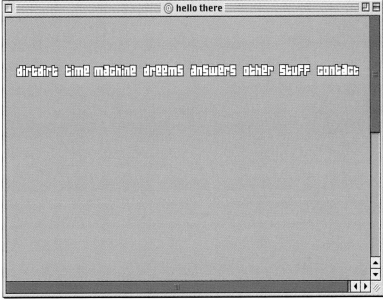

WWW.DIRTDIRT.COM
D: CHRIS STANGLAND, C: CHRIS STANGLAND
M: CHRIS@DIRTDIRT.COM

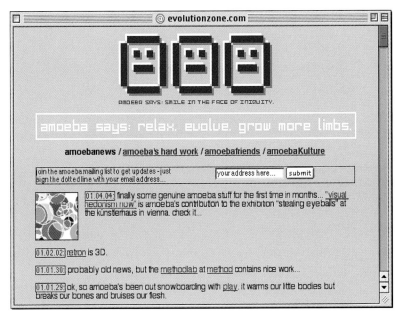

WWW.EVOLUTIONZONE.COM
D: MARIUS WATZ
M: AMOEBA@EVOLUTIONZONE.COM

WWW.BIGB.COM
D: BRAD VASSEY
M: BVASSEY@YAHOO.COM

WWW.TWOTHIRTY.COM
D: PAUL JARVIS, C: PAUL JARVIS
M: INFO@TWOTHIRTY.COM

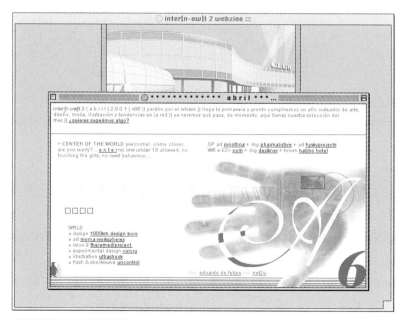

WWW.NET2UONLINE.COM/INTERNOWT
D: EDUARDO DE FELIPE, C: EDUARDO DE FELIPE
A: NET2U, M: EFELIPE@SVALERO.ES

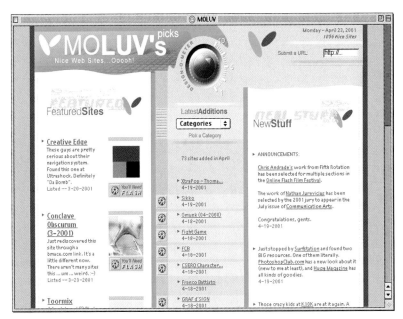

WWW.MOLUV.COM
C: MAURICE WRIGHT, P: MAURICE WRIGHT
M: MAURICE@MOLUV.COM

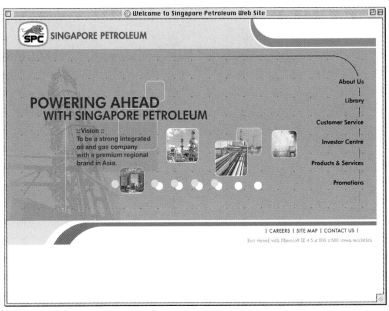

WWW.SPC.COM.SG
D: IVAN M P TAN, C: JOSOPHINE POH
M: IVAN.TAN@ARETAE.COM

WWW.TAIYUP.COM
M: TYK70@TAIYUP.COM

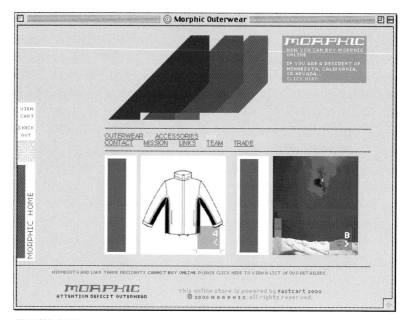

WWW.MORPHIC1.COM
D: MIKE CINA
M: INFO@TRUEISTRUE.COM

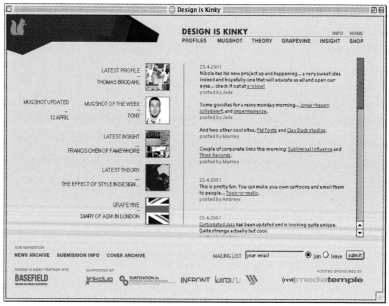

WWW.DESIGNISKINKY.NET/INDEX_MAIN.HTML
D: ANDREW JOHNSTONE
M: INSIGHT@DESIGNISKINKY.NET, DIK@DESIGNISKINKY.NET

WWW.DADAKO.COM
D: HAWKEN BRIGHT-ROBERTS
M: HAWKEN@DADAKO.COM

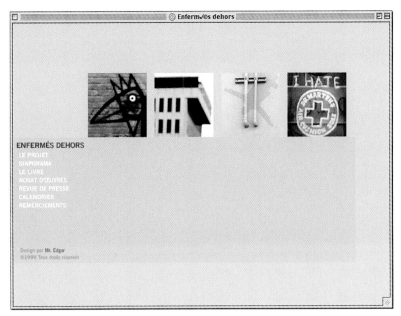

WWW.MR-EDGAR.COM/ENFERMES
D: MR.EDGAR
M: CONTACT@MR-EDGAR.COM

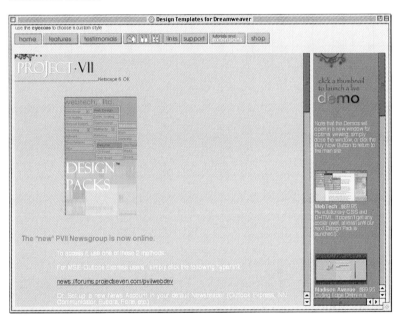

WWW.PROJECTSEVEN.COM/MAGIC
D: AL SPARBER

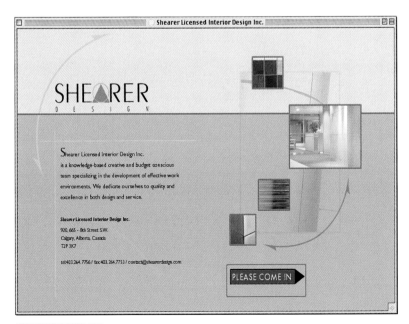

WWW.SHEARERDESIGN.COM
D: JAMES LEAL-VALIAS, **C:** JAMES LEAL-VALIAS
M: JAMES@TAG-ADVERTISING.COM

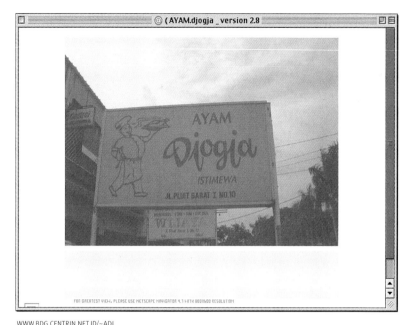

WWW.BDG.CENTRIN.NET.ID/~ADJ
C: DANIEL YANG, P: DANIEL YANG
A: ORANGECIRCLE, M: DANIEL@ORANGECIRCLE.NET

WWW.JAPON.TO/@/
D: YUSUKE ANZAI
A: FONTSTUDIO @, M: ANZAI@JAPON.TO

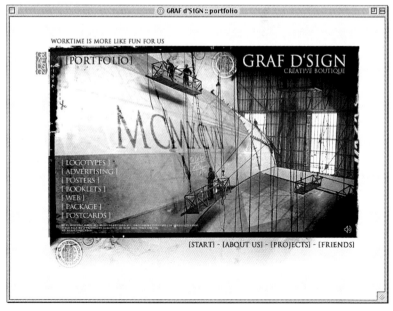

WWW.GDSCB.COM/ENGLISH/PORTFOLIO/INDEX.HTML
A: GRAF D'SIGN, M: INBOX@GDSCB.COM

WWW.LESSRAIN.DE
C: THOMAS MEYER, P: THOMAS MEYER
A: LESS RAIN, M: LARS@LESSRAIN.COM

WWW.ETC.ETC.FREE.FR/LOLITA.HTM
D: GILLES RAYNALDY

WWW.WEBPRODUCTIONS.COM
D: STEVE GIOVINCO
M: INFO@WEBPRODUCTIONS.COM

149

WWW.SPORT-UND-KULTURMARKETING.DE
D: DIRK PÄTZOLD, C: THOMAS LANGE, P: NETRESEARCH GMBH & CO KG
A: NETRESEARCH GMBH & CO KG, M: MA@NETRESEARCH.DE

WWW.MARC-KLEIN.COM/FS_HOME.HTML
D: MARC KLEÍN
M: CREATOR@MARC-KLEIN.COM

WWW.KEMPERS.NET/NAVIGATION
A: MORE INTERACTIVE, M: INFO@MOREINTERACTIVE.DE

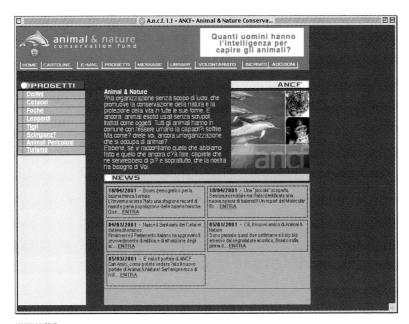

WWW.ANCF.IT
D: GUERINO DELFINO
M: DELFINO@HYPHEN.IT

WWW.160-ZEICHEN.DE
D: HARALD MÜLLER
M: HARALD@MULLER.DE

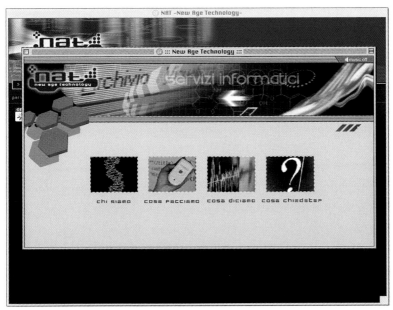

WWW.NAT.IT
C: OSCAR ANTINO, P: NEW AGE TECHNOLOGY
M: OSCAR@NAT.IT

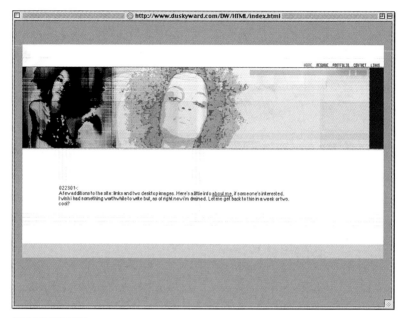

WWW.DUSKYWARD.COM
C: JOEL KELLEY
M: RAYROBINSON@MEDIAONE.NET

WWW.SOUNTAIN.COM/BRO/INDEX.HTML
D: YOUSUKE ABE
M: INFO@SOUNTAIN.COM

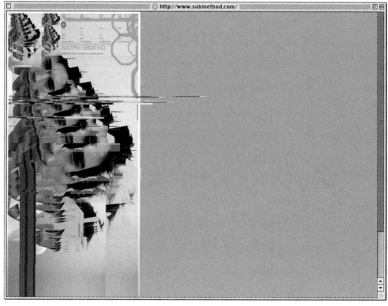

WWW.SUBMETHOD.COM
D: MIKE YOUNG
A: DESIGNGRAPHIK, M: MIKE@DESIGNGRAPHIK.COM

WWW.STEREOLAB.CO.UK
D: KLEBER

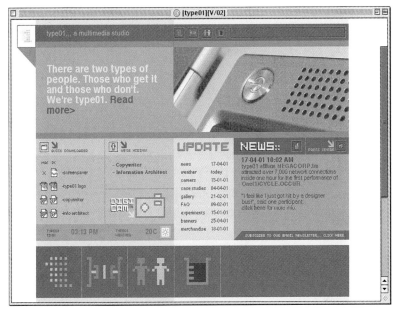

WWW.TYPE01.COM
D: DAMIAN STEPHENS
A: TYPE01, M: INFO@TYPE01.COM

WWW.EINHORN.DE/START.HTML
D: SEBASTIAN SCHIER
M: BASTI@AGI.DE

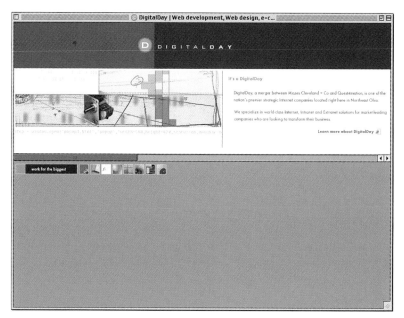

WWW.DIGITAL-DAY.COM
D: HOWARD CLEVELAND
M: HOWARDC@DIGITAL-DAY.COM

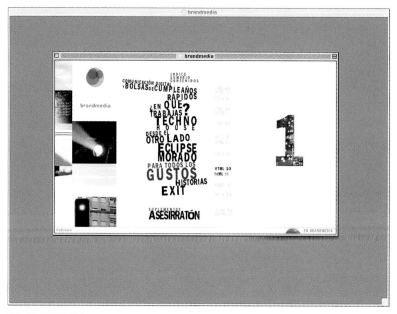

WWW.BRANDMEDIA.COM
A: EQUIPO BRANDMEDIA, M: INFO@BRANDMEDIA.COM

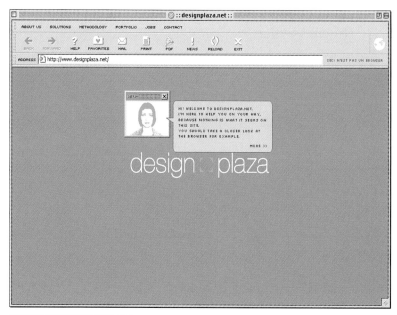

WWW.DESIGNPLAZA.NET/BROWSER.HTM
D: HERMAN VAN DURME
M: HERMAN.VAN.DURME@BE.ARTHURANDERSEN.COM

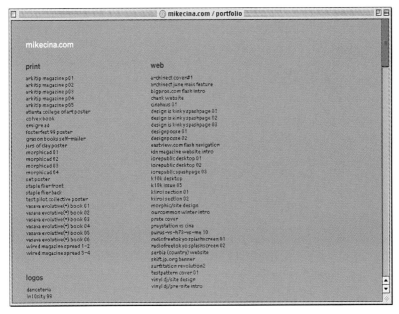

WWW.MIKECINA.COM/INDEX2.HTML,
D: MIKE CINA
M: INFO@TRUEISTRUE.COM

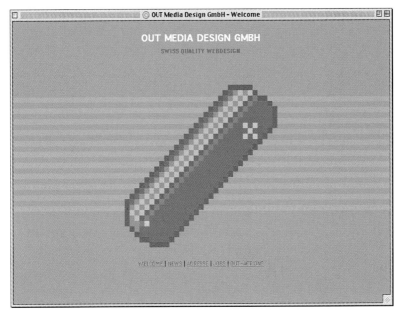

WWW.OUT.TO
D: URS MEYER, **C:** URS MEYER, **P:** OUT MEDIA DESIGN GMBH
M: URS@OUT.TO

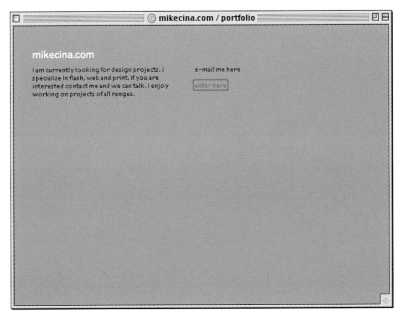

WWW.MIKECINA.COM
D: MICHAEL CINA
M: INFO@TRUEISTRUE.COM

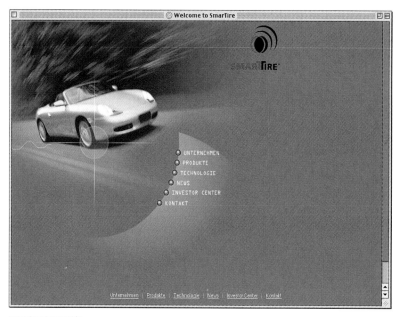

WWW.SMARTIRE.COM/FL
A: AXIS INTERACTIVE DESIGN INC., M: DESIGN@AXIS-MEDIA.COM

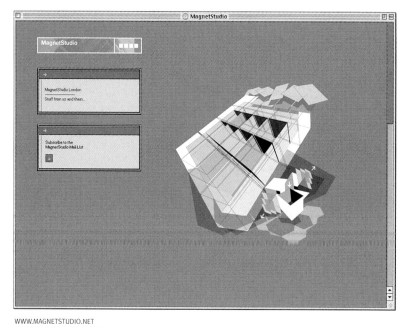

WWW.MAGNETSTUDIO.NET
D: JON BLACK, C: JON BLACK
A: MAGNET DESIGN, M: JON@MAGNETSTUDIO.NET

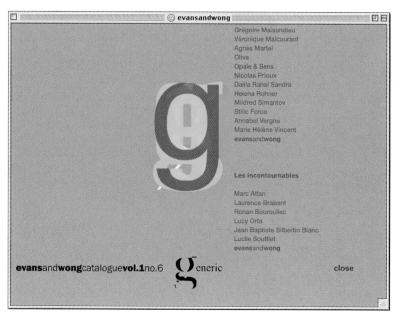

WWW.EANDW.COM
A: SPILL INDUSTRIES, M: CONTACT@SPILL.NET

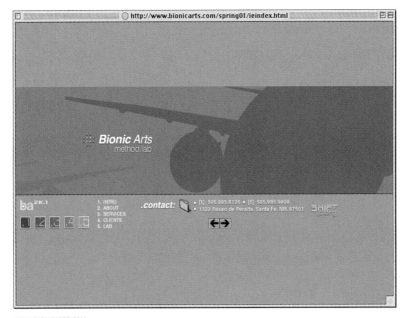

WWW.BIONICARTS.COM
D: ERIN STAFFEL
A: BIONIC ARTS INC., M: ERIN@BIONICARTS.COM

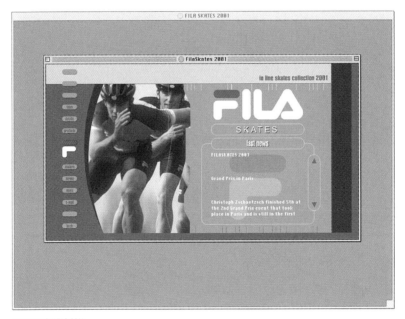

WWW.FILASKATES.COM
D: MICHELE GUGLIELMIN
A: SEVEN S.R.L.

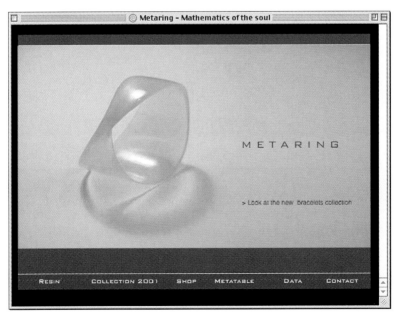

WWW.METARING.COM
D: PHILIPP MOHR
A: METARING INC, M: INFO@METARING.COM

WWW.LINDKVIST.COM/MAIN.HTML
D: ANDREAS LINDKVIST
M: ANDREAS@LINDKVIST.COM

WWW.GANODESIGN.IT
D: GANO, C: GANO, P: GANODESIGN
A: GANODESIGN, M: GANO@GANODESIGN.IT

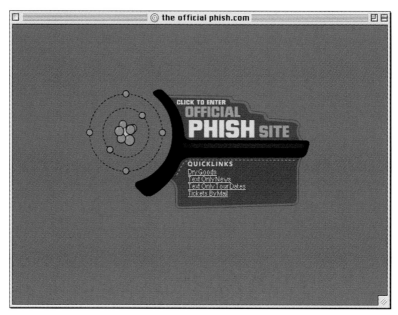

WWW.PHISH.COM
D: MATTHEW RICHMOND, C: TOBY BOUDREAUX, P: KEITH PIZER
M: DARLEEN@CHOPPINGBLOCK.COM

158

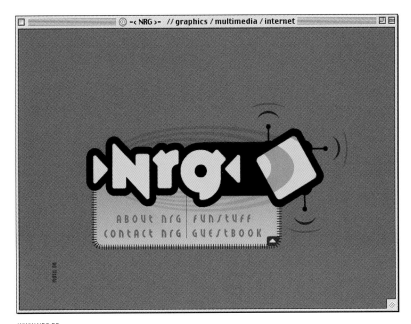

WWW.NRG.BE
D: PETER VAN DEN WYNGAERT
M: PETER@NRG.BE

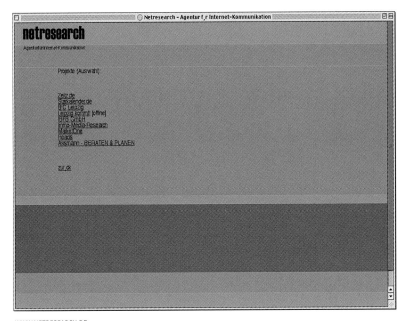

WWW.NETRESEARCH.DE
D: DIRK PÄTZOLD, **C:** THOMAS LANGE, **P:** NETRESEARCH GMBH & CO KG
A: NETRESEARCH GMBH & CO KG, **M:** MA@NETRESEARCH.DE

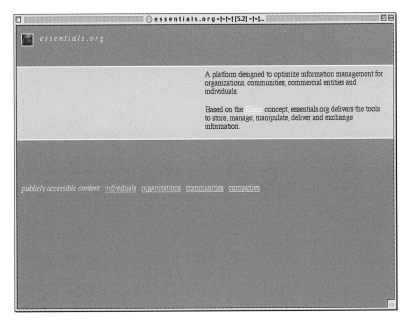

WWW.ESSENTIALS.ORG
A: ARIAS WEB DESIGN, **M:** GOOSE@ESSENTIALS.ORG

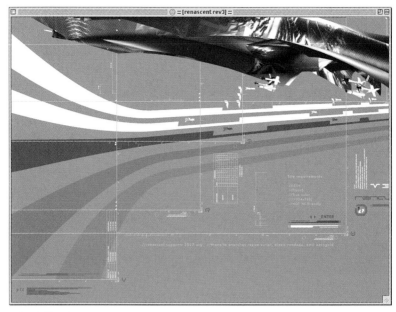

WWW.RENASCENT.NL
D: JOOST KORNGOLD
M: JKORNGOLD@FCICONNECT.COM

WWW.DECO-VISION.DE
M: ANDREW@DECO-VISION.DE

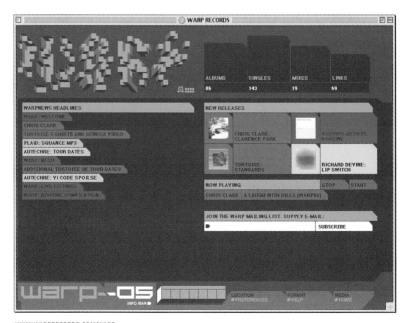

WWW.WARPRECORDS.COM/WARP
D: THE DESIGNERS REPUBLIC & KLEBER
M: CAROLINE@KLEBER.NET

WWW.ALVEZEXPRESIONES.CJB.NET
D: ANNA MARIA LOPEZ LOPEZ, C: ANNA MARIA LOPEZ LOPEZ
M: ANNA@FASHIONMAS.COM

WWW.VASAVA.ES/MINIWEB
A: VASAVA ARTWORKS, M: VASAVA@VASAVA.ES

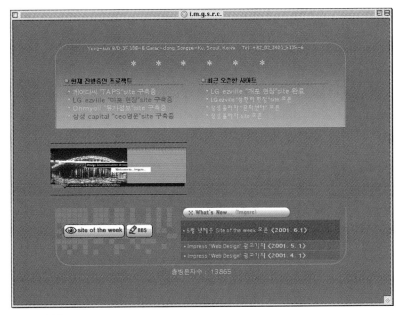

WWW.IMGSRC.CO.KR
D: JUNG HEA, PEANG, C: JUNG HEA, PEANG
A: IMGSRC, M: IMGSRC@IMGSRC.CO.KR

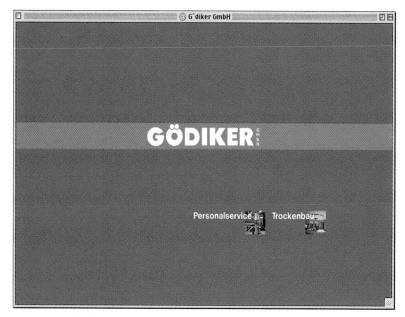

WWW.GOEDIKER.DE/FLASH/INDEX.HTML
D: UWE HEMMEN, **C:** UWE HEMMEN
M: HEMMEN@WORLDS4.COM

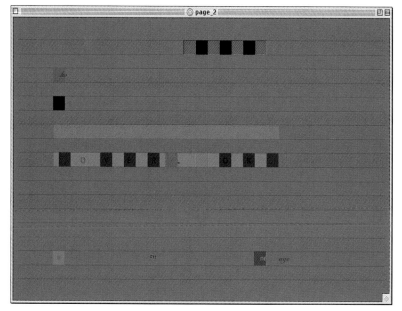

WWW.RE-MADE.COM
D: PHILIPPE LEJEUNE
M: LEJEUNE@CAPE.COM

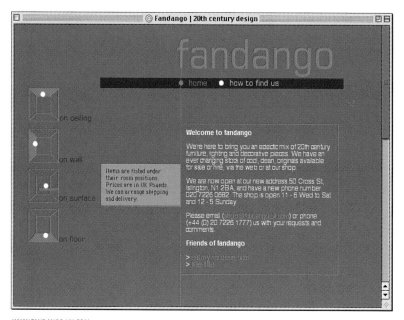

WWW.FANDANGO.UK.COM
D: MARIE EMMOTT, **C:** TRALIA DIGITAL
M: ADMIN@TRALLADIGITAL.CO.UK

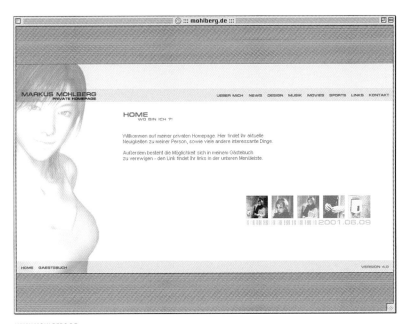

WWW.MOHLBERG.DE
D: MARKUS MOHLBERG, C: MARKUS MOHLBERG

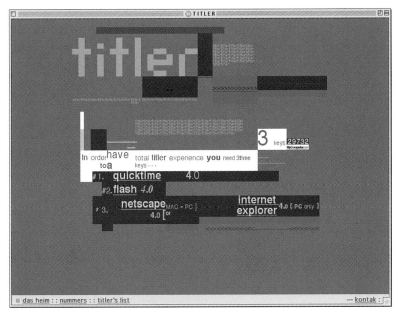

WWW.TITLER.COM
D: MURAT BODUR
A: WWW.MURATDESIGN.COM, M: MURAT@MURATDESIGN.COM

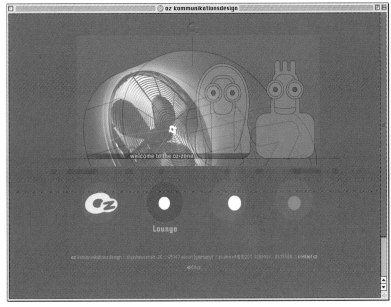

WWW.OZ-ZONE.DE
D: K+C BRACKMANN, C: K+C BRACKMANN, P: K+C BRACKMANN

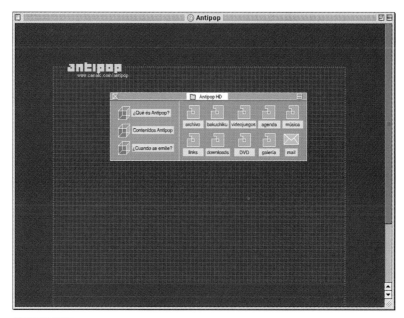

WWW.CANALC.COM
A: VASAVA ARTWORKS, M: VASAVA@VASAVA.ES

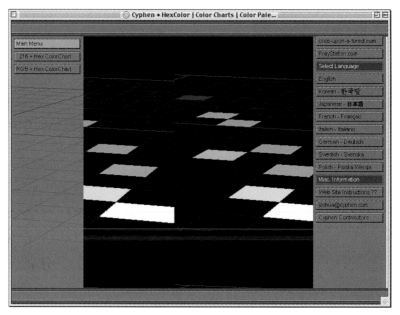

WWW.CYPHEN.COM/INDEX_POPUP.HTML
D: JOSHUA DAVIS
M: JOSHUA@CYPHEN.COM

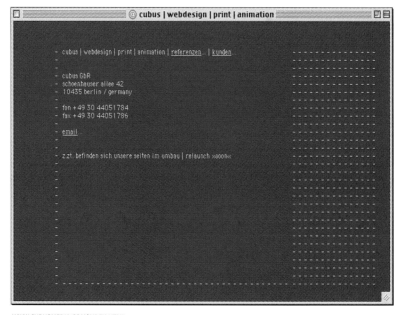

WWW.CUBUSMEDIA.COM/INDEX.HTML
A: CUBUSIMEDIA, M: CUBUS@CUBUSMEDIA.COM

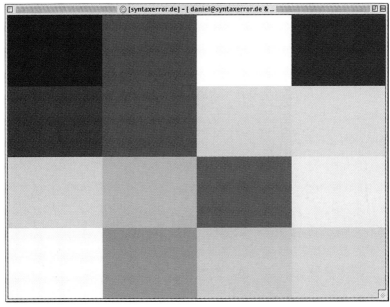

WWW.SYNTAXERROR.DE
D: DANIEL LETTMAYER
M: DANIEL@SYNTAXERROR.DE, KAI@SYNTAXERROR.DE

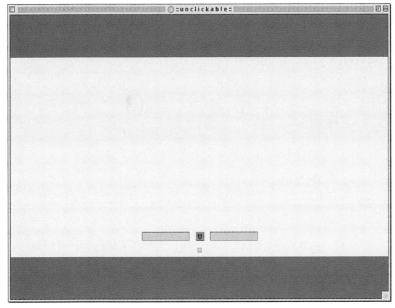

WWW.UNCLICKABLE.COM
A: UNCLICKABLE, LTD., M: CLICK@UNCLICKABLE.COM

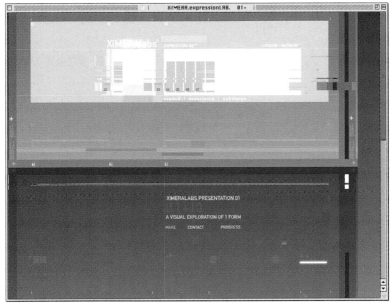

WWW.XIMERALABS.COM/PLUS01.HTML
A: XIMERA, M: DAVIDJOHNSSON@YAHOO.COM

WWW.SUTURE.NET
D: RICKY COX
A: SUTURE NET,, M: INFO@SUTURE.NET

WWW.PULLBEAR.COM
A: VASAVA ARTWORKS + XNOGRAFICS, M: VASAVA@VASAVA.ES

WWW.JOHNSTEINBERGHAIR.COM/FLA/INDEXB.HTML
A: STUDIO:CMD [ACTIVE MEDIA], M: INFO@STUDIOCMD.COM

WWW.ARHAUS.COM/FRAMESET.HTML
D: HOWARD CLEVELAND
M: HOWARDC@DIGITAL-DAY.COM

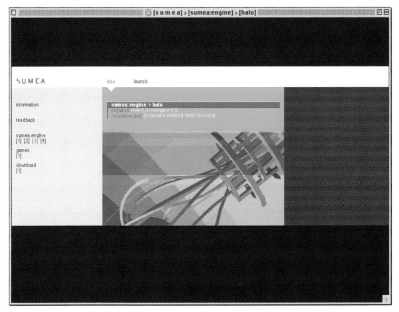

WWW.SUMEA.COM
D: SAMI AROLA
M: SAMI@SUMEA.COM, JARKKO@SUMEA.COM

WWW.BEERFOTO.COM/PORTRAITS
D: PACO LA LUCA, C: PACO LA LUCA
A: BAMBOO-PRODUCTIONS BCN, M: OFFICE.BCN@BAMBOO-PRODUCTIONS.COM

167

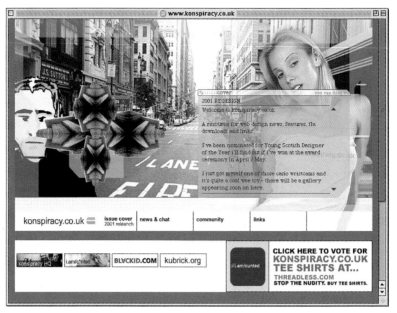

WWW.KONSPIRACY.CO.UK
D: AARON HARPER, C: AARON HARPER
A: KONSPIRACY.CO.UK, M: AARON@KONSPIRACY.CO.UK

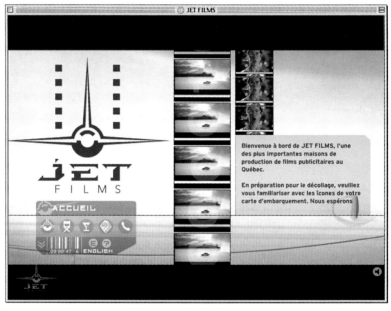

WWW.JETFILMS.COM
D: MR. EDGAR
M: CONTACT@MR-EDGAR.COM

WWW.DAVIDBEAN.NET
D: DAVID BEAN, C: DAVID BEAN
A: DAVIDBEAN.NET

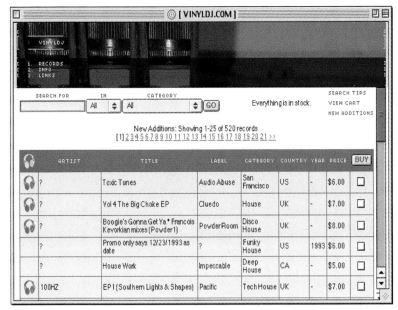

WWW.VINYLDJ.COM
D: MIKE CINA
M: INFO@TRUEISTRUE.COM

WWW.GETOUTTHERE.BT.COM/INDEX2.CFM
A: WWW.SASDESIGN.CO.UK, M: HROBERTS@SASDESIGN.CO.UK

WWW.WORLD-DIRECT.COM/GIA
D: MARKUS HÜBNER, C: MARKUS HÜBNER
A: WORLD-DIRECT.COM, M: OFFICE@WORLD-DIRECT.COM

WWW.LIVINGLUXURY.COM
D: ANDREAS GUMM
M: AGUMM@LIVINGLUXURY.DE

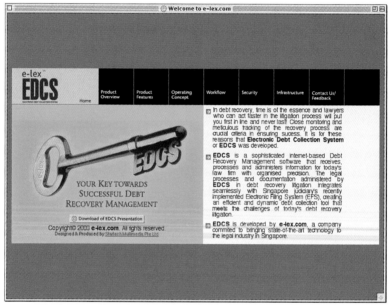

WWW.E-LEX.COM.SG
A: STARTECH MULTIMEDIA PTE LTD., M: EUGENE@STARTECHMM.COM

WWW.SOULBATH.COM/WALLS/WALLo8.HTML
D: JUDSON FRONDORF
M: FRONDORF@APS.EDU

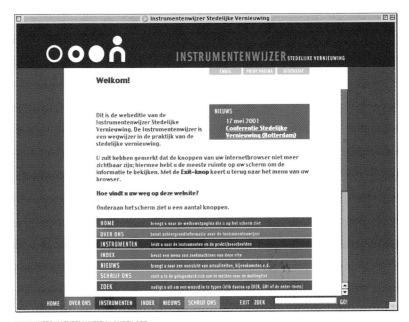

WWW.INSTRUMENTENWIJZER.NL/INDEX.ASP
D: SOLAR, C: MARINUS KUIVENHOVEN, P: BRAM CRINS
A: REALDESIGN, M: YUNG@GENP.NL

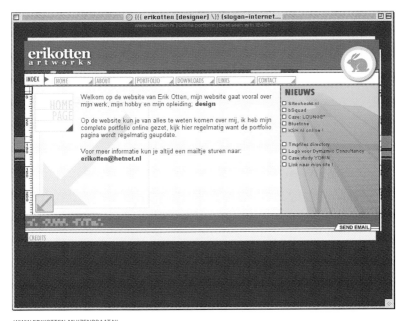

WWW.ERIKOTTEN.MUIZENPRAAT.NL
D: ERIKOTTEN, C: SJEEMZ, P: ERIKTOTTEN
M: ERIKOTTEN@HETNET.NL

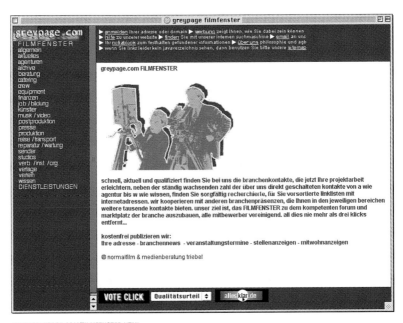

WWW.GREYPAGE.COM/FILMFENSTER.HTML
D: MICHAEL GROOTE, C: DIRK S. TRIEBEL
A: MEDIENBERATUNG TRIEBEL, M: WWW.MEDIENBERATUNG.DE

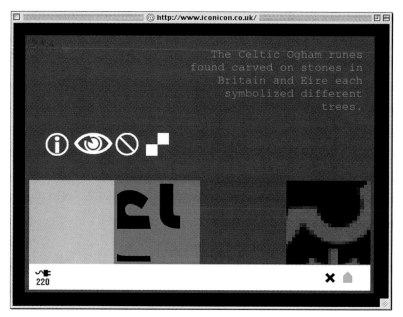

WWW.ICONICON.CO.UK
D: CHRISTOPHER ROBBINS, C: CHRISTOPHER ROBBINS
A: GROGRAPHICS, M: FOSOTIMA@HOTMAIL.COM

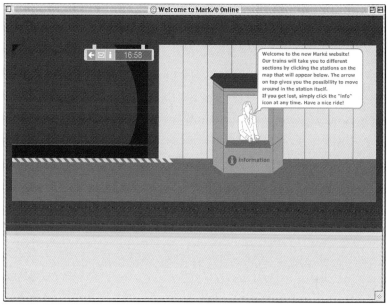

WWW.MARKEE.BE
D: REGINALD VAN DE VELDE, JERONIMO FANTINI
A: MARKÉ, M: INFO@MARKEE.BE

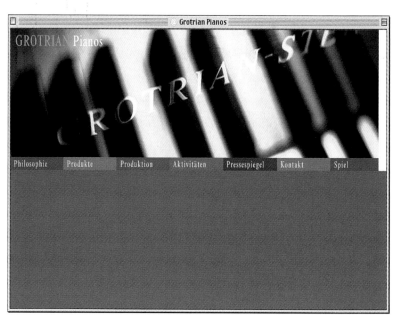

WWW.GROTRIAN.DE
D: GESINE GROTRIAN, C: MAUSS, BRÜGGEMANN, P: GROTRIAN-STEINWEG
A: FONS HICKMANN, M: HICKMANN@KAIROS.TO

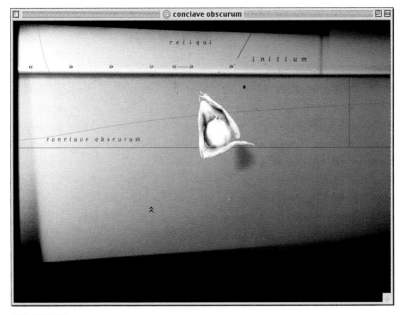

CMART.DESIGN.RU
D: OLEG G. PASCHENKO
M: CMART@DESIGN.RU

WWW.BROOKLYNFOUNDRY.COM
A: BROOKLYN DIGITAL FOUNDRY, **M:** SZOT@BROOKLYNFOUNDRY.COM

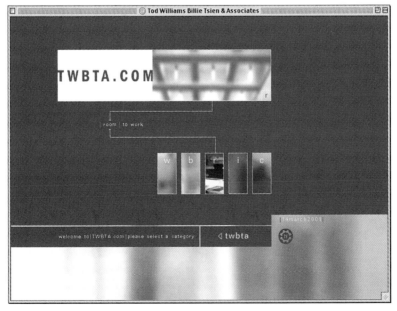

WWW.TWBTA.COM
D: PHILIP RYAN, **C:** PHILIP RYAN
M: RYAN@BROOKLYNFOUNDRY.COM

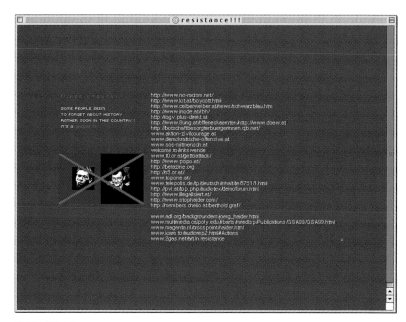

WWW.RE-MOVE.ORG

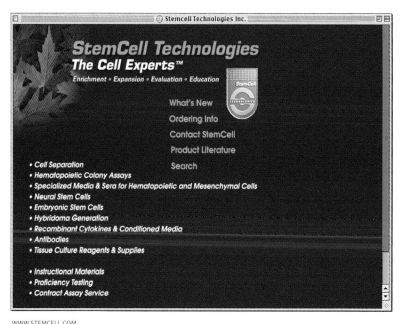

WWW.STEMCELL.COM
A: AXIS INTERACTIVE DESIGN INC., **M:** DESIGN@AXIS-MEDIA.COM

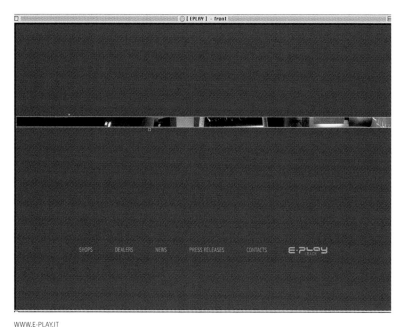

WWW.E-PLAY.IT
D: ALESSANDRO ORLANDI, **P:** SEVEN S.R.L.
M: SONIA.MARTINI@SEVEN.IT

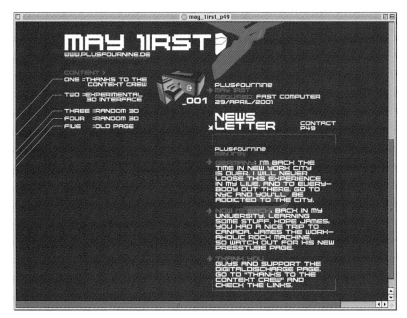

WWW.PLUSFOURNINE.DE
C: MARTIN HESSELMEIER
M: P49@GMX.DE

WWW.DESIGNERSHOCK.COM
A: DESIGNERDOCK®GROUP, M: STEFAN@DESIGNERSHOCK.COM

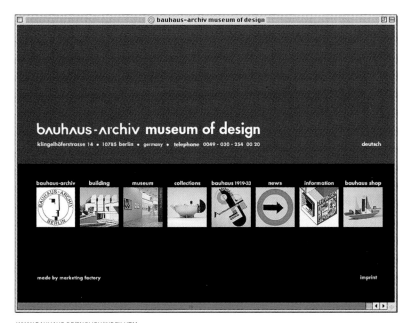

WWW.BAUHAUS.DE/ENGLISH/INDEX.HTM
D: JOANNE MOAR
M: INFO@MARKETING-FACTORY.DE

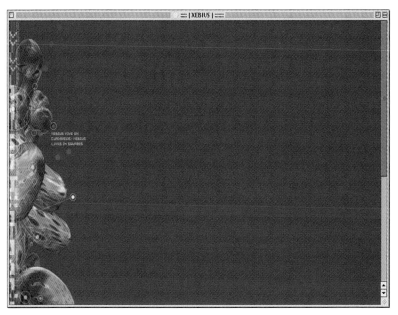

WWW.XEBIUS.COM
D: MANUEL CAMINO MÁRQUEZ, C: MANUEL CAMINO MÁRQUEZ
M: XEBIUS@XEBIUS.COM

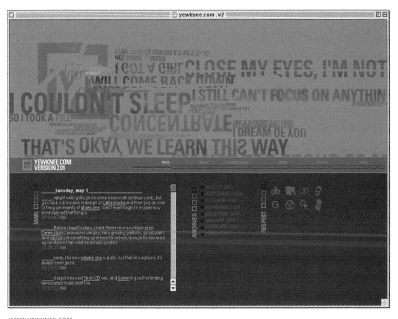

WWW.YEWKNEE.COM
D: MICHAEL EADES
M: MICHAEL@YEWKNEE.COM

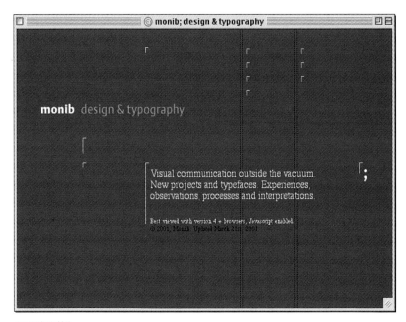

WWW.MONIB.COM
D: MONIB MAHDAVI, C: MONIB MAHDAVI
M: INFO@MONIB.COM

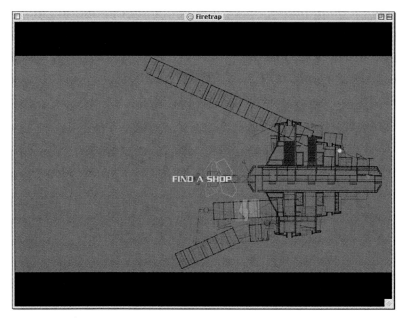

WWW.FIRETRAP.NET/FIRETRAP.HTM
D: ANNE FLOWER
M: FIRETRAP@WDT.CO.UK

WWW.KIMVESTOR.COM
D: PETER VAN DEN WYNGAERT
M: PETER@NRG.BE

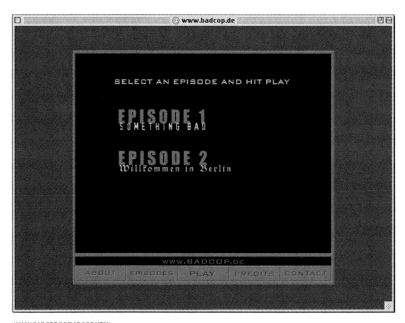

WWW.BADCOP.DE/BADCOP.HTML
A: CUBUS|MEDIA, M: CUBUS@CUBUSMEDIA.COM

WWW.HHECWORLD.COM/HANDLOOMS/INDEX.HTML
C: RAKESH SINGH, P: HHEC
M: RAKESHSINGH@INDIAMART.COM

WWW.CAFE-GOURMET.COM.AR
D: MERCEDES LOUGE, C: ALEJANDRO JARANDILLA, P: ALEJANDRO JARANDILLA
A: PUBLILAND, M: ALEJANDRO@PUBLILAND.COM.AR

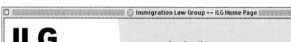
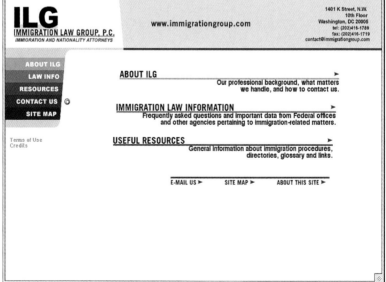

WWW.IMMIGRATIONGROUP.COM/MAIN.HTM
A: SPILL INDUSTRIES, M: CONTACT@SPILL.NET

WWW.COMPUTERPLANETITALY.IT
D: FABIO TINELLI, C: FABIO TINELLI
A: INTERNET2U, M: INFO@INTERNET2U.IT

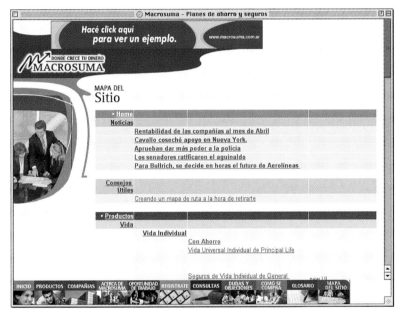

WWW.MACROSUMA.COM.AR
D: MERCEDES LOUGE, C: ALEJANDRO JARANDILLA, P: ALEJANDRO JARANDILLA
A: PUBLILAND, M: ALEJANDRO@PUBLILAND.COM.AR

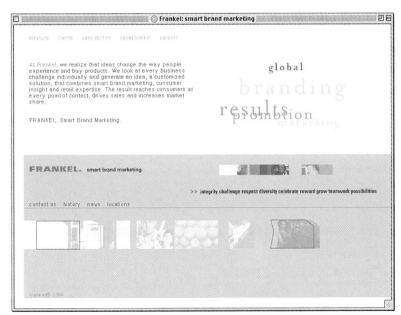

WWW.FRANKEL.COM
A: DESIGNKITCHEN, INC., M: SCOTTY@DESIGNKITCHEN.COM

179

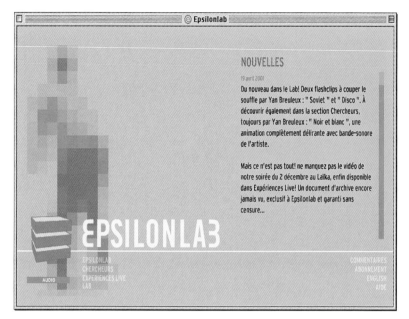

WWW.EPSILONLAB.COM
D: MR.EDGAR
M: CONTACT@MR-EDGAR.COM

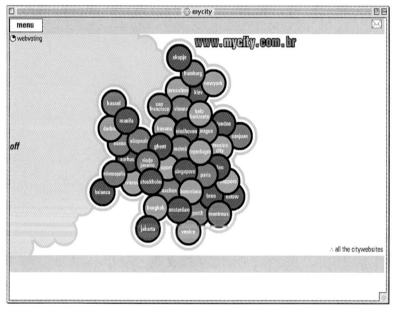

WWW.MYCITY.COM.BR
D: JAIR DE SOUZA
M: MYCITY@GBL.COM.B

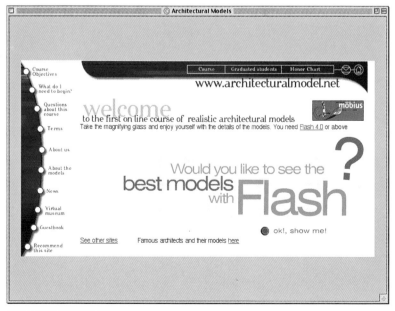

WWW.ARCHITECTURALMODEL.NET
A: WWW.GLOBALRED.COM, M: INFO@MAQUETASDEARQUITECTURA.COM

WWW.GRASS-ONIONS.NET
A: GRASSONIONS, M: NAYA@GRASS-ONIONS.NET

WWW.MAGAZINE-MUSIC.DE
D: ANDREAS F. SPERWIEN, C: ANDREAS F. SPERWIEN
A: SPERWIEN DESIGN, M: INFO@HHCONCEPT.DE

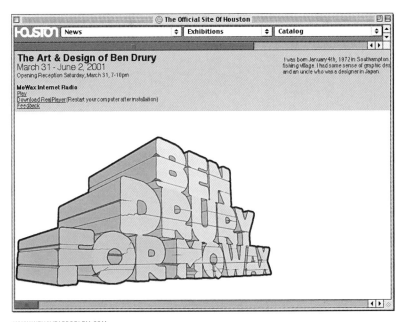

WWW.WEHAVEAPROBLEM.COM
D: MATT HOUSTON
M: HOUSTON@WEHAVEAPROBLEM.COM

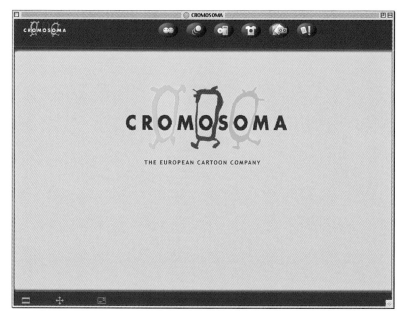

WWW.CROMOSOMA.COM
D: TONI RICART
A: WWW.MULTISTUDIO.COM, M: WILLY@CROMOSOMA.COM

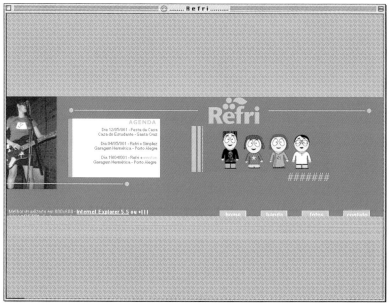

WWW.REFRIROCK.CJB.NET
D: FABIAN UMPIERRE, C: FABIAN UMPIERRE
M: VALERIA.BARROS@MTV.COM.BR

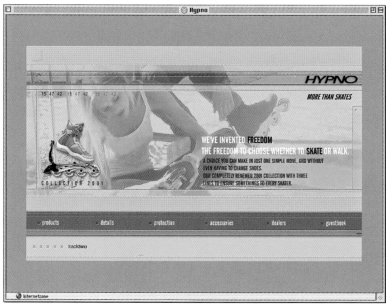

WWW.HYPNO.IT
D: MIRKO CACCARO, MICHELE GUGLIELMIN (AD)

WWW.KNO-VA.DE
D: ANDREA BRÄUNING
M: BRÄUNING@BEAUFORT8.DE

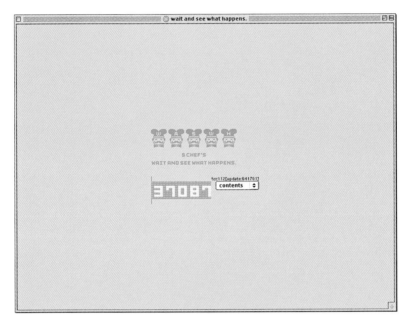

WWW1.ODN.NE.JP/~AAA69890
D: AYAKO HIRAKATA
M: AYK@POP02.ODN.NE.JP

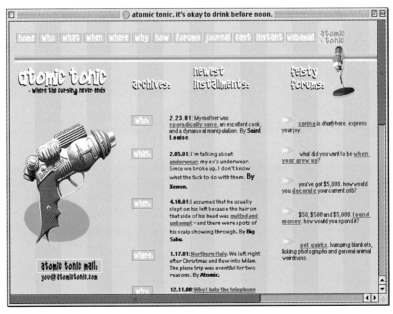

WWW.ATOMICTONIC.COM
D: DELUXEINDUSTRIES.COM.
M: ATOMIC@ATOMICTONIC.COM

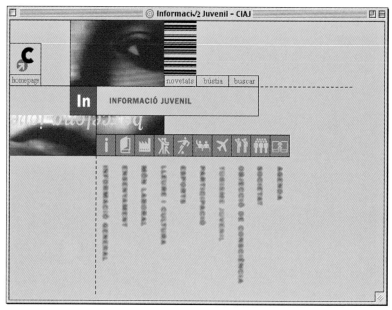

WWW.BCN.ES/CIAJ
D: ORIOL ARMEGOU
A: TOORMIX, M: INFO@TOORMIX.COM

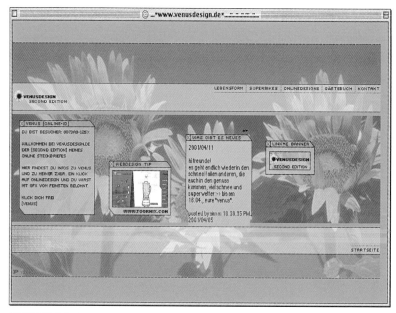

WWW.VENUSDESIGN.DE
A: PIXELIZER, M: WEBMASTER@VENUSDESIGN.DE

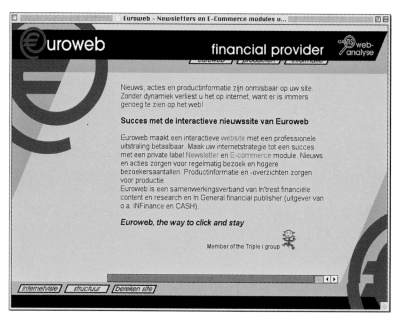

WWW.EUROWEB.TO/PORTAL
D: ARNOUD VAN DELDEN, C: ARNOUD VAN DELDEN
M: EUROWEB@WHIZZWEB.NL

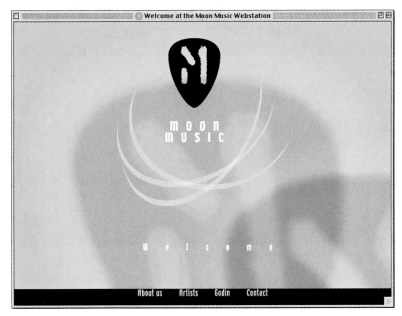

WWW.MOON-MUSIC.CH
D: URS MEYER, **C**: OLIVER ZAHORKA, **P**: BODO SUSS, MOON MUSIC
M: URS@OUT.TO

WWW.AGENTEN-UND-FREUNDE.DE
P: AGENTEN-UND-FREUNDE
M: ERDOEDY@POWART.DE

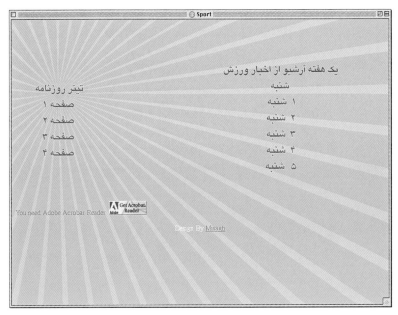

WWW.KHABARS.COM
D: MISAGH CO.
A: MISAGH GRAPHIC, **M**: INFO@SMISAGH.COM

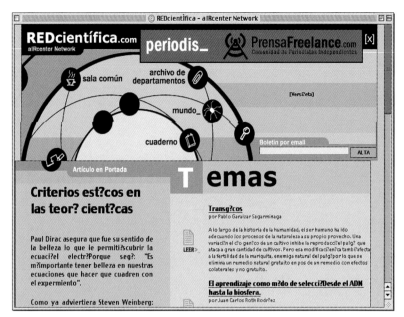

WWW.REDCIENTIFICA.COM
D: DAVID NAVARRO GÓMEZ, C: DAVID NAVARRO GÓMEZ
A: ENK3 COMUNICACIÓN, M: NAVARRO@ENK3.COM

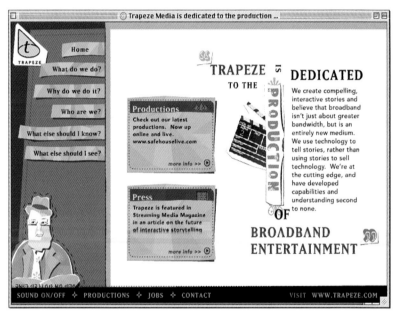

WWW.TRAPEZE.COM
A: TRAPEZE, M: INFO@TRAPEZE.COM

WWW.MODELSHOW.COM.AR
D: MERCEDES LOUGE, C: ALEJANDRO JARANDILLA, P: ALEJANDRO JARANDILLA
A: PUBLILAND, M: ALEJANDRO@PUBLILAND.COM.AR

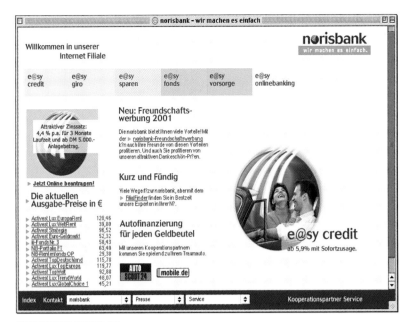

WWW.NORISBANK.DE/INDEX1.ASP
A: MORE INTERACTIVE, M: INFO@MOREINTERACTIVE.DE

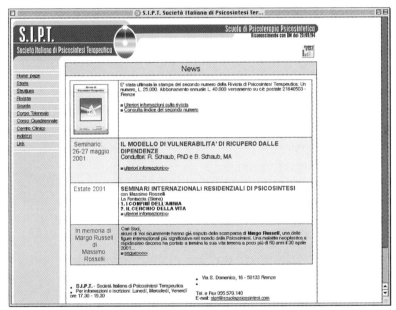

WWW.SCUOLAPSICOSINTESI.COM
D: FRANCESCA MORBIDELLI, C: FRANCESCA MORBIDELLI
M: FRANCESCA.MOR@TIN.IT

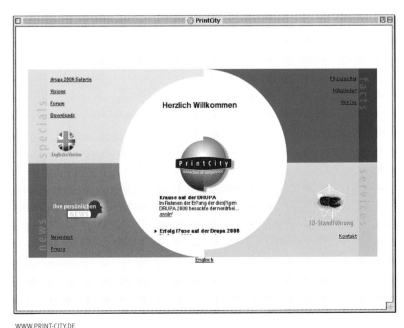

WWW.PRINT-CITY.DE
A: MORE INTERACTIVE, M: INFO@MOREINTERACTIVE.DE

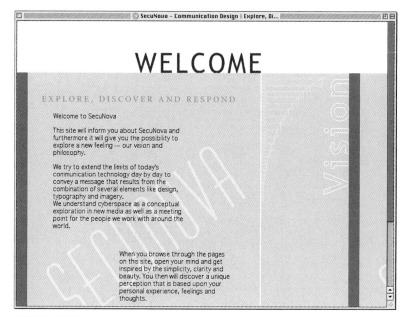

WWW.SECUNOVA.COM
D: MARKUS HÜBNER, C: MARKUS HÜBNER
A: SECUNOVA COMMUNICATION DESIGN, M: OFFICE@SECUNOVA.COM

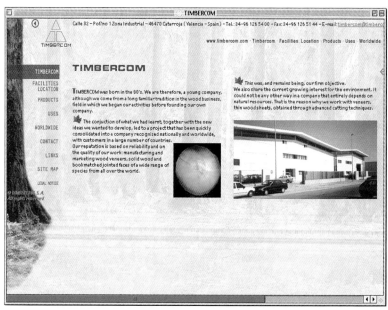

WWW.TIMBERCOM.COM
D: ADOLFO VENTURA, C: ADOLFO VENTURA
A: TALLER DIGITAL, M: ADOLFO@TALLERDIGITAL.COM

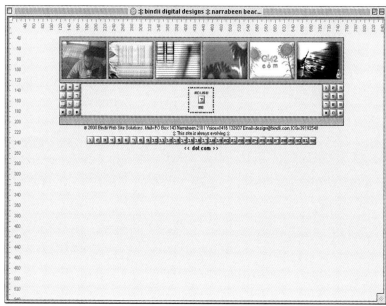

WWW.BINDII.COM
D: PAUL O'NEILL
A: BINDII WEB SITE SOLUTIONS, M: OUCH@BINDII.COM

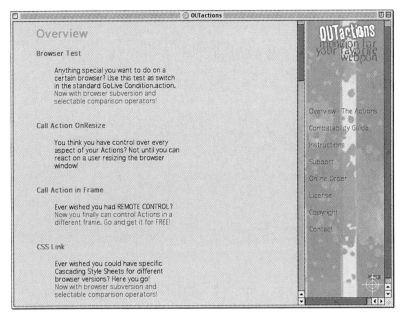

WWW.OUTACTIONS.COM
D: OLIVER ZAHORKA, **C:** OLIVER ZAHORKA, **P:** OUT MEDIA DESIGN GMBH
M: URS@OUT.TO

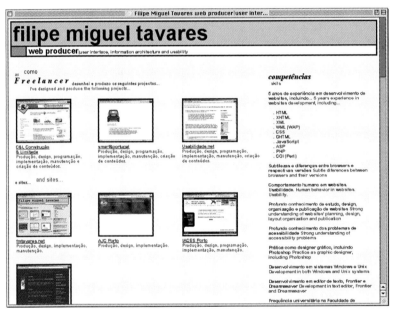

WWW.FMTAVARES.NET
D: FILIPE MIGUEL TAVARES
A: MASMADERA.NET, **M:** FMT@FMTAVARES.NET

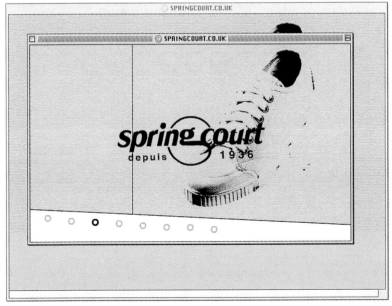

WWW.SPRINGCOURT.CO.UK
D: MARK DANIELS, **C:** LUDO PELLÉ, **P:** WESTSIDE GROUP
A: WESTSIDE GROUP, **M:** LUDO@WESTSIDEGROUP.COM

189

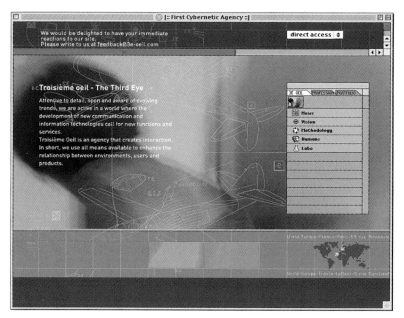

WWW.3E-OEIL.COM/SITE/UK/FRAME/INDEX.HTML
D: CHRISTIAN LECOUBLE
M: CHRIS@3E-OEIL.COM

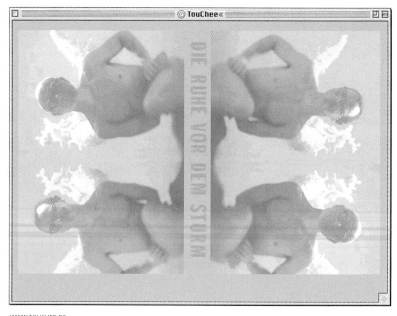

WWW.TOUCHEE.DE
D: WALTER MÖSSLER, C: PACO LALUCA
A: TOUCHEE, M: WMOESSLER@TOUCHEE.DE

WWW.THINKJUSTWEB.COM
D: KIT, C: KIT
A: JUST WEB DESIGN CENTRE, M: KITYO@THINKJUSTWEB.COM

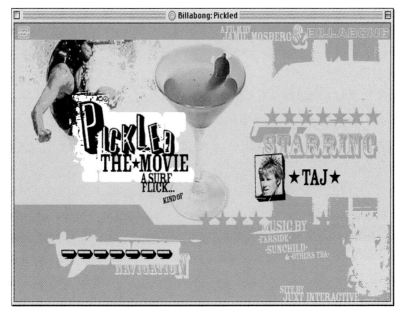

WWW.PICKLED.TV/MAIN.HTML
D: TODD PURGASON, C: JEFF KEYSER
A: JUXT INTERACTIVE, M: INFO@JUXTINTERACTIVE.COM

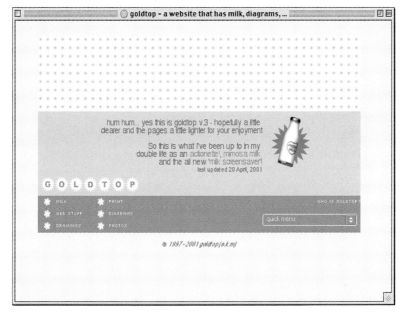

WWW.GOLDTOP.ORG
D: EMERALD MOSLEY
M: GOLDTOP@GOLDTOP.ORG

WWW.NATUREMEETINGS.COM
D: MARTA ANDREZ, C: GIL CORREIA
M: DESIGN@NETAMORPHOSE.PT

WWW.PLANETOFTHEDRUMS.COM
D: MIKE YOUNG
M: MIKE@DESIGNGRAPHIK.COM

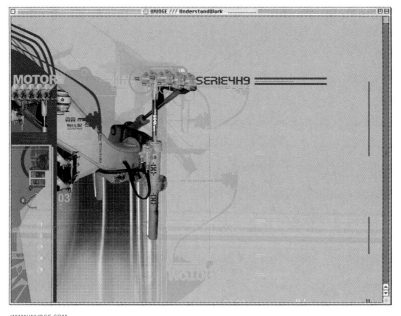

WWW.WUDGE.COM
D: EMMANUEL MOUAZAN
A: XZESSLAB, **M:** CONTACT@WUDGE.COM

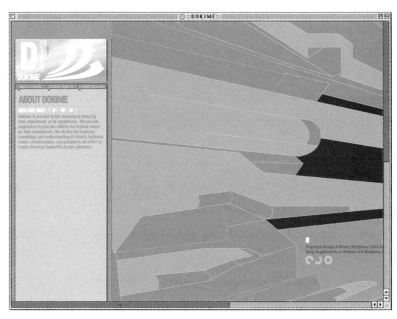

WWW.DOKIME.COM
D: CHADWICK SHAO
A: DOKIME, **M:** MINH@DOKIME.COM

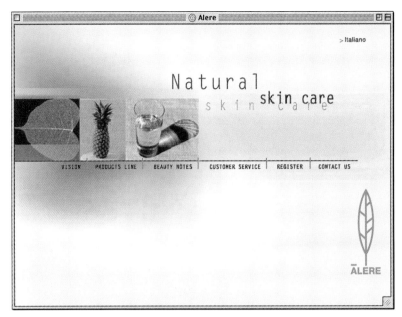

WWW.ALERE.IT/HOME.HTML
D: GUERINO DELFINO
M: DELFINO@HYPHEN.IT

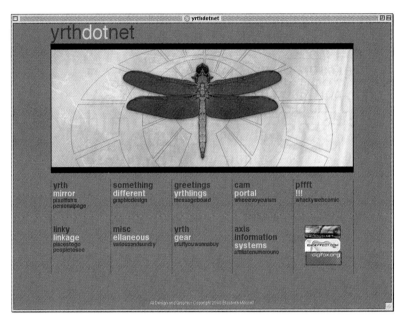

WWW.YRTH.NET
D: ELIZABETH MITCHELL
M: NYRDGIRL@HOTMAIL.COM

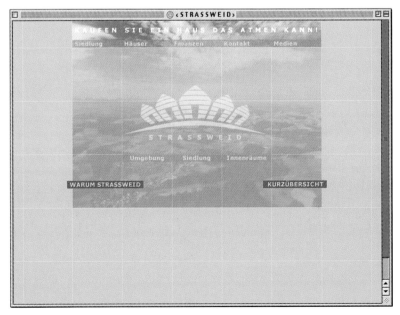

WWW.STRASSWEID.CH
D: OLIVER ZAHORKA, **C:** OLIVER ZAHORKA, **P:** GENOSSENSCHAFT SIEDLUNG STRASSWEID
A: OUT MEDIA DESIGN GMBH, **M:** URS@OUT.TO

193

WWW.SALADCREAM.COM/HTML/INDEX1.HTM
D: AL FOX
A: FI SYSTEM BRAND NEW MEDIA, **M:** INFO@BNM.CO.UK

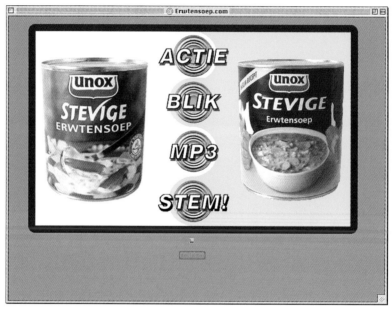

WWW.ERWTENSOEP.COM
D: JASPER VAN KUIJK
M: JASPER@VANKUIJK.COM

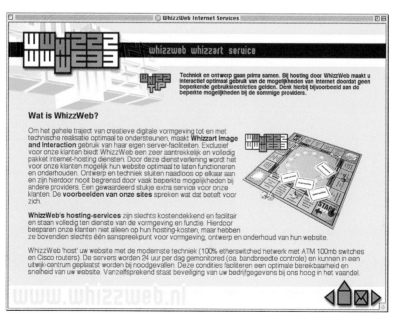

WWW.WHIZZWEB.NL
D: ARNOUD VAN DELDEN, **C:** ARNOUD VAN DELDEN

WWW.HELLOLOGAN.COM
A: LOGAN, M: INFO@HELLOLOGAN.COM

WWW.JENETT.COM
A: JENETT.COM, M: DANIEL@JENETT.COM

WWW.WAHNSIGNAL.DE
D: FABU, C: FABU
M: FABU@WAHNSIGNAL.DE

WWW.ORBIT8.NET
D: ANDY, C: ANDY
M: MATTHEW@FEAROFSPEED.COM

WWW.KNOW-US.CO.UK
A: BLACK ID, M: BLACK@BLACKID.COM

WWW.LINKDESIGN.NET
D: LIAM FITZGERALD, C: LIAM FITZGERALD
A: LINK:DESIGN, M: LIAM@LINKDESIGN.NET

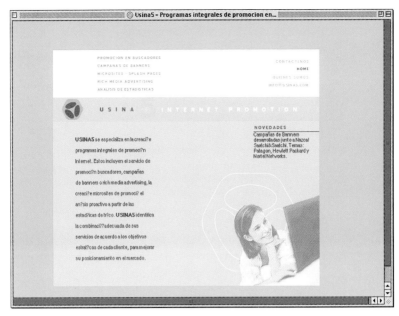

WWW.USINA5.COM
D: JUAN MARTÍN CUCURULO, **C:** AGUSTÍN GÓMEZ VEGA, **P:** DIEGO FERRARO
M: ESTUDIO@INTERAR.COM.AR

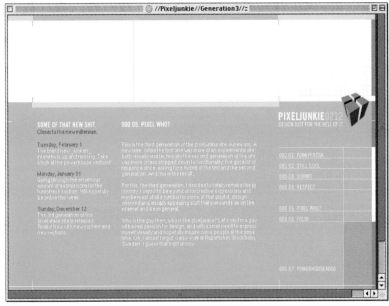

WWW.PIXELJUNKIE.COM/05.HTML
D: JANNE STARSKY
M: JANNE@STARSKY.COM

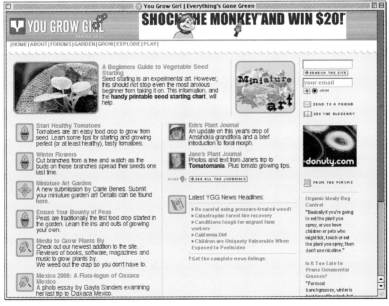

WWW.YOUGROWGIRL.COM
D: GAYLA SANDERS
M: GAYLA@YOUGROWGIRL.COM

197

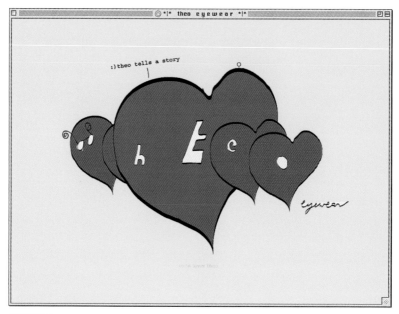

WWW.THEO.BE
D: PAUL DE SCHUTTER, **C:** PAUL DE SCHUTTER
A: VOLTA, **M:** PAUL@VOLTA.BE

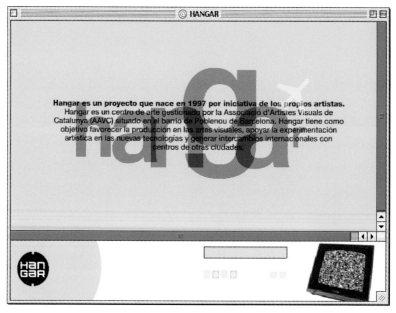

WWW.HANGAR.ORG
A: VASAVA ARTWORKS, **M:** VASAVA@VASAVA.ES

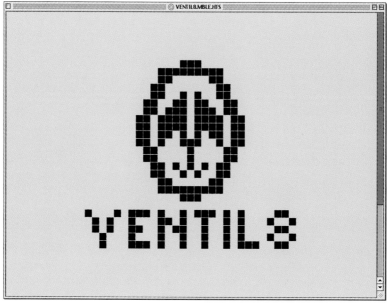

WWW.VENTIL8.NET
A: VENTIL8, **M:** INFO@VENTIL8.NET

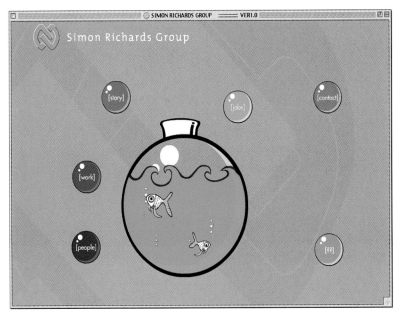

WWW.SRGROUP.COM.AU/FLASH.HTML
A: ARTICHOKE, M: ALES@ARTICHOKEDESIGN

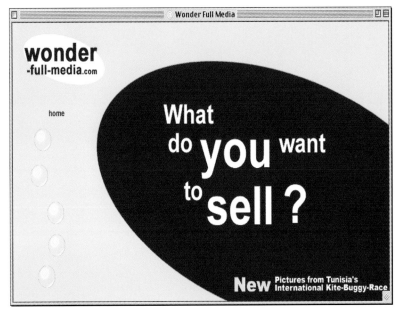

WWW.WONDER-FULL-MEDIA.COM
D: SUSANNE BEHNKE, C: CHRISTIAN SCHLIEHE, P: SUSANNE BEHNKE
M: SB@WONDER-FULL-MEDIA.COM

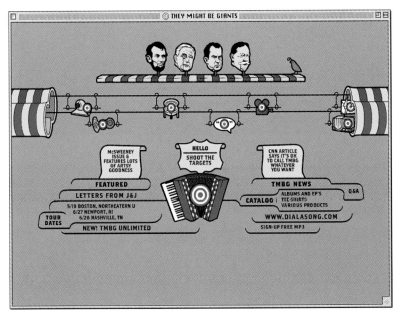

WWW.TMBG.COM
D: TOM ROMER, C: CHANDLER MCWILLIAMS, P: KEITH PIZER
M: DARLEEN@CHOPPINGBLOCK.COM

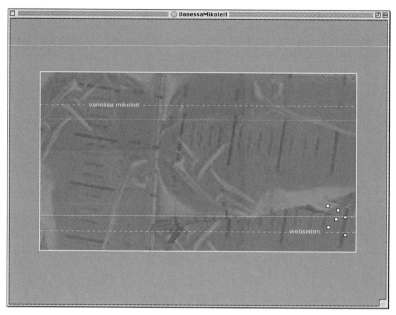

WWW.TALKNET.DE/~V.MIKOLEIT
D: VANESSA MIKOLEIT, C: VANESSA MIKOLEIT
M: JAVAN@GMX.DE

WWW.JZY001.HOME.CHINAREN.COM
D: JZY, C: NO, P: JZY
A: JZY, M: JZYJZYJZY@163.NET

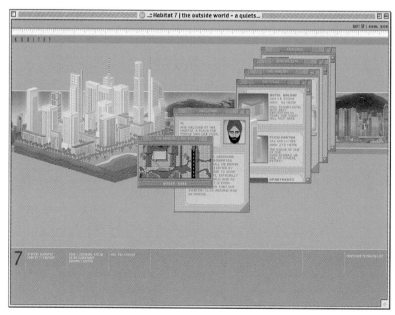

WWW.HABITAT7.DE/DESIGN2/INDEXIE.HTM
D: STEFFEN SCHAEFER
A: HABITAT 7, M: FOUNDER@HABITAT7.DE

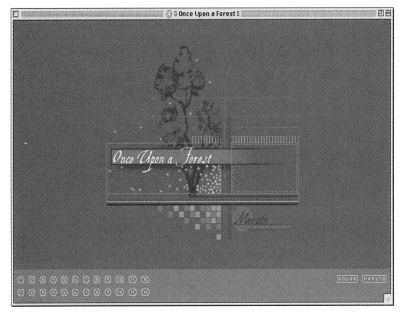

WWW.ONCE-UPON-A-FOREST.COM/MAY-99/MAY-99.HTML
D: JOSHUA DAVIS
A: ANTIWEB-CHAOS

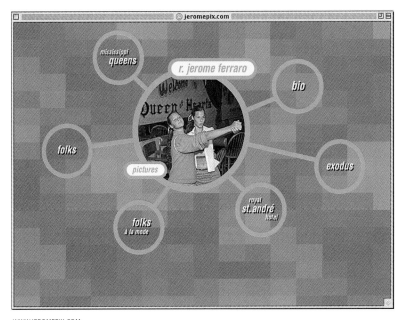

WWW.JEROMEPIX.COM
D: JEROME FERRARO
M: JEROME@JEROMEPIX.COM

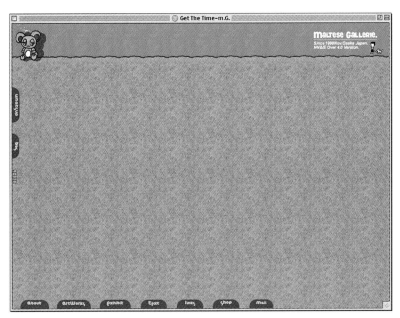

WWW.KCAT.ZAQ.NE.JP/HARDCORE/MG04/INDEX.HTML
A: MALTESE GALLERIE, **M:** HARDCORE@KCAT.ZAQ.NE.JP

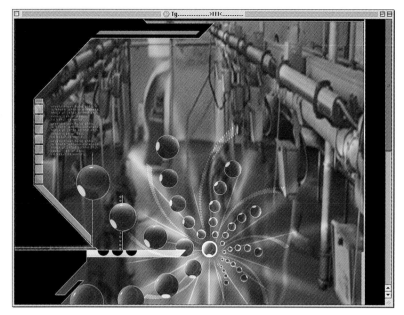

WWW.TOGUESS.NET
D: POUTEAU CYRIL, P: POUTEAU CYRIL
A: POUTEAU CYRIL, M: TOGUESS76@HOTMAIL.COM

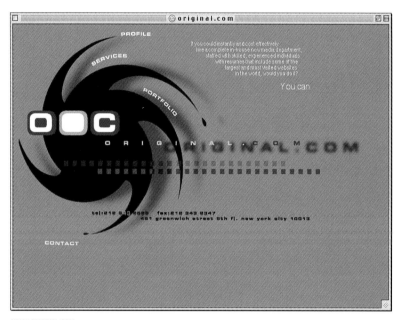

WWW.ORIGINAL.COM
D: BRADFORD SCHMIDT
A: ORIGINAL.COM, M: BRAD@BRADFORDSCHMIDT.COM

WWW.E-LLUMINATION.NET
A: E-LLUMINATION TEAM, M: DAVIDJOHNSSON@YAHOO.COM

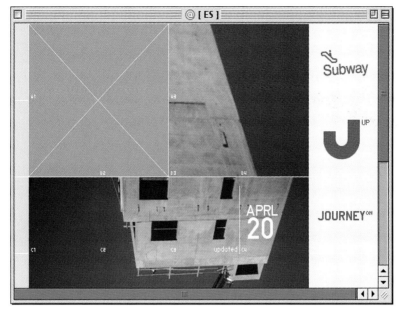

WWW.ELIXIRSTUDIO.COM
D: ARNAUD MERCIER
M: AMERCIER@BLASTRADIUS.CO

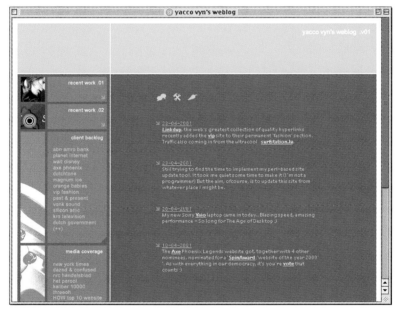

WWW.YACCO.NET
D: YACCO VYN, C: YACCO VYN
A: SKIP_INTRO DIGITAL MEDIA, M: YACCO@YACCO.NET

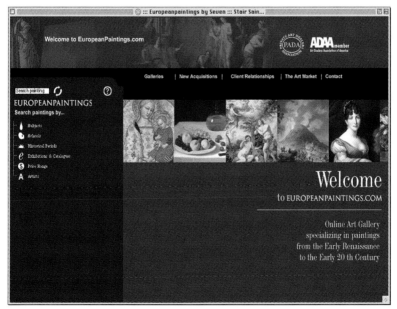

WWW.EUROPEANPAINTINGS.COM
D: MATTEO GIURICIN, C: SIMONE MOREALI, P: SEVEN S.R.L.
A: SEVEN S.R.L., M: SONIA.MARTINI@SEVEN.IT

WWW.ALIENSKIN.COM
D: JERRY PEMBERTON

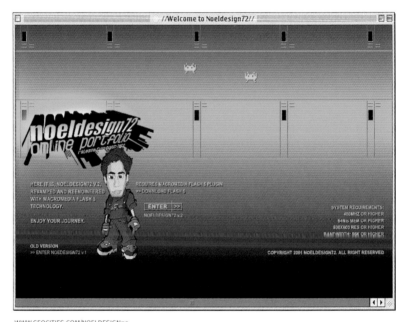

WWW.GEOCITIES.COM/NOELDESIGN72
D: NOEL, C: NA, P: NA
A: NA, M: NOELTTS@HOTMAIL.COM

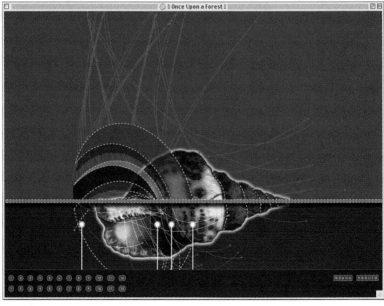

WWW.ONCE-UPON-A-FOREST.COM/OCT-99/OCT-99.HTML
D: JOSHUA DAVIS
M: CHAOS@PRAYSTATION.COM

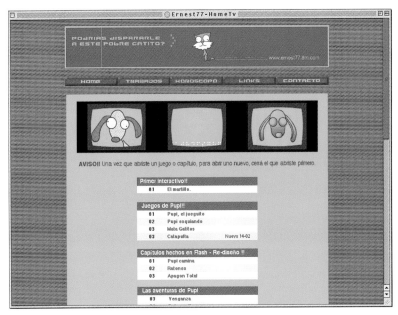

WWW.USUARIOS.SION.COM/ERNEST77
M: ERNESTO@BASEHEAD.COM.AR

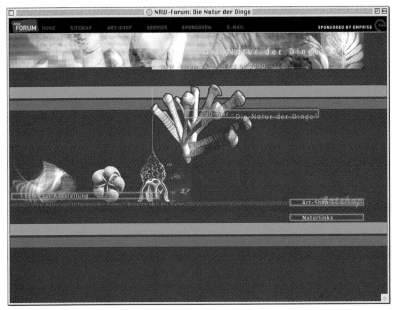

WWW.NRW-FORUM.DE/DEUTSCH/NATUR/INDEX.HTM
D: KATRIN BRACKMANN, C: MATTHIAS KOSLOWSKI, P: WERNER LIPPERT
A: ONLINE RELATIONS, M: KA@OZ-ZONE.DE

WWW.COCA-COLA.BE
D: NICOLAS JANDRAIN, C: VERONIQUE MULLER, P: BRICE LE BLEVENNEC
A: EMAKINA, M: NICOLAS.JANDRAIN@PI.BE

WWW.FLUID.COM
D: ANDREW SIROTNIK, MELISSA CROWLEY
A: FLUID INC.

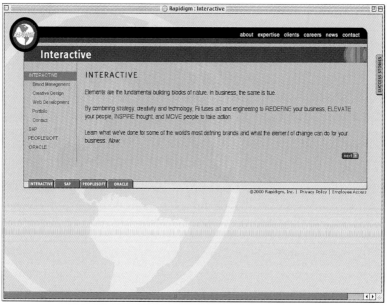

WWW.RAPIDIGM.COM/INTERACTIVE/INDEX.PHP3
D: TODD GRECO
M: TGRECO@RAPIDIGM.COM

WWW.CAFFEMOCHA.COM/SUZUKI
D: ANDY "ENUE" SCHAAFCREATIVE LEAD , C: MARK "SUSHI" ARCENAL
A: TRANSITLAB.COM, M: CONCERNEDBEING@CAFFEMOCHA.COM

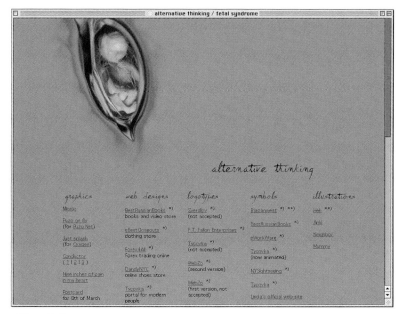

WWW.TIVANOV.COM
C: ALEXANDER TIVANOV, P: ALEXANDER TIVANOV
M: ALEXANDER@TIVANOV.COM

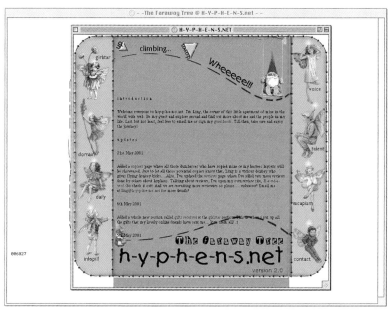

WWW.H-Y-P-H-E-N-S.NET
C: CHENG SHUNLING, P: CHENG SHUNLING
M: LING@H-Y-P-H-E-N-S.NET

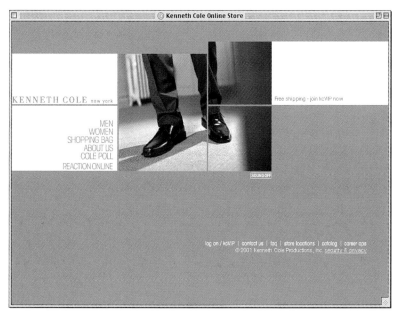

WWW.KENNETHCOLE.COM
D: KENNETH COLE
A: IN-HOUSE DESIGN, M: MEMBERS@KENNETHCOLE.COM

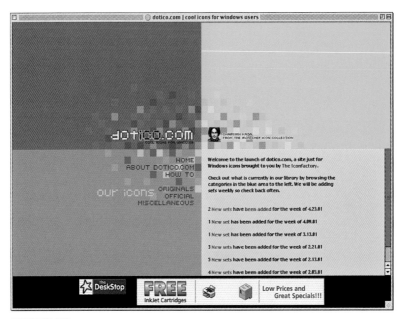

WWW.DOTICO.COM
A: THE ICONFACTORY, M: WEBMASTER@ICONFACTORY.COM

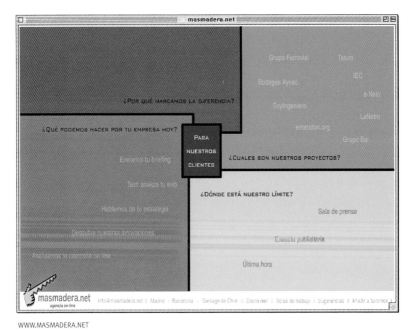

WWW.MASMADERA.NET
D: FILIPE MIGUEL TAVARES
A: MASMADERA.NET, M: JLDOMINGUEZ@MASMADERA.NET

WWW.VITRA.COM
D: SONJA SCHÄFER
A: VIRTUAL IDENTITY AG, KNOW IDEA GMBH

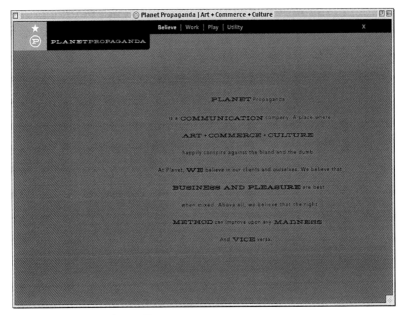

WWW.PLANETPROPAGANDA.COM/INDEX2.ASP
D: KEVIN WADE
A: PLANET PROPAGANDA, M: HANK@PLANETPROPAGANDA.COM

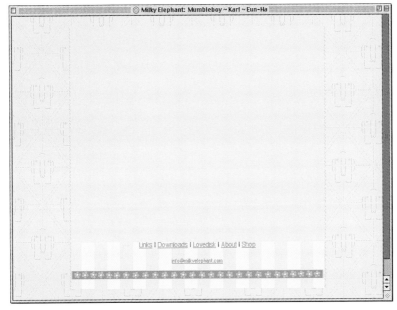

WWW.MILKYELEPHANT.COM/MILKYMENU.HTML
D: EUN-HA PAEK
A: MILKYELEPHANT, M: HI@MILKYELEPHANT.COM

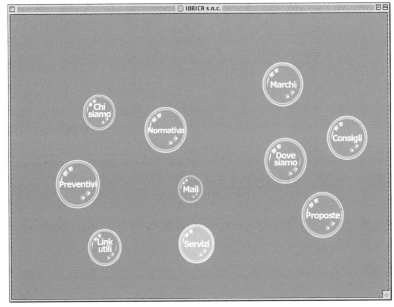

WWW.IDRICA.COM
D: FABIO TINELLI, C: FABIO TINELLI
A: INTERNET2U, M: INFO@INTERNET2U.IT

WWW.HOUSE-OF-MUSIC.DE
D: MICHAEL MAUCH
A: LOGOPILOT, M: MAUCH@LOGOPILOT.DE

WWW.DAWNWEB.COM
D: JULIO LOAYZA, C: FRANCOIS CASTRO, P: MARCOS BELLO
A: DIGITAL DAWN, M: WEBMASTER@DAWNWEB.COM

WWW.PAPASDALINGUA.COM.BR
D: TATIANA BRUGALLI, C: GLADIMIR DUTRA, P: FABIANO DE ANDRADE
A: ALDEIA DESIGN, M: FABIANO@ALDEIADESIGN.COM.BR

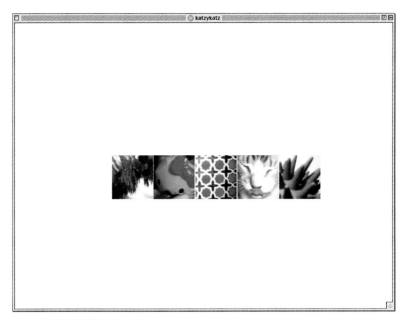

WWW.MUTILATEDLIPS.COM
A: KATZYKATZ, M: KATY@MUTILATEDLIPS.COM

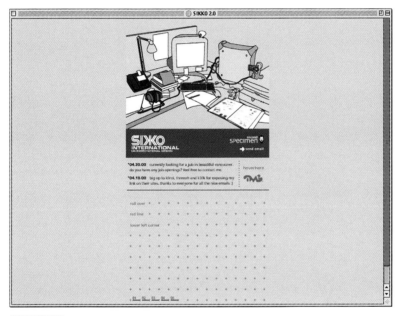

WWW.SIKKO.COM
D: HANNES OTTAHAL AKA SIKKO*
M: SIKKO@SIKKO.COM

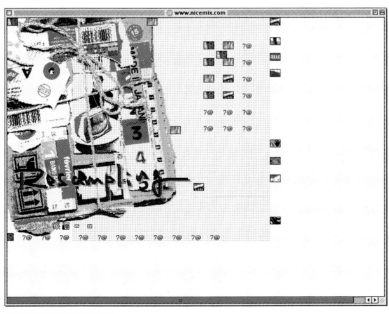

WWW.NICEMIX.COM/INDEX_R.HTML
D: ASAMI HIRAI
M: INFO@NICEMIX.COM

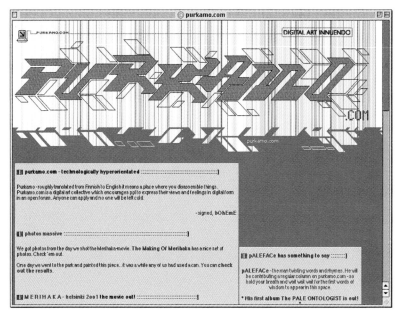

WWW.PURKAMO.COM
D: ANSSI JOHANSSON A.K.A BOHEME
M: BOHEME@PURKAMO.COM

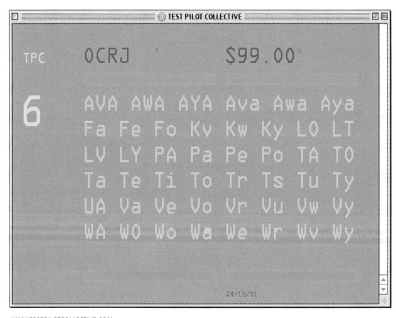

WWW.TESTPILOTCOLLECTIVE.COM
A: TEST PILOT COLLECTIVE, M: INFO@TESTPILOTCOLLECTIVE.COM

WWW.JENETT.COM/BORN/HTM/FRAME.HTM
A: JENETT.COM, M: DANIEL@JENETT.COM

WWW.LIVINGATHOME.DE
D: SABINE BRUNKE-REUBOLD
M: NFO@LIVINGATHOME.DE

WWW.GRAFICA-ONLINE.COM
C: DANIELE VANONCINI, P: DANIELE VANONCINI
M: WEBMASTER@GRAFICA-ONLINE.COM

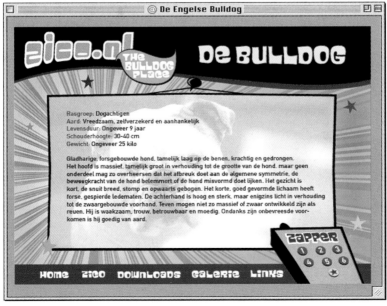

WWW.ZICO.NL
D: MARIO BERENDSEN, C: MARIO BERENDSEN
M: ZICODINHO@PLANET.NL

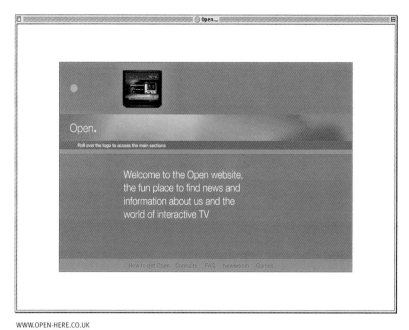

WWW.OPEN-HERE.CO.UK
D: SIMON SANKARAYYA
A: DIGIT, M: DELYTH@DIGITLONDON.COM

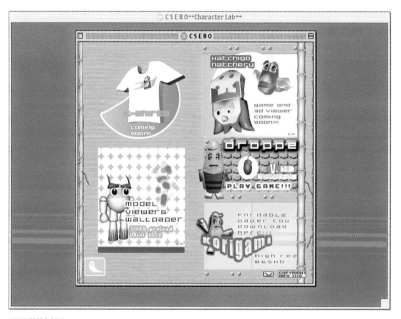

WWW.CSERO.COM
D: IAN STOKES
A: CSERO CHARACTER LAB, M: CYBORG@CSERO.COM

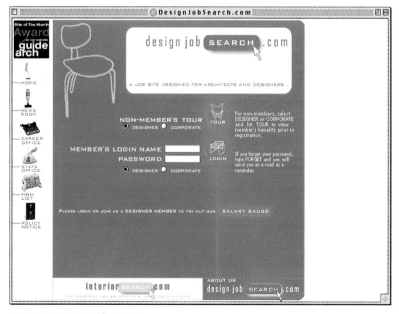

WWW.DESIGNJOBSEARCH.COM/INDEX1.ASP
D: BEN WONG
M: MAIL@DESIGNJOBSEARCH.COM

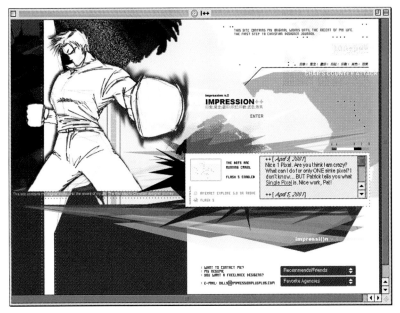

WWW.IMPRESSIONPLUSPLUS.COM
D: BILLY KWAN
M: BILLY@IMPRESSIONPLUSPLUS.COM

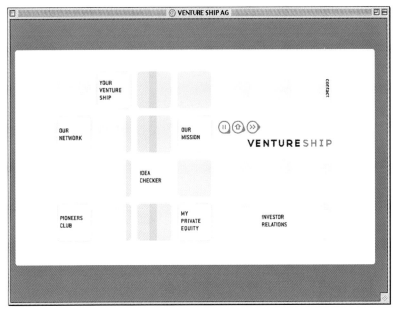

WWW.VENTURESHIP.DE/NONFLASH.HTM
A: IN(CORPORATE, M: INFO@INCORPORATE.DE

WWW.BAKERLAW.COM/DEFAULT.ASP
D: HOWARD CLEVELAND
M: HOWARDC@DIGITAL-DAY.COM

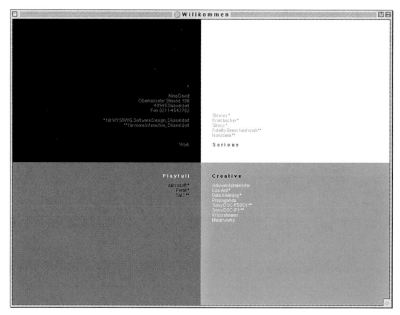

WWW.NINADAVID.DE/WORK/INDEX.HTML
D: NINA DAVID
M: ICH@NINADAVID.DE

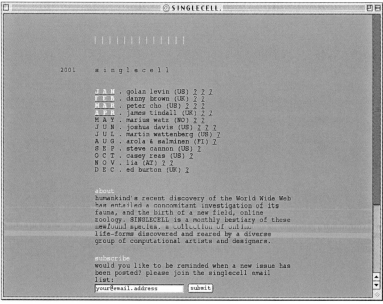

WWW.SINGLECELL.ORG
A: WWW.SINGLECELL.ORG, M: ZOOKEEPER@SINGLECELL.ORG

WWW.BEAT106.COM
A: BLACK ID, M: BLACK@BLACKID.COM

216

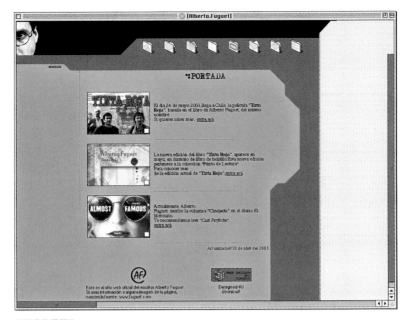

WWW.FUGUET.COM
D: SONICO, **C:** SONICO
A: EVOLUCIONA, **M:** SONICO@FUGUET.COM

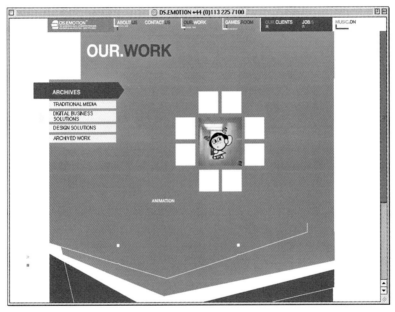

WWW.DSEMOTION.COM
A: DS EMOTION, **M:** JAY@DSEMOTION.COM

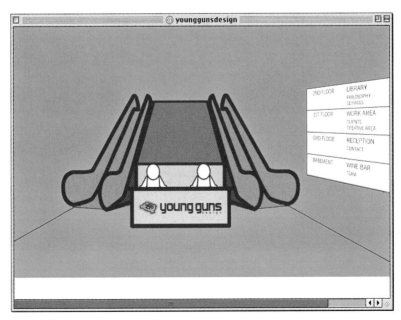

WWW.YOUNGGUNSDESIGN.COM
A: YOUNG GUNS DESIGN, **M:** INFO@YOUNGGUNSDESIGN.COM

WWW.EGOMEDIA.COM
D: EGO MEDIA
M: INFO@EGOMEDIA.COM

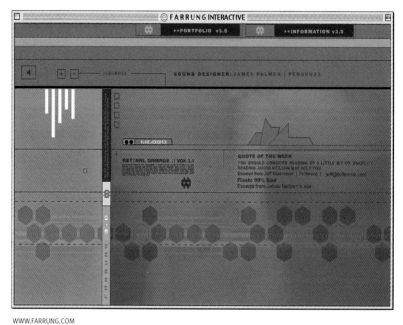

WWW.FARRUNG.COM
D: JAMES GLADDEN
A: FARRUNG INTERACTIVE, M: JGLADDEN@HOTMAIL.COM

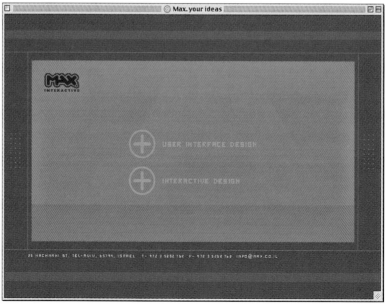

WWW.MAX.CO.IL
D: RUTH KIKIN
A: MAX INTERACTIVE LTD. , M: RUTH@MAX.CO.IL

WWW.LOCTEAM.COM
D: ELENA PALLEJÀ, **C:** ROSA ROMEU
M: MAIL@LOCTEAM.COM

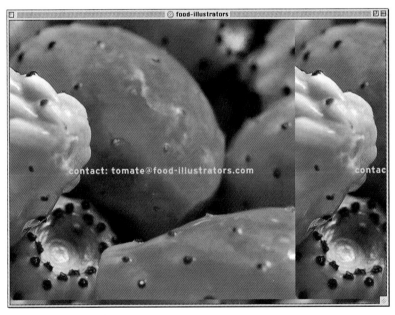

WWW.FOOD-ILLUSTRATORS.COM
D: PACO LALUCA
A: WWW.BAMBOO-PRODUCTIONS.COM, **M:** OFFICE.BCN@BAMBOO-PRODUCTIONS.COM

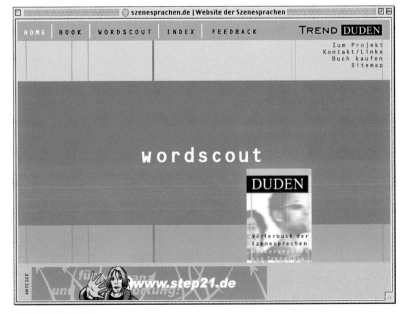

WWW.SZENESPRACHEN.DE
D: SUSANNE REIZLEIN.
M: INFO@TRENDBUERO.DE

WWW.CHASNDAVE.FREESERVE.CO.UK
D: DAVE DAY
M: WEBMASTER@CHASNDAVE.CO.UK

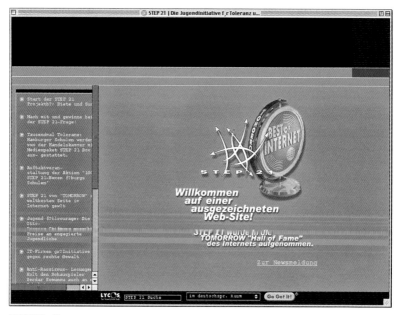

WWW.STEP21.DE
A: TURBO D3 GMBH, M: DOENHOFF.PHILIP@STEP21.DE

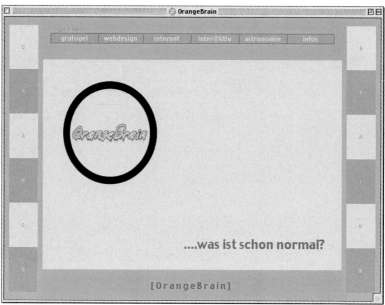

WWW.ORANGEBRAIN.DE
C: CHRISTIAN HILL, P: CHRISTIAN BETTINGER
A: MATRIX WEBDESIGN, M: WEBMASTER@ORANGEBRAIN.DE

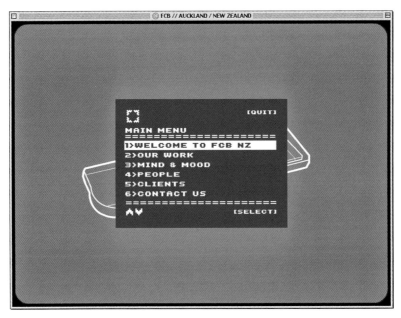

WWW.FCB.CO.NZ
D: SIMON CHESTERMAN, C: EBONY CHARLTON, P: PETE HIBBERDINE
A: UNIFORM, M: SIMON@TEAMUNIFORM.NET

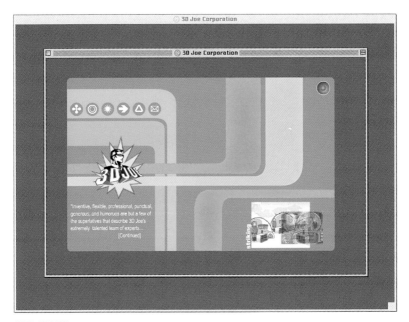

WWW.3DJOE.COM
D: RENAUD TERNYNCK, C: IAN STOKES, P: BRIAN ALMASHIE
A: 3D JOE, M: BRIAN@3DJOE.COM

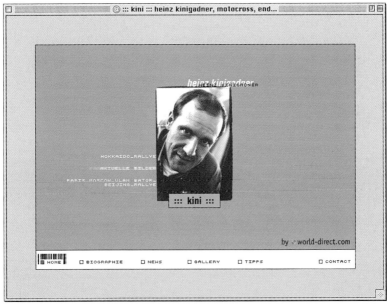

WWW.KINIGADNER.COM
D: MARKUS HÜBNER, C: LUKAS TUSCH, P: LUKAS TUSCH
A: WORLD-DIRECT.COM, M: OFFICE@WORLD-DIRECT.COM

WWW.BESTFLASHSITES.DE/ARCHIV.HTML
D: DIRK BEHLAU
M: DIRK@PIXELEYE.DE

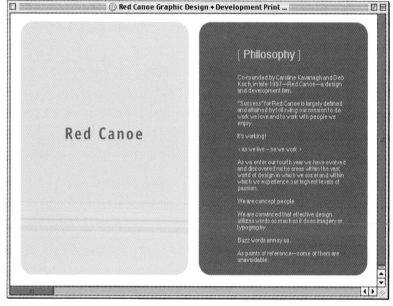

WWW.REDCANOE.COM
D: CAROLINE KAVANAGH, C: DEBORAH KOCH
A: RED CANOE

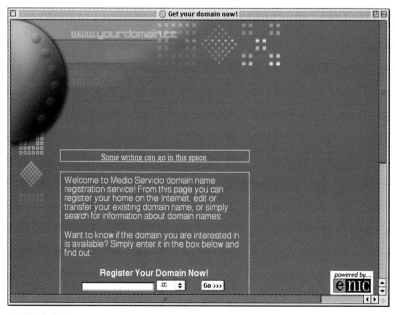

WWW.MEDIO.COM
D: MICHAEL KERN
M: MKERN@MEDIO.COM

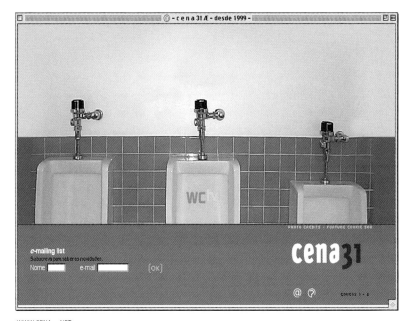

WWW.CENA31.NET
D: FILIPE OLIVEIRA
M: FILIPEDIGITAL@CENA31.NET

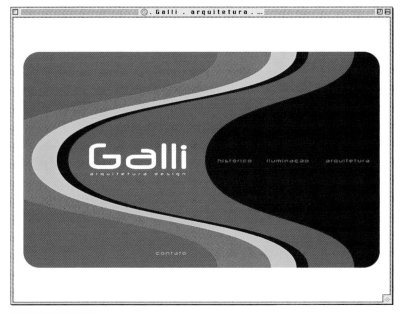

WWW.GALLIDESIGN.COM.BR
D: LUCIENE CALABRIA, **C:** LUCIENE CALABRIA
A: DOLCE VITA COMUNICAÇÃO, **M:** LCALABRIA@ITAUCULTURAL.ORG.BR

WWW.HYPHEN.IT
D: GUERINO DELFINO
M: DELFINO@HYPHEN.IT

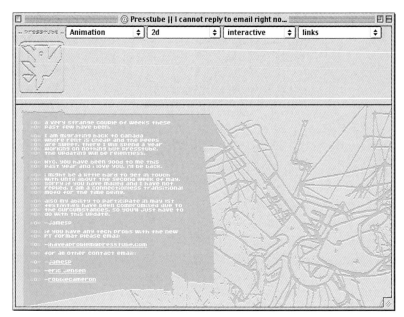

WWW.PRESSTUBE.COM
D: JAMES PATERSON
M: JAMES@PRESSTUBE.COM

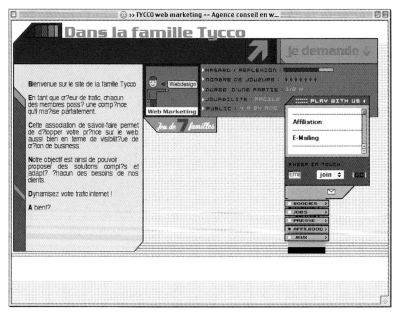

WWW.TYCCO.COM
D: JP WOZNIAK, C: MATTHIAS, P: TYCCO
M: WEBMARKETING@TYCCO.NET

WWW.THEBRIGHTON.DEMON.CO.UK
D: EUGENE GELLMANN
M: GENIE@THEBRIGHTON.DEMON.CO.UK

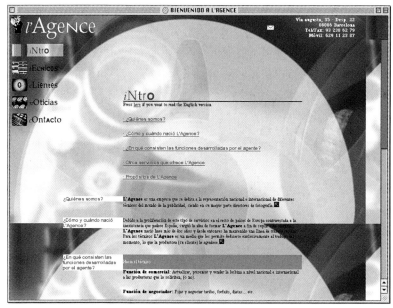

WWW.LAGENCE-IMAGE.COM
D: ADOLFO VENTURA, **C:** ADOLFO VENTURA
A: TALLER DIGITAL, **M:** ADOLFO@TALLERDIGITAL.COM

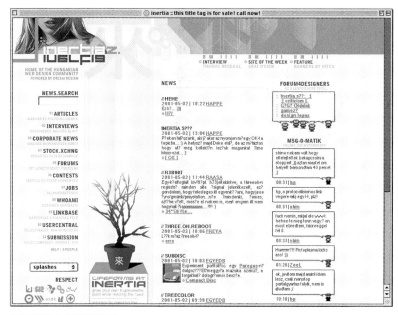

WWW.INERTIA.D2.HU/INDEX.PHTML
A: DREAM.DESIGN INTERACTIVE LTD., **M:** INFO@DREAM.HU

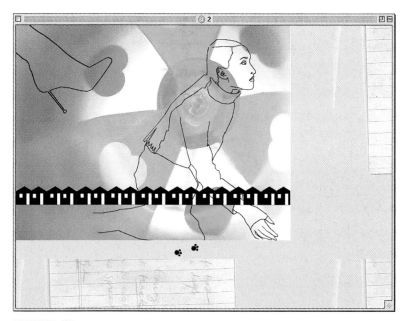

WWW.DREAM7.COM
D: MARGARET PENNEY
M: INFO@DREAM7.COM

225

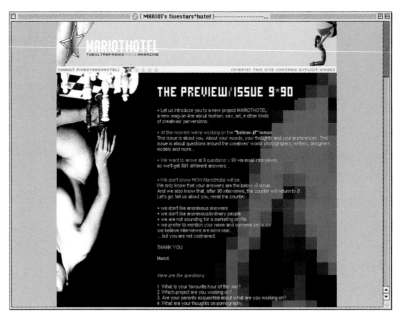

WWW.THEMARIOTHOTEL.COM
D: FRANCESCO BERTELLI
M: INFO@THEMARIOTHOTEL.COM

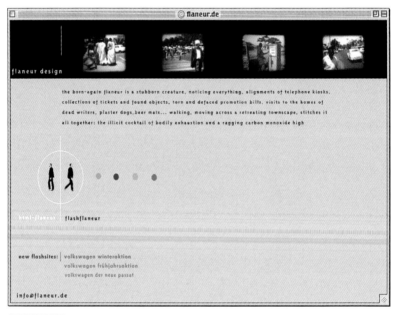

WWW.FLANEUR.DE
D: HELGE WINDISCH, C: HELGE WINDISCH
A: FLANEUR DESIGN, M: INFO@FLANEUR.DE

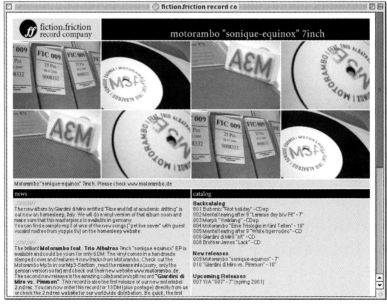

WWW.FICTIONFRICTION.COM
D: JOHANNES SCHARDT
M: SOMEBODY@FICTIONFRICTION.COM

WWW.BALANCE-MUENCHEN.DE
D: BRIGITTA ERDÖDY
A: POWART-MULTIMEDIA, **M:** ERDOEDY@POWART.DE

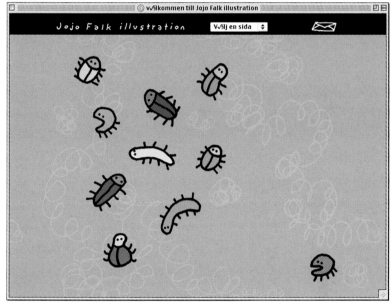

WWW.LABORATORIET.COM/JOJO/ENG/ENGELSKA.HTML
D: JOJO FALK
M: INFO@LABORATORIET.COM

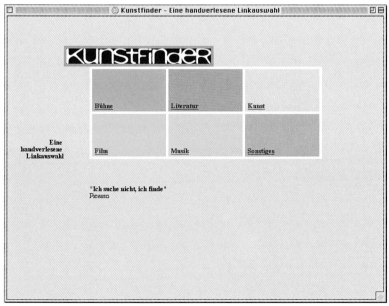

WWW.KUNSTFINDER.DE
D: HARTMUT SCHRÖTER, **C:** HARTMUT SCHRÖTER
A: SCHRÖTER-DESIGN, **M:** SCHROETERDESIGN@WEB.DE

WWW.SHAPESQUAD.COM/WHOWE/OFFICE.HTML
A: SHAPE SQUAD, **M:** INFO@SHAPESQUAD.COM

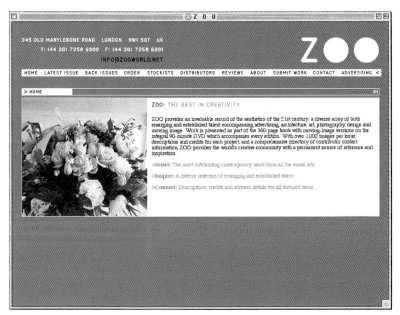

WWW.PURPLEHOUSE.COM/HOME.HTML
D: SIMON BAKER
M: INFO@ZOOWORLD.NET

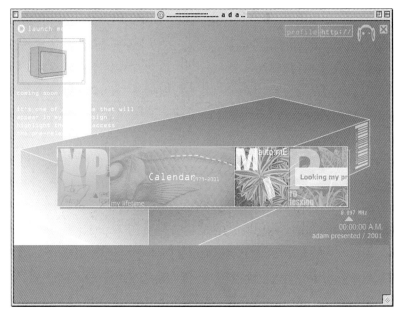

WWW.ADAMDOM.COM
D: ADAM LEE
M: ADAM@ADAMDOM.COM

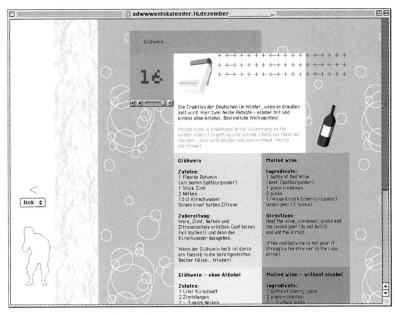

WWW.ADWWWENTSKALENDER.DE/WINTER00/16.HTML
D: NINA DAVID
M: ICH@NINADAVID.DE

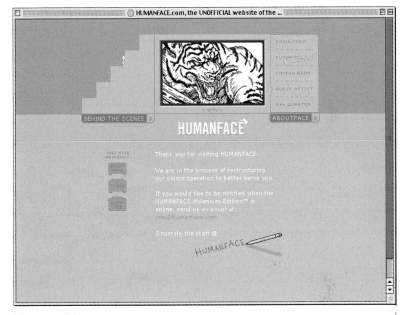

WWW.HUMANFACE.COM
D: PAUL KIM
M: INFO@HUMANFACE.COM

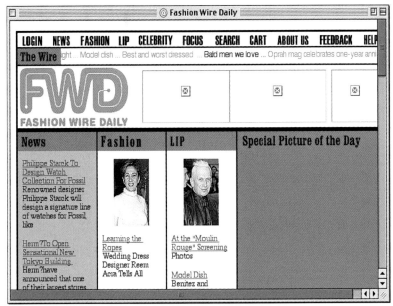

WWW.FASHIONWIREDAILY.COM/FWD/OPENING.ASP
D: IRWIN DRUKER
M: SALES@DIGINK.COM

WELCOME.SINGTEL.COM/MOVIE/DEFAULT.ASP
D: IVAN M.P. TAN
A: ARETAE LTD, M: IVAN.TAN@ARETAE.COM

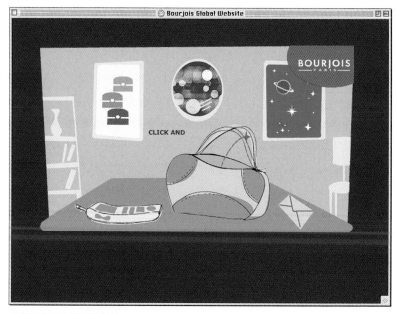

WWW.BOURJOIS.COM/BOURJOIS.CGI
A: WWW.SASDESIGN.CO.UK, M: HROBERTS@SASDESIGN.CO.UK

WWW.METHOD.COM
A: METHOD, M: INFO@METHOD.COM

WWW.ANYMO.COM/RYOKO
D: ADAM CHAN
M: ADAM@ANYMO.COM

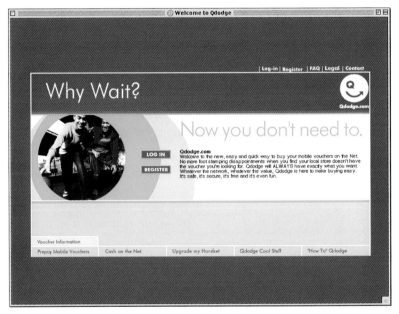

WWW.QDODGE.COM
A: BLACK ID, M: BLACK@BLACKID.COM

WWW.FASHIONEAST.CO.UK
D: OVEN DIGITAL, C: OVEN DIGITAL
A: OVEN DIGITAL LONDON, M: TOKE@OVEN.COM

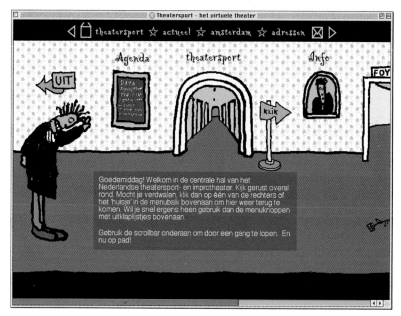

WWW.THEATERSPORT.NL
D: ARNOUD VAN DELDEN, **C:** ARNOUD VAN DELDEN
M: WEBMASTER@THEATERSPORT.NL

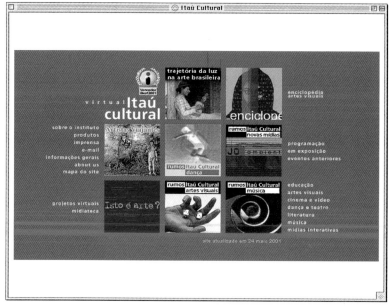

WWW.ITAUCULTURAL.ORG.BR
D: RICARDO RIBENBOIM, **C:** MARCOS CUZZIOL, **P:** JESUS DE PAULA ASSIS
A: ITAÚ CULTURAL, **M:** LUCIENE@ITAUCULTURAL.ORG.BR

WWW.BURGERKING.CO.UK
A: BLACK ID, **M:** BLACK@BLACKID.COM

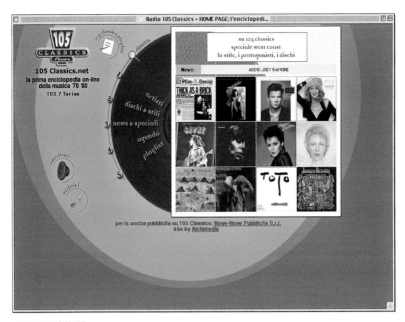

WWW.105CLASSICS.NET
D: ALESSANDRO AMODIO, C: ROBERTO FIORILI, P: ALESSANDRO AMODIO
A: ALCHIMEDIA S.R.L., M: AAMODIO@ALCHIMEDIA.COM

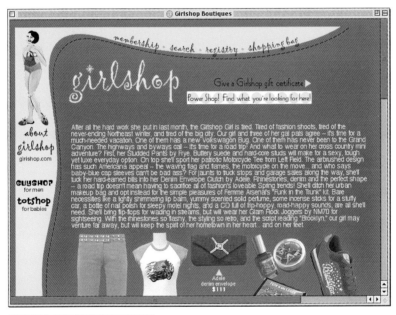

WWW.GIRLSHOP.COM/SHOP/GIRLS/DEFAULT.ASP
D: LAURA EISMAN
M: FEEDBACK@GIRLSHOP.COM

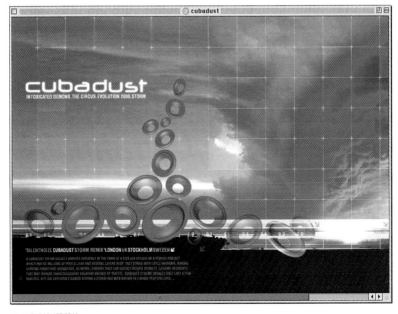

WWW.CUBADUST.COM
D: JONAS STRANDBERG-RINGH
M: HAGA@HOME.SE

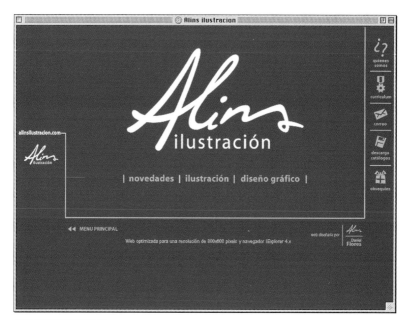

WWW.ALINSILUSTRACION.COM
C: DANIEL FLORES JIMÉNEZ
M: SONIAALINS@ALINSILUSTRACION.COM

WWW.PANTONEUNIVERSE.COM
A: SPILL INDUSTRIES, M: CONTACT@SPILL.NET

WWW.AGENTPROVOCATEUR.COM
A: WAX, M: JAMES.GHANI@WAX.CO.UK›

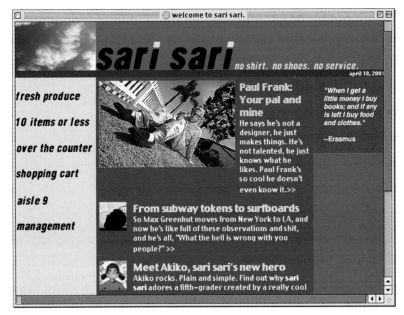

SARISARI.ORG/INDEX2.HTML
D: CHRISTINE CASTRO
M: CHRISTINE@SARISARI.ORG

WWW.JAMSHOES.COM
A: ATTIK.COM, M: TRACEYT@ATTIK.COM

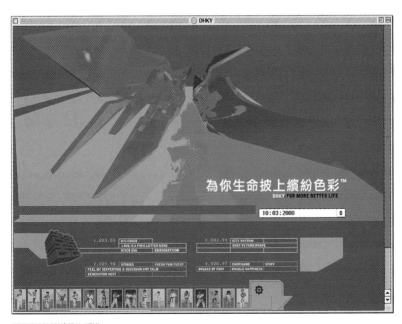

WWW.DHKY.COM/VIRAL.HTML
D: DAVID YU
M: SIFU@DHKY.COM

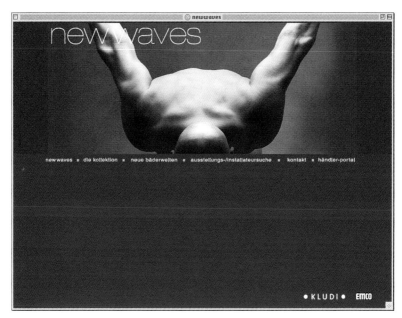

WWW.NEW-WAVES.DE
A: SCHLASSE GMBH, M: SCHUMACHER@SCHLASSE.DE

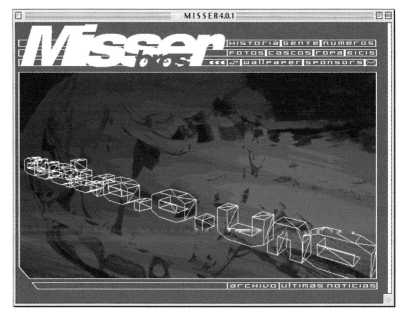

WWW.MISSERBROS.N3.NET
D: PAU MISSER, C: PAU MISSER
A: PM, M: ES.PAU@TERRA.ES

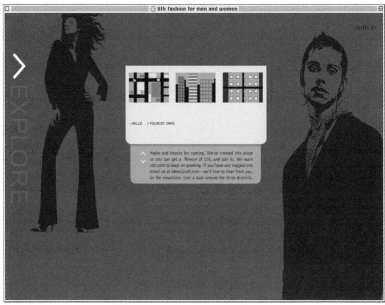

WWW.UTH.COM
A: WWW.SASDESIGN.CO.UK, M: HROBERTS@SASDESIGN.CO.UK

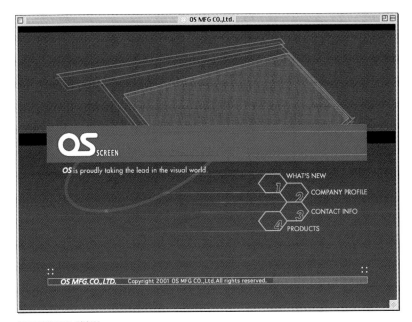

WWW.OSCORP.CO.JP/E/MFG
D: SYU SHIMAZAKI, **C:** SYU SHIMAZAKI, **P:** TAKAHARU ITO
A: OFFICE-I/O, **M:** ITO@OFFCE-IO.CO.JP

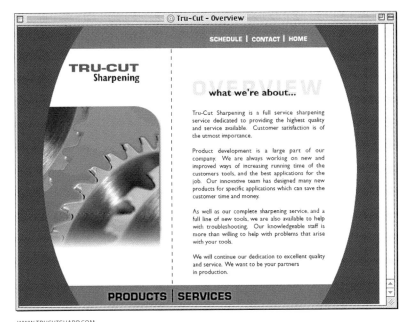

WWW.TRUCUTSHARP.COM
D: DAVID EDIGER
A: AXIS-MEDIA, **M:** DEDIGER@AXIS-MEDIA.COM

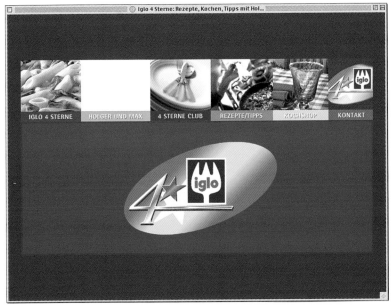

WWW.HOLGERUNDMAX.DE
D: MR HEIKO QUANT, MS HILKE HARTMANN

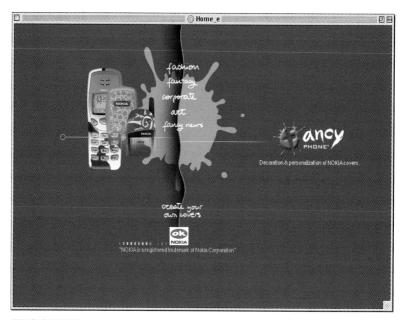

WWW.FANCYPHONE.ES
D: SANTI SALLÉS, **C:** SANTI SALLÉS
A: TUNDRABCN, **M:** INFO@TUNDRABCN.COM

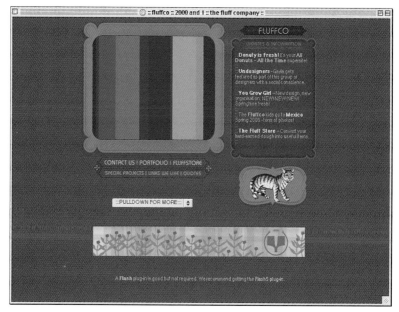

WWW.FLUFFCO.COM
D: DAVIN RISK / GAYLA SANDERS
M: DESIGN@FLUFFCO.COM

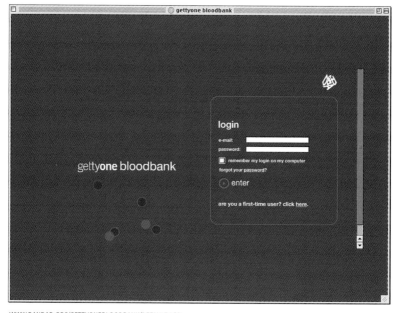

WWW.DANDAD.ORG/GETTYONEBLOODBANK/DEFAULT.ASP
D: CHRIS THOMPSON
M: CHRIS@DANDAD.CO.UK

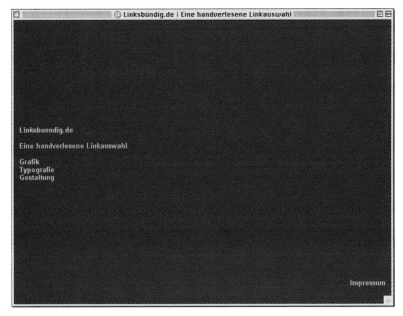

WWW.LINKSBUENDIG.DE
D: HARTMUT SCHRÖTER, C: HARTMUT SCHRÖTER
A: SCHRÖTER-DESIGN, M: SCHROETERDESIGN@WEB.DE

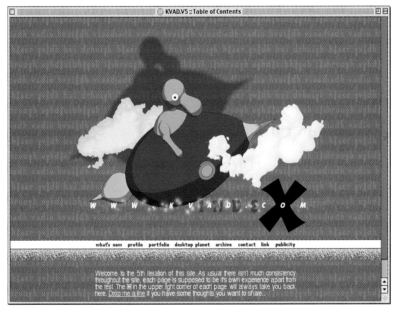

WWW.KVAD.COM/V5/TOC.HTML
D: KJETIL VATNE
M: VATNE@ONLINE.NO

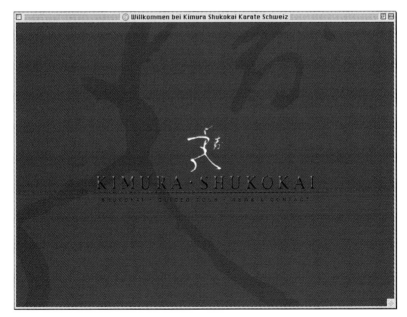

WWW.SHUKOKAI.CH
D: URS MEYER, C: OLIVER ZAHORKA, P: SHUKOKAI KARATESCHULEN SCHWEIZ
M: URS@OUT.TO

WWW.BRICK-BY-BRICK.COM
D: CAROLINE KAVANAGH, **C**: BENJAMIN KAUBISCH
A: RED CANOE

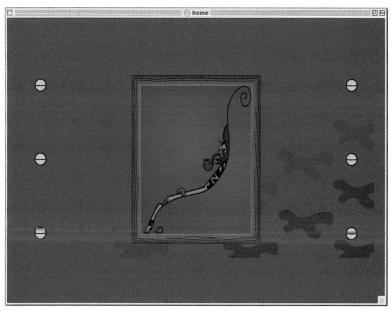

WWW.FOWLERISM.NET/GIRL.HTML
D: SIMON PIKE
A: BROAD SNOUT, **M**: SIMON@BROADSNOUT.COM

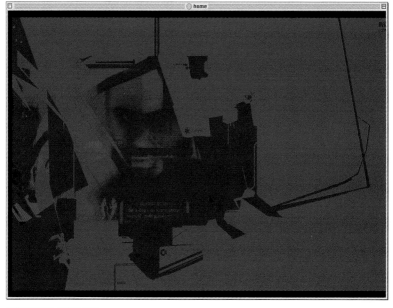

WWW.OVERAGE4DESIGN.COM
D: DAVID RONDEL
M: DRC@OVERAGE4DESIGN.COM

WWW.DOLOMITE.IT/ENGLISH.HTM
D: VALERIO TEDESCO
M: INFO@OOTWORLD.COM

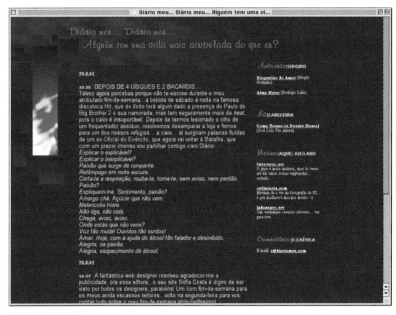

WWW.DIARIOMEU.COM
D: FILIPE MIGUEL TAVARES
A: MASMADERA.NET, M: FMT@FMTAVARES.NET

WWW.GEOCITIES.COM/VICTORIACONTRERAS
D: VICTORIA CONTRERAS FLORES
M: VCONT@MAIL.ONO.ES

WWW.AUSTRALIANINFRONT.COM.AU
D: MATTHEW WILLIS
M: INFRONT@AUSTRALIANINFRONT.COM.AU

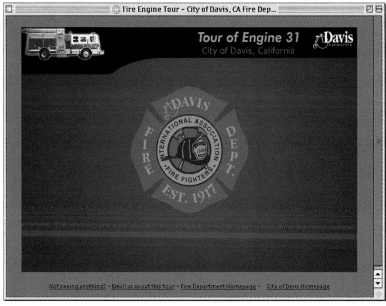

WWW.CITY.DAVIS.CA.US/FIRE/TOUR
D: SETH DUFFEY
M: SDUFFEY@CI.DAVIS.CA.US

WWW.KNNBCCB.COM/LOVE_IE.HTML
D: HOWE CHOON TANG
A: D:CHOTOMY, **M:** HOWE@KNNBCCB.CO

WWW.CHOPPINGBLOCK.COM
D: TOM ROMER, C: TOBY BOUDREAUX, P: KEITH PIZE
M: DARLEEN@CHOPPINGBLOCK.COM

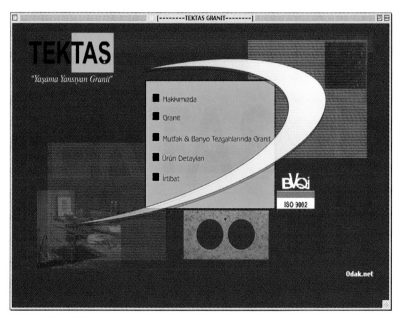

WWW.TEKTASGRANIT.COM
A: ODAK NET, M: KORAY@ODAK.NET

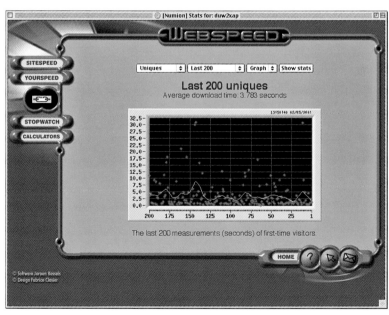

WWW.NUMION.COM
D: FABRICE CLOSIER, JEROEN KESSELS
A: ZUIDZIJDE RECLAME BUREAU, M: JEROEN@NUMION.COM

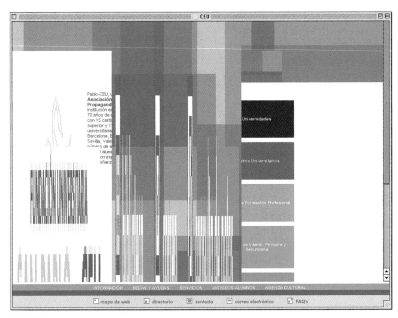

WWW.CEU.ES
A: EQUIPO BRANDMEDIA, M: INFO@BRANDMEDIA.COM

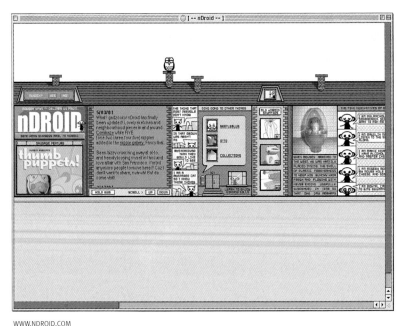

WWW.NDROID.COM
A: NDROID, M: GIRL@NDROID.COM

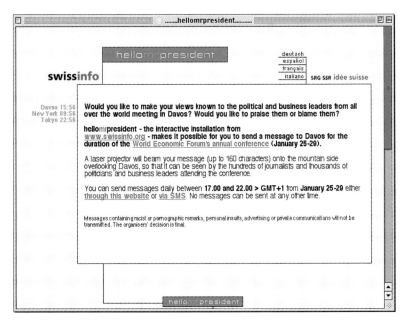

WWW.HELLOMRPRESIDENT.COM
D: CALC, C: CALC, P: JOHANNES.GEES
A: CALC, M: OMI@LAS.ES

244

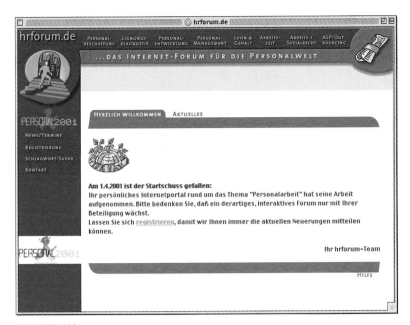

WWW.HRFORUM.DE
D: MICHAEL MAUCH
A: LOGOPILOT, M: MAUCH@LOGOPILOT.DE

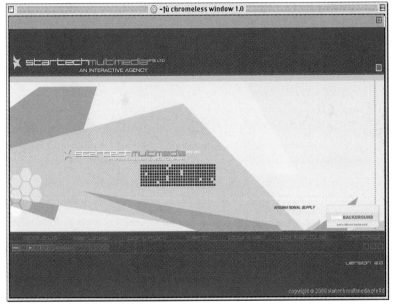

WWW.STARTECHMM.COM
A: STARTECH MULTIMEDIA PTE LTD., M: EUGENE@STARTECHMM.COM

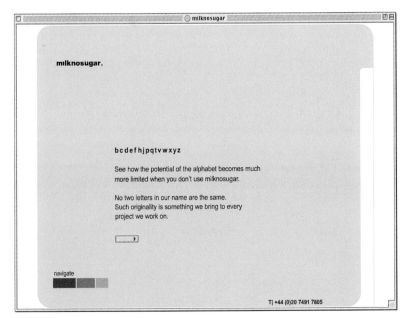

WWW.MILKNOSUGAR.COM/FLASH/INDEX.HTM
A: NAVYBLUE NEW MEDIA, M: NEWMEDIA@NAVYBLUE.COM

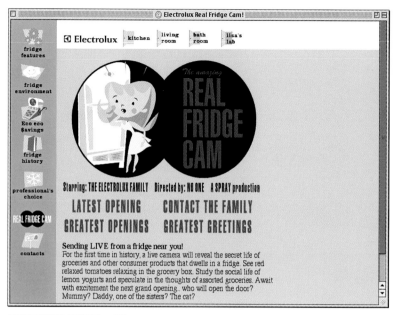

WWW.ELECTROLUX.COM/NODE230.ASP
A: ANDERS EDHOLM, M: ANDERS.EDHOLM@ELECTROLUX.SE

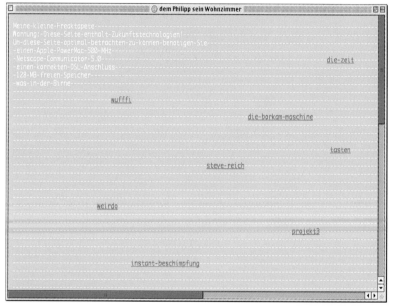

WWW.FH-TRIER.DE/~SCHILLIP
C: PHILIPP SCHILLING, P: PHILIPP SCHILLING
M: PIL.S@WEB.DE

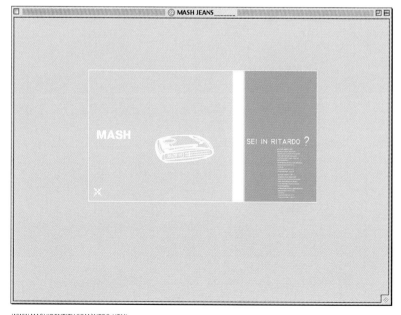

WWW.MASHIDENTITY.COM/INTRO.HTML
D: VALERIO TEDESCO
M: INFO@OOTWORLD.COM

WWW.DISRITMIA.COM.BR
D: ROGERIO RIBEIRO, **C:** ROGERIO RIBEIRO, **P:** MARCO VIDAL
A: ROGERIO RIBEIRO, **M:** INFOR@DISRITMIA.COM.BR

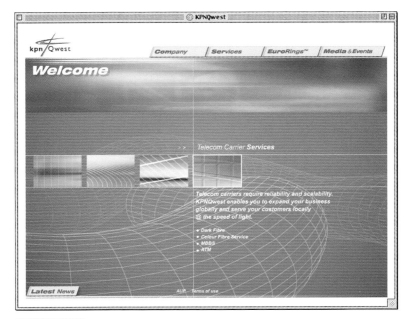

WWW.KPNQWEST.COM
D: MICHEAL O'SULLIVAN
M: MICHEAL@EGOMEDIA.COM

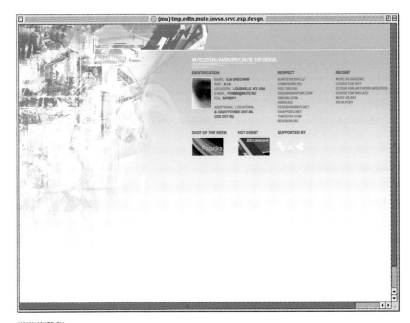

WWW.MUTE.RU
C: ILIA OVECHKIN, **P:** ILIA OVECHKIN
M: FORMS@MUTE.RU

WWW.FIFTIESWEB.COM
D: CANDACE RICH
A: RICH DESIGN STUDIOS, **M:** CANDACE@FIFTIESWEB.COM

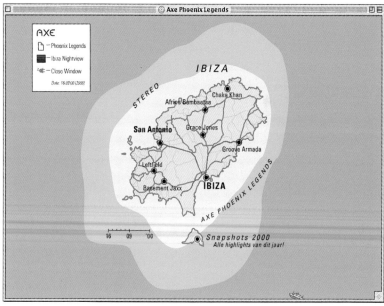

WWW.AXE.NL
D: YACCO VIJN, **C:** YACCO VIJN
M: YACCO@OZLO.NL

WWW.CAMENZINDGRAFENSTEINER.COM
D: STEFAN CAMENZIND
A: CAMENZIND GRAFENSTEINER, **M:** INFO@CAMENZINDGRAFENSTEINER.COM

WWW.EBOY.COM
A: EBOY, **M:** T@EBOY.COM

WWW.ELGIROENELEJE.ORG/INDEX.HTM
D: GABRIEL [-DHIJO-]
M: DIJO@JET.ES

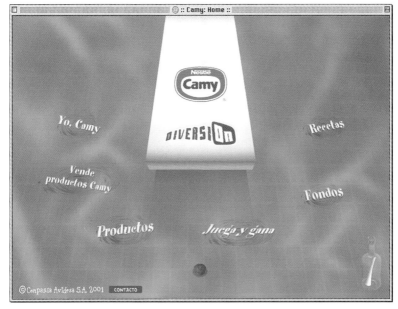

WWW.CAMY.ES
A: ARISTA INTERACTIVA

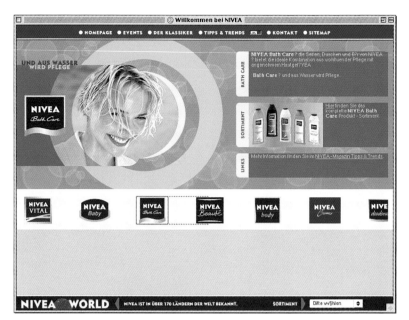

WWW.NIVEA.DE
D: ANDREW SINN
A: FORK UNSTABLE MEDIA, M: INFO@FORK.DE

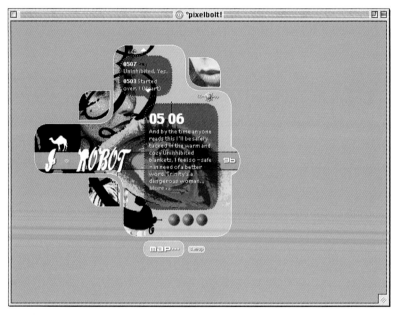

LEGLESS.INFECTIVE.NET
D: NEVR IOTA THESLEFF, C: NEVR IOTA THESLEFF
M: LINOTTE77@HOTMAIL.COM

WWW.SNEAKERBUILDER.COM/GALLERY_FSET.HTML
A: SIARON, M: SIARON@SNEAKERBUILDER.COM

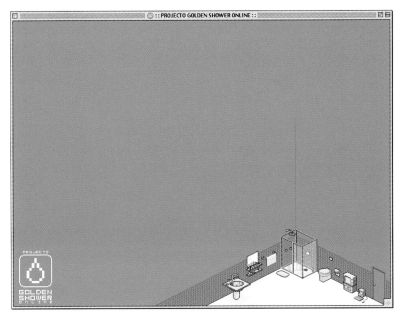

WWW.GOLDENSHOWER.GS/E/HOME.HTML
D: CARLOS BÊLA
M: CARLOSBELA@UIA.COM.BR

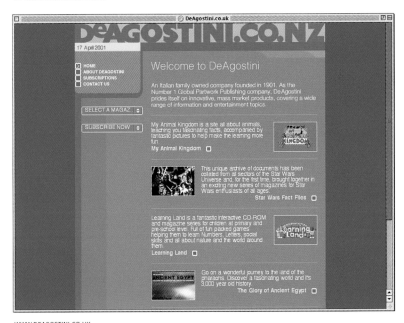

WWW.DEAGOSTINI.CO.UK
A: BLACK ID, **M:** BLACK@BLACKID.COM

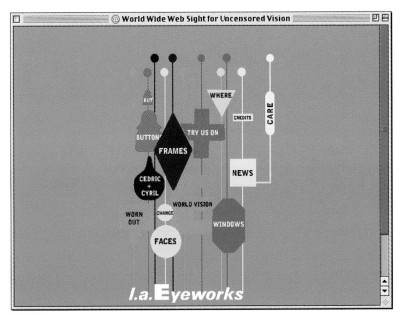

WWW.LAEYEWORKS.COM/INTERFACE.HTML
D: MICHAEL WORTHINGTON
M: MAXFISH@EARTHLINK.NET

WWW.ZOUKCLUB.COM/BASE.HTM
A: BLACK ID, M: BLACK@BLACKID.COM

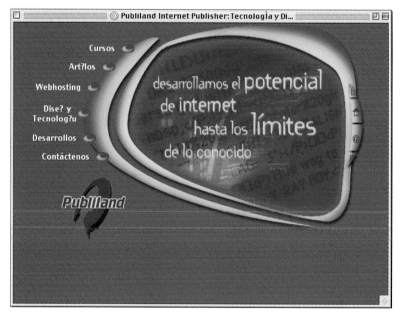

WWW.PUBLILAND.COM.AR
D: MERCEDES LOUGE, C: ALEJANDRO JARANDILLA, P: ALEJANDRO JARANDILLA
A: PUBLILAND, M: ALEJANDRO@PUBLILAND.COM.AR

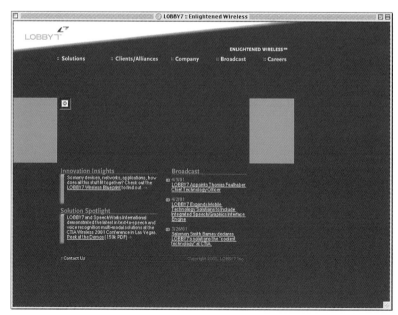

WWW.LOBBY7.COM
D: WWW.CATAPULTTHINKING.COM, WWW.JASONPRINCE.COM
M: J@JASONPRINCE.COM

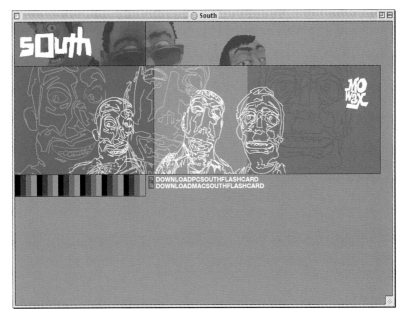

WWW.MOWAX.COM/SOUTH/SOUTH.HTML
D: BEN DRURY
A: TUI, M: MOWAX@ALMAROAD.CO.UK

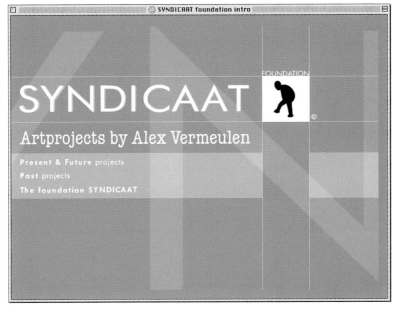

WWW.SYNDICAAT.ORG
D: HARTMAN
M: M.HARTMAN@WITHARTMAN.COM

WWW.OZ-ZONE.COM/PORTFOLIO/ECC/INDEX.HTM
D: KATRIN BRACKMANN, C: KATRIN BRACKMANN, P: ECC
M: KA@OZ-ZONE.DE

WWW.YOMIKO.COM
D: PAUL JASON, C: PAUL JASON
A: PAUL JASON, M: SUZETTE.NG@SPIKE.COM.AU

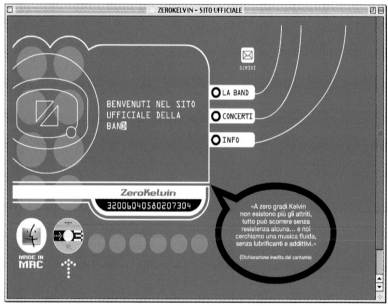

WWW.ZEROKELVIN.IT
D: MARCELLO BELLETTI
M: MARCELLO_BELLETTI@ONDE.NET

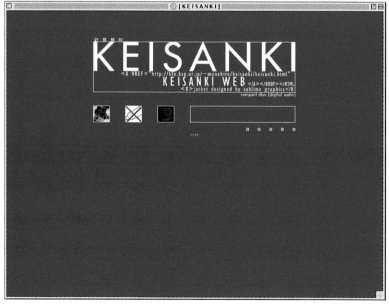

KFN.KSP.OR.JP/~MUNEHIRO/KEISANKI/KEISANKI.HTML
D: KEITA MATSUBARA
M: INFO@SUBLIMEGRAPHICS.COM

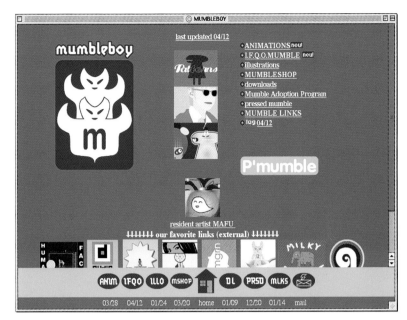

WWW.MUMBLEBOY.COM
D: MUMBLEBOY
M: MUMBLEBOY@MAIL.EARTHLINK.NET

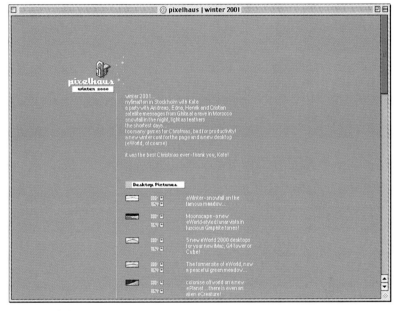

WWW.PIXELHAUS.COM
D: DAVE BRASGALLA
M: WEBMASTER@PIXELHAUS.COM

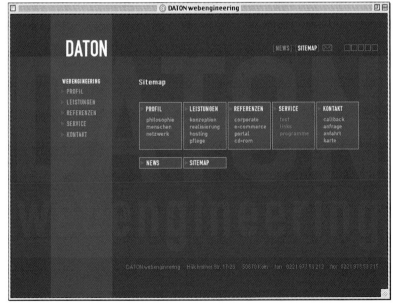

WWW.DATON.DE
D: A. HUHMANN
A: DATON, M: INFO@DATON.DE

WWW.ROMANDSON.COM
M: ANDYC@ROMANDSON.COM

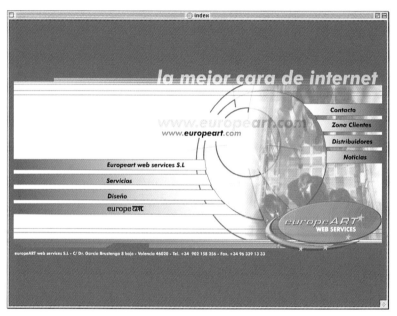

WWW.EUROPEART.COM
C: JOSE IBAÑEZ SORIA, P: EUROPEART WEB SERVICES S.L.
A: EUROPEART WEB SERVICES S.L., M: JOSE@EUROPEART.COM

WWW.SCOTTISHCANALS.CO.UK
A: BLACK ID, M: BLACK@BLACKID.COM

WWW.KICKZ.COM
D: CHRISTIAN GROSSE
A: KICKZ AG, M: GROSSE@KICKZ.COM

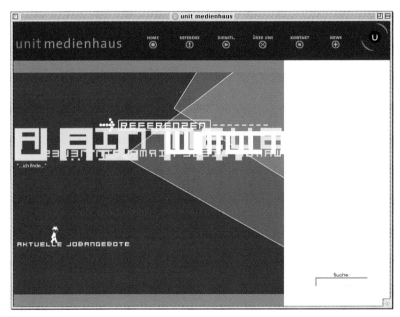

WWW.UNIT-MEDIENHAUS.DE
D: DIETMAR SCHMIDT, C: FRANK MÜLLER, P: KINGMEDIA
M: SCHMIDT@UNIT-MEDIENHAUS.DE

WWW.OXYGIZER.COM
D: MARKUS HÜBNER, C: MARKUS HÜBNER
A: WORLD-DIRECT.COM, M: OFFICE@WORLD-DIRECT.COM

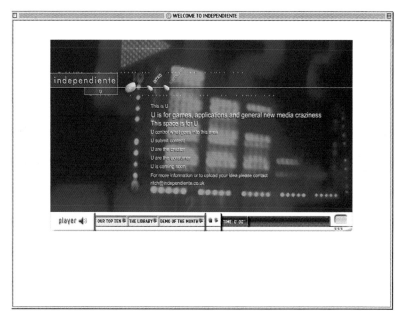

WWW.INDEPENDIENTE.CO.UK
D: BRAD SMITH
A: DIGIT, M: DELYTH@DIGITLONDON.COM

WWW.PHILIPS.COM.BR
P: BERNARDO SARTORI
M: FVIEIRACOURA@MODEMMEDIA.COM

WWW.PUBLISHERS.ASN.AU
D: MICHAEL SIGNAL
A: ARTICHOKE WEB DESIGN, M: MIKE@ARTICHOKEDESIGN.COM.AU

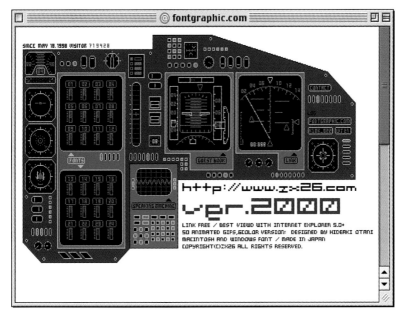

WWW.ZX26.COM
D: HIDEAKI OHTANI
M: ZX26@ZX26.COM

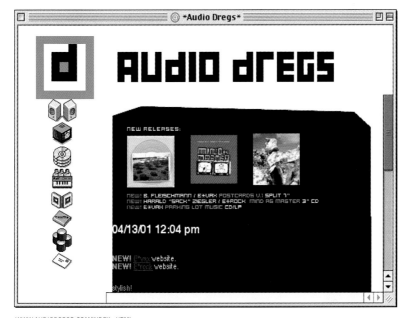

WWW.AUDIODREGS.COM/INDEX2.HTML
D: BROTHERS E*ROCK & E*VAX
M: EROCK@AUDIODREGS

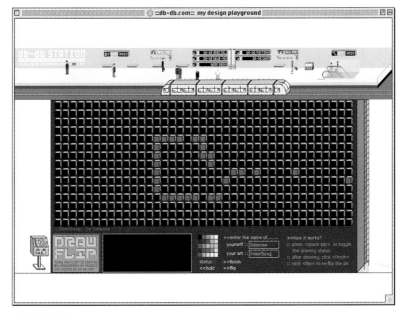

WWW.DB-DB.COM
D: FRANCIS LAM
M: FRANCIS@DB-DB.COM

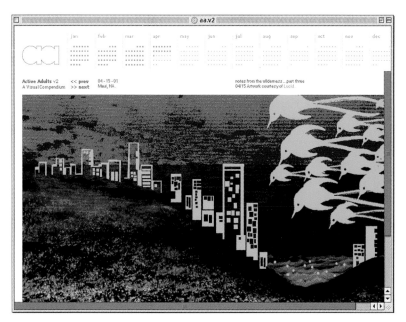

WWW.ACTIVEADULTS.NET
M: HEADOFFICE@ACTIVEADULTS.NET

WWW.VENTILATORMAG.COM
D: RACHEL LIPSITZ
M: ROLLERBALL@IONIX.NET

WWW.SCREENARIO.DE
D: VERENA SEGERT, **C:** VERENA SEGERT
M: VS@SCREENARIO.DE

WWW.SEBASTIAN-INTL.COM/WEB
D: MIRCO PASQUALINI
M: INFO@OOTWORLD.COM

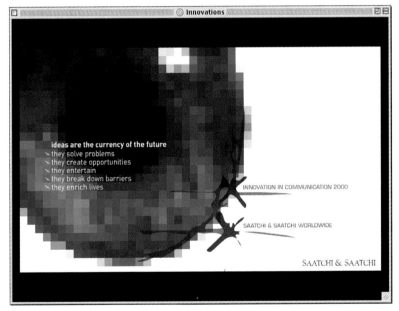

WWW.SAATCHI-SAATCHI.COM/INNOVATION/LAUNCH.HTML
A: AMAZE

WWW.MAXIBON.NESTLE.IT
D: SERGIO VALSECCHI, C: MIRIAM ALBANESE, P: ICONMEDIALAB
A: ICONMEDIALAB, M: SERGIO.VALSECCHI@ICONMEDIALAB.IT

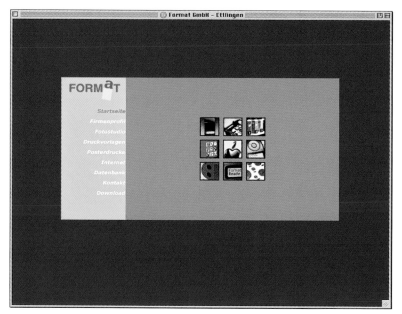

WWW.FORMATGMBH.DE
D: WOLFGANG KOPF, C: MARC BRODT
M: INFO@FORMATGMBH.DE

WWW.UBD-KOELN.DE
D: DIETMAR SCHMIDT, C: FRANK MÜLLER, P: KINGMEDIA
M: SCHMIDT@UNIT-MEDIENHAUS.DE

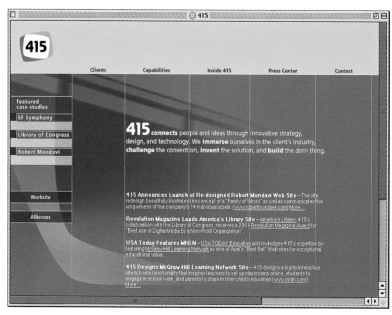

WWW.415.COM
A: 415 INC. COPYRIGHT © THE MCGRAW-HILL COMPANIES, M: INFO@415.COM

WWW.SIQUEIRACAMPOS.COM
D: TATIANA BRUGALLI, C: GLADIMIR DUTRA, P: FABIANO DE ANDRADE
A: ALDEIA DESIGN, M: FABIANO@ALDEIADESIGN.COM.BR

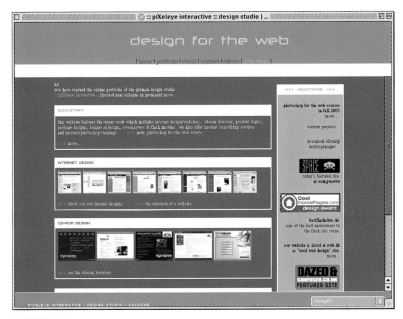

WWW.PIXELEYE.NET
D: DIRK BEHLAU
M: DIRK@PIXELEYE.DE

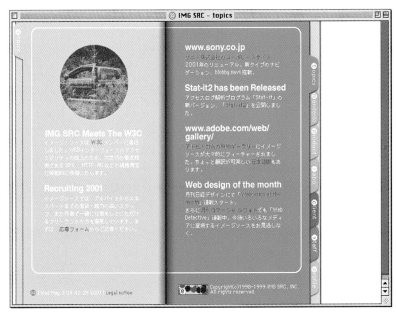

WWW.IMGSRC.CO.JP
A: IMG SRC, INC., M: INFO@IMGSRC.CO.JP

WWW.ODAK.NET
A: ODAK NET, **M:** KORAY@ODAK.NET

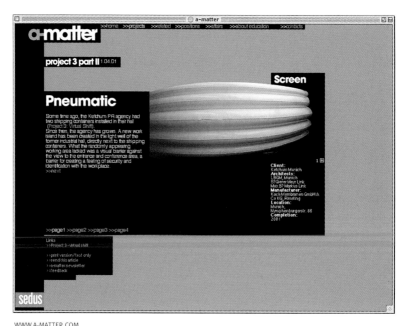

WWW.A-MATTER.COM
D: FRANK THIELE
A: FACTOR PRODUCT , **M:** F.THIELE@FACTOR-PRODUCT.COM

WWW.MORAT-KG.COM
D: FRANK MILKAU
A: SURFERS PARADISE SITE-FACTORY, **M:** INFO@FRAMO-MORAT.COM

WWW1.KTBOXING.COM
D: MICHAEL SIGNAL
A: ARTICHOKE WEB DESIGN

WWW.EXPANETS.COM/SITE/DEFAULT.HTM
A: OOTWORLD, M: INFO@OOTWORLD.COM

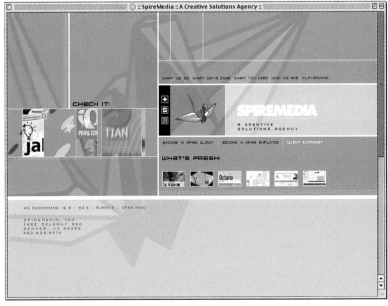

WWW.SPIREMEDIA.COM/INDEX2.CFM
D: PAUL SCHRANK
A: SPIREMEDIA, M: PAUL@SPIREMEDIA.COM

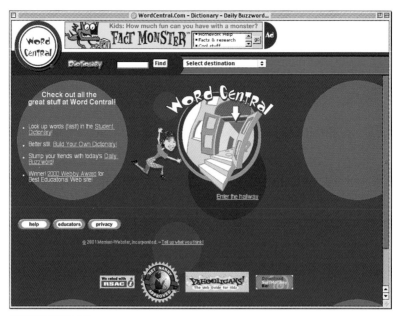

WWW.WORDCENTRAL.COM
D: URBAN OASIS
M: SFAVRE@URBANOASIS.NET

WWW.SNOWEXPERTS.AT/F_EXPERTEN...1.HTML
D: PETER HUMMEL, C: JOHANNES B., P: TISCOVER AG
A: PLATFORM-C, M: PETER.HUMMEL@PLATFORM-C.CH

WWW.ALTEA-ONLINE.COM
D: KATRIN BRACKMANN, C: BERND BRAUN, P: ALTEA
A: ONLINE RELATIONS, M: KA@OZ-ZONE.DE

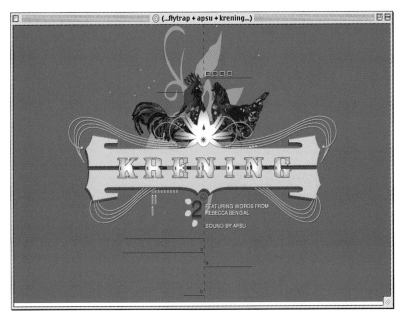

WWW.BARSHOW.CO.UK
D: AUDRA FRANCIS
M: INFO@DALZIEL-POW.CO.UK

WWW.BARSHOW.CO.UK
M: INFO@DALZIEL-POW.CO.UK

WWW.CONCEPTOSURBANOS.COM
D: MICHAEL IRIZARRY, C: LESSER DEMARCHENA, P: MICHAEL REDONDO
A: SIXTHLIGHT STUDIOS CORP., M: FLASHWAVE2K@HOTMAIL.COM

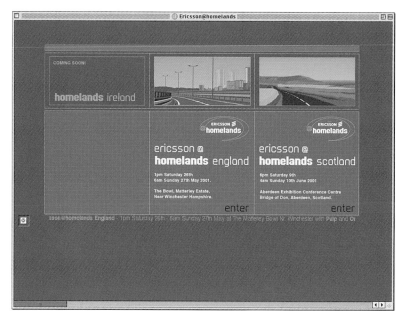

WWW.HOMELANDS.CO.UK
A: BLACK ID, M: BLACK@BLACKID.COM

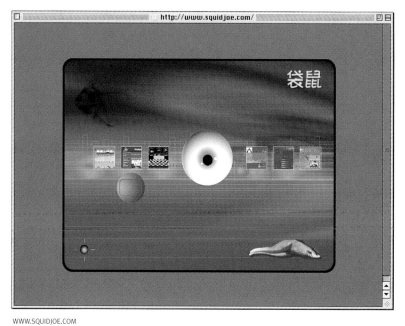

WWW.SQUIDJOE.COM
D: JOE, C: JOE
M: SQUIDJOE@HOTMAIL.COM

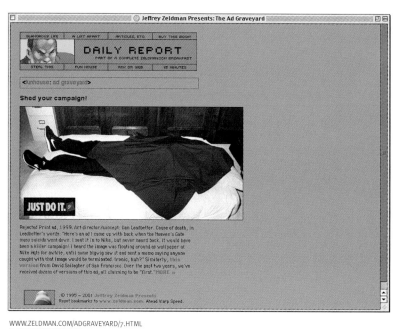

WWW.ZELDMAN.COM/ADGRAVEYARD/7.HTML
A: WWW.ZELDMAN.COM/

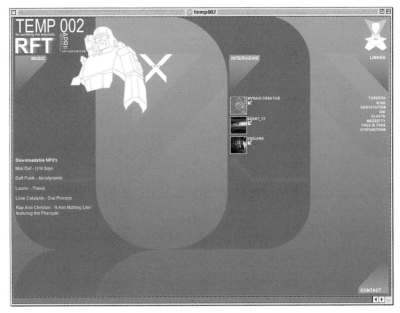

WWW.RADIOFREETOKYO.COM
D: SETH ERICKSON
M: INFO@RADIOFREETOKYO.COM

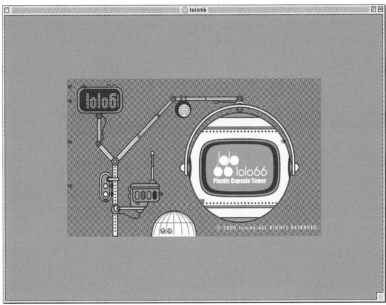

HOME8.HIGHWAY.NE.JP/LOUNGE/TOP-F/INDEX.HTML
D: TORU KONO [LOLO66]
M: LOOSE@PI.HIGHWAY.NE.JP

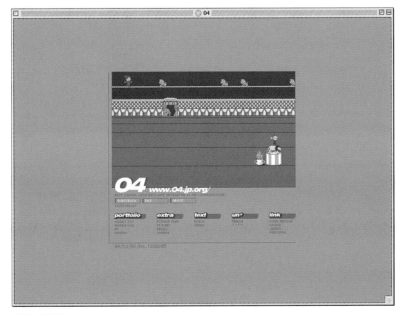

WWW.o4.JP.ORG
D: YUJI OSHIMOTO
M: o4@JP.ORG

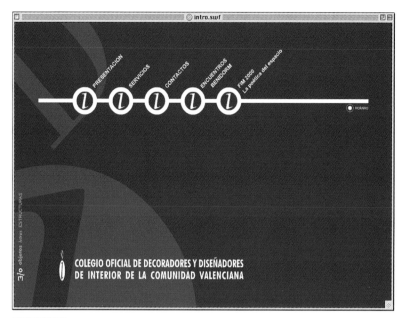

WWW.CDICV.COM
D: VICENTE REVERT, **C:** VICENTE REVERT TATAY
M: OLECOMUNICACION@TERRA.ES

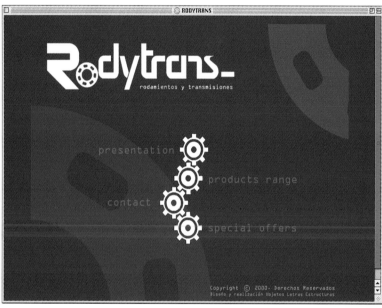

WWW.RODYTRANS.ES
D: VICENTE REVERT, **C:** VICENTE REVERT TATAY
M: OLECOMUNICACION@TERRA.ES

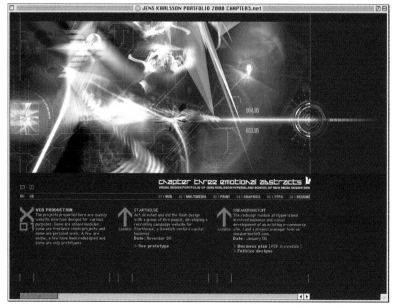

WWW.CHAPTER3.NET
C: JENS KARLSSON, **P:** JENS KARLSSON
M: JENS@CHAPTER3.NET

WWW.LAWOFTHEJUNGLE.COM.AU
A: ARTICHOKE, M: ALES@ARTICHOKEDESIGN

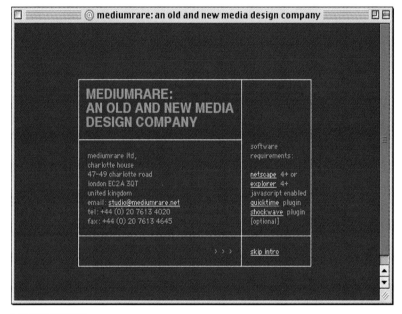

WWW.MEDIUMRARE.NET
D: TOBY STOKES, C: GARY HILL, P: TOBY STOKES
A: MEDIUMRARE, M: CHRISTIAN@MEDIUMRARE.NET

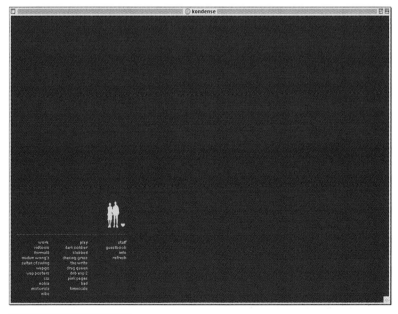

WWW.KONDENSE.COM/MAINFRAME.HTM
D: KENNY KENTAN
M: KENTAN@KONDENSE.COM

WWW.THELIGHTHOUSE.CO.UK/HOME.HTML
A: NAVYBLUE NEW MEDIA, M: NEWMEDIA@NAVYBLUE.COM

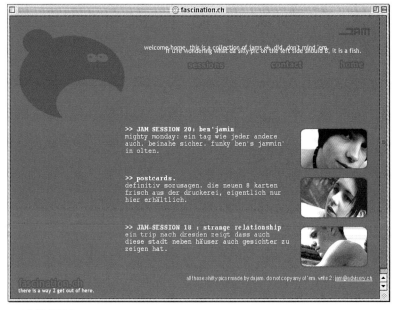

WWW.FASCINATION.CH
D: JAM, JVO A.MAURER
M: FISCHIMGLAS@SOUTHPOLE.CH

WWW.FLOU.IT/HTML/COMMON/WIZARD
A: ORCHESTRA S.R.L, M: INFO@FLOU.IT

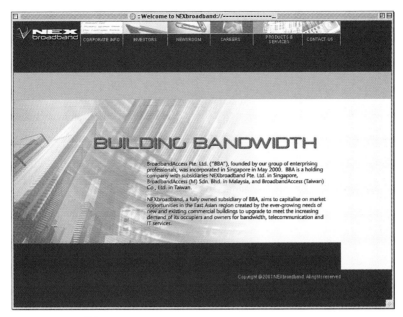

WWW.NEXBROADBAND.COM
A: STARTECH MULTIMEDIA PTE LTD., M: EUGENE@STARTECHMM.COM

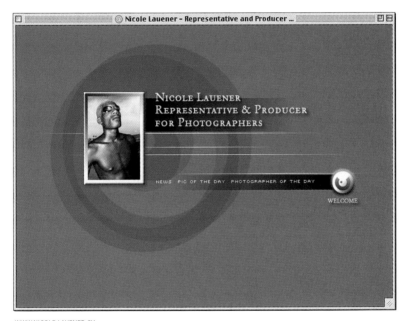

WWW.NICOLE-LAUENER.CH
D: URS MEYE, C: OLIVER ZAHORKA, P: NICOLE LAUENER
M: URS@OUT.TO

WWW.CITTADELLARTE.IT
D: CALC, C: CALC
A: CALC, M: OMI@LAS.ES

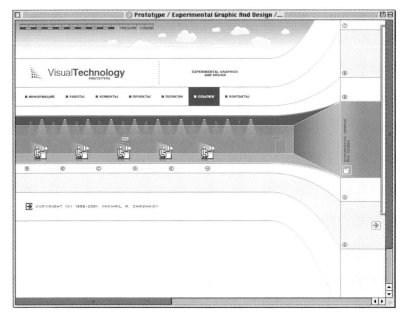

WWW.PROTOTYPE.RU
C: ROMAN GRIGOROVICH, P: MIKHAIL A. ZHSHKOV
M: PROTOTYPE@HOTBOX.RU

WWW.ZYTRONIC.CO.UK
D: CHRIS JONES, C: CHRIS JONES
A: CLOCKWORK DESIGN, M: INFO@CLOCKWORK-DESIGN.CO.UK

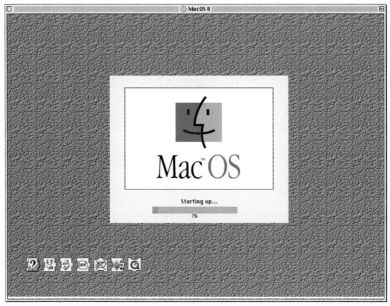

WWW.YAROMAT.COM/MACOS8
D: JARO VON FLOCKEN
A: WWW.N-IMAGE.COM

274

WWW.MARTINAWINTER.DE
D: MICHAEL FEUERBACHER, C: MICHAEL FEUERBACHER
M: MICK@FEUERBACHER.DE

WWW.DREADA.DE/FLASHSITE/MITK5.HTML
D: WALTER MÖSSLER, C: PACO LALUCA
A: TOUCHEE, M: WMOESSLER@TOUCHEE.DE

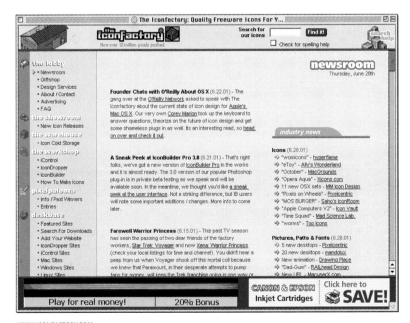

WWW.ICONFACTORY.COM
D: GEDEON MAHEUX
M: GEDEON@ICONFACTORY.COM

WWW.HUMONGOUS.COM
D: REBECCA FUHRMAN
M: WEBMASTER@HUMONGOUS.COM

WWW.GAZZETTA.IT
D: SERGIO VALSECCHI, C: MIRIAM ALBANESE, P: ICONMEDIALAB
A: ICONMEDIALAB, M: SERGIO.VALSECCHI@ICONMEDIALAB.IT

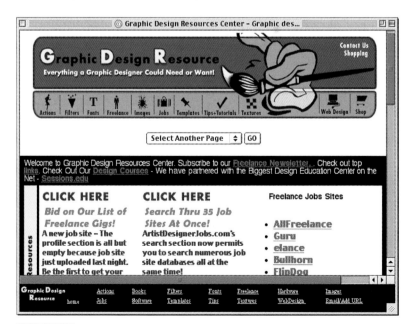

WWW.DEEZIN.COM
D: RACHEL GOLDSTEIN
M: DEEZIN2@AOL.COM

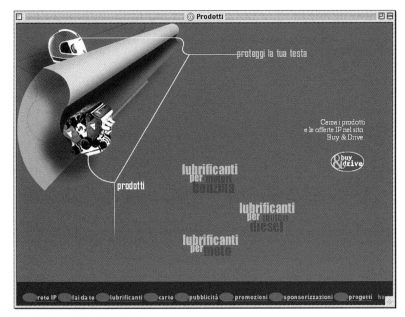

WWW.AGIPPETROLI.IT/IP/PRODOTTI.HTML
D: GUERINO DELFINO
M: DELFINO@HYPHEN.IT

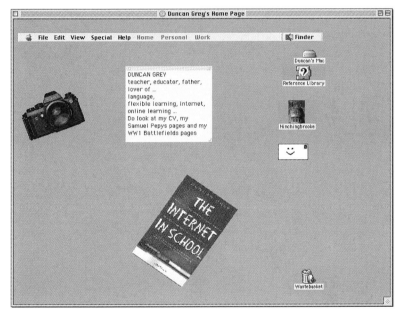

WWW.HINCHBK.CAMBS.SCH.UK/DUNK/DUNK.HTML
D: DUNCAN GREY, **C:** DUNCAN GREY
A: DUNCAN GREY, **M:** DSG@POST.COM

WWW.MIB.IT
D: RIZZA MASSIMILIANO, **C:** RIZZA MASSIMILIANO
M: MIB@MIB.IT

WWW.GOTREK.COM.AU/GOTREK/INDEX.HTML
D: MICHAEL SIGNAL
A: ARTICHOKE WEB DESIGN, M: MIKE@ARTICHOKEDESIGN.COM.AU

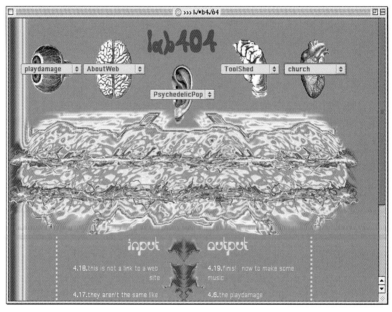

WWW.LAB404.COM
D: CURT CLONINGER
M: CURT@LAB404.COM

WWW.TROJE.NL
D: ARNOUD VAN DELDEN, C: ARNOUD VAN DELDEN
M: TROJE@WHIZZWEB.NL

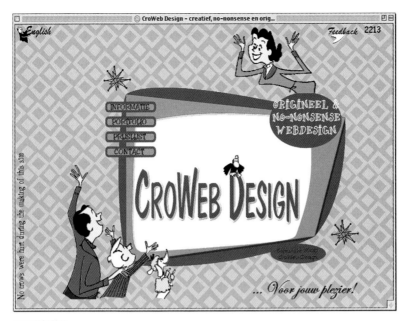

WWW.CROWEB.NL
D: CAROLINE VAN DEN BERG
A: CROWEB DESIGN, M: INFO@CROWEB.NL

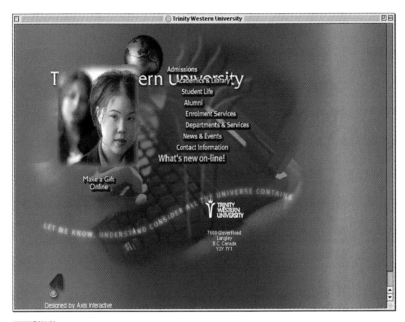

WWW.TWU.CA
A: AXIS INTERACTIVE DESIGN INC., M: DESIGN@AXIS-MEDIA.COM

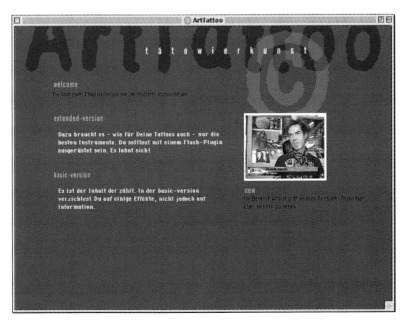

WWW.ARTTATTOO.CH
D: URS MEYER, C: OLIVER ZAHORKA, P: HENRIK AMAIS
M: URS@OUT.TO

WWW.CELINETTE.COM
D: CÉLINE CLANET
M: CELINE.CLANET@NOOS.FR

WWW.TWELVEFIRE.COM
C: FLORIAN WEBER, P: FLORIAN WEBER
M: CSSHSH@STRUCTBENCH.COM

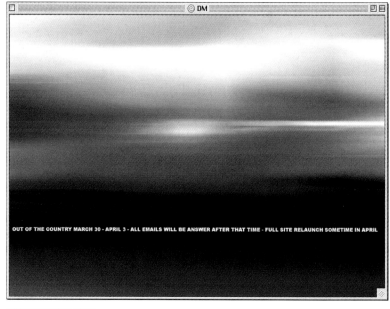

WWW.DESIGNMONTAGE.COM
D: ROIBBIE HIRSCH, C: ROBBIE HIRSCH, P: ROBBIE HIRSCH
M: R@DESIGNMONTAGE.COM

TWELVEFIRE.COM/TWELVEFIRE.HTML
D: FLORIAN WEBER
A: **TWELVEFIRE, M:** INFO@TWELVEFIRE.COM

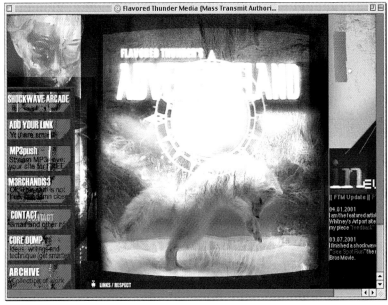

WWW.FLAVOREDTHUNDER.COM/INDEX9-2000.SHTML
D: MARK DAGGETT
M: MARK@FLAVOREDTHUNDER.COM

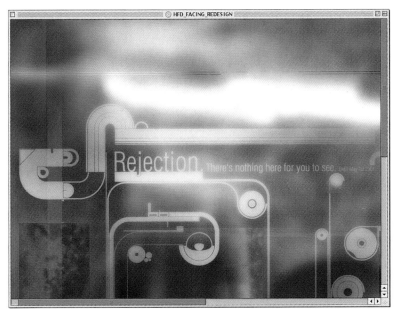

WWW.HUNGRYFORDESIGN.COM
D: NANDO COSTA
M: NANDO@ICONOLOGIC.COM

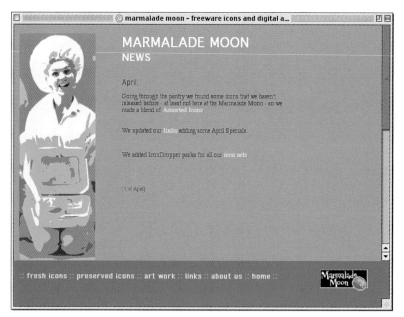

WWW.MARMALADEMOON.COM
D: CATHARINA ENGLAND
M: WEBMISTRESS@MARMALADEMOON.COM

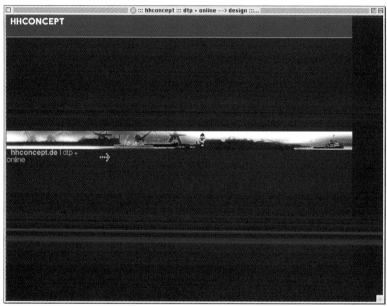

WWW.HHCONCEPT.DE
D: ANDREAS F. SPERWIEN, C: ANDREAS F. SPERWIEN
A: SPERWIEN DESIGN, M: INFO@HHCONCEPT.DE

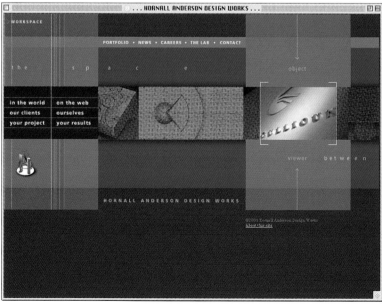

WWW.HADW.COM
D: CHRIS SALLQUIST, P: HALLIE BOWKER
A: HORNALL ANDERSON DESIGN WORKS, INC., M: INFO@HADW.COM

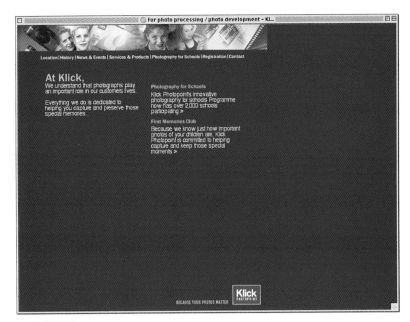

WWW.KLICK.CO.UK
A: BLACK ID, M: BLACK@BLACKID.COM

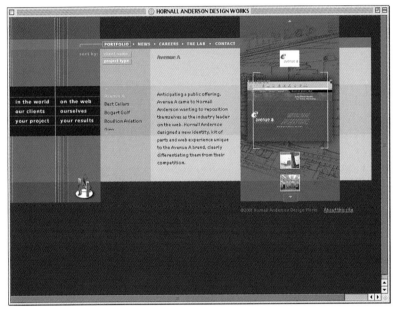

WWW.HORNALLANDERSON.COM/PORTFOLIO.PHP
D: MARGARET LONG, P: HALLIE BOWKER
A: HORNALL ANDERSON DESIGN WORKS, INC., M: INFO@HADW.COM

WWW.UTENTI.TRIPOD.IT/ECAMPAN
A: CAMPANER ENRICO WEB, M: ECAMPANER@HOTMAIL.COM

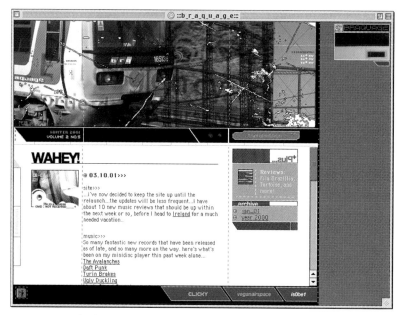

WWW.BRAQUAGE.COM/BRQ/INDEX.HTM
A: VP HOLLERAN, M: VPH@BRAQUAGE.COM

WWW.BOSKAR.COM
A: ODAK.NET, M: KORAY@ODAK.NET

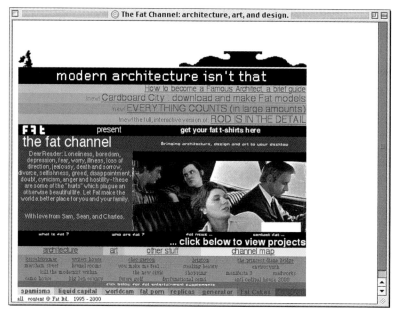

WWW.FAT.CO.UK
A: FAT, M: FAT@FAT.CO.UK

WWW.NAKEDHOLIDAY.COM
D: MAT POPROCKI
A: NAKED HOLIDAY, M: SEX@NAKEDHOLIDAYC.OM

WWW.PRENSAFREELANCE.COM
D: DAVID NAVARRO GÓMEZ, C: DAVID NAVARRO GÓMEZ
A: ENK3 PROYECTOS DE COMUNICACIÓN, M: NAVARRO@PRENSAFREELANCE.COM

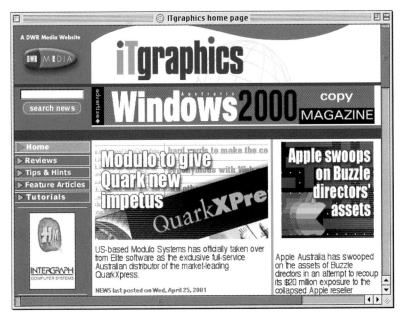

WWW.ITGRAPHICS.COM
A: DWR MEDIA PTY LTD., M: DWR@DWR.COM.AU

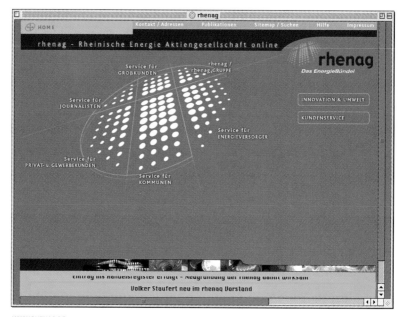

WWW.RHENAG.DE
D: KATRIN BRACKMANN, C: KATRIN BRACKMANN, P: RHENAG
A: ONLINE RELATIONS, M: KA@OZ-ZONE.DE

WWW.BUYAROCK.COM/INDEX_01.HTML
D: DARLEEN SCHERER
M: DARLEEN@CHOPPINGBLOCK.COM

WWW.BIJENKORF.NL
D: MIREILLE KOEKELIS, C: RAOUL BRAHIM
M: MIREILLE.KOEKELIS@BIT-IC.NL

WWW.MATIM.COM
D: MATTHIAS, C: MATTHIAS,
M: MATIM@CARAMAIL.COM

WWW.LS-D.DE/START.HTML
D: SVEN NIKOLAUS RUSCHEK
A: IN(CORPORATE COMMUNICATION+DESIGN, M: INFO@INCORPORATE.DE

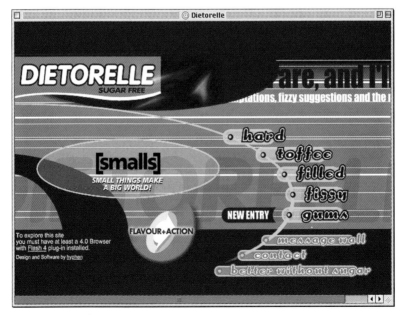

WWW.DIETORELLE.IT/ING/HOME.HTML
D: GUERINO DELFINO
M: DELFINO@HYPHEN.IT

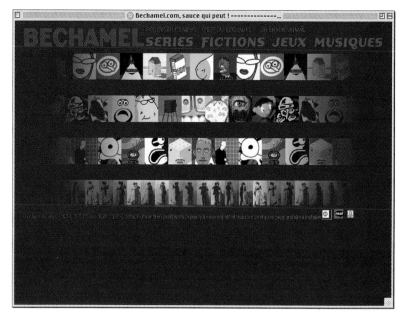

WWW.BECHAMEL.COM
D: GUILLAUME JOIRE, SOPHIE ESTIVAL
A: BECHAMEL.COM, M: DITES-NOUS-TOUT@BECHAMEL.COM

WWW.KJURSTEKA.YO.LV
D: ILZE CIMOSKA, C: ILZE CIMOSKA
A: KJURSTEKA, M: ILZE@INTERBALTIKA.COM

WWW.REYFELIPE.COM
D: AITOR AYESA, C: AITOR AYESA
A: AYSER - DESARROLLOS INFORMÁTICOS, M: DIGGER@AYSER.COM

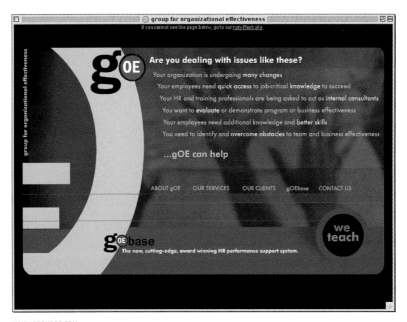

WWW.GROUPOE.COM
D: HOWARD CLEVELAND
M: HOWARDC@DIGITAL-DAY.COM

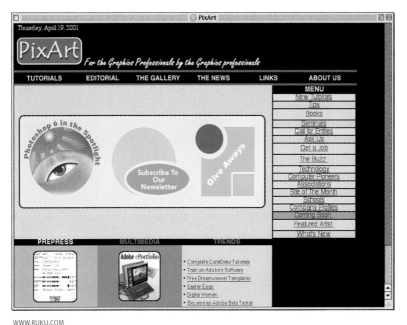

WWW.RUKU.COM
D: JOE WILLIAMS
M: PIXART@RUKU.COM

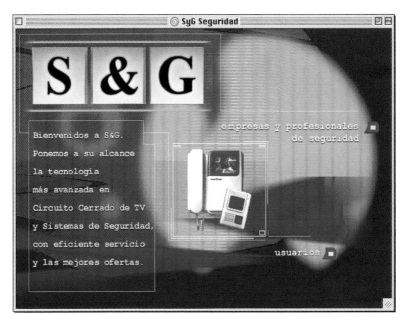

WWW.SYGSEGURIDAD.COM.AR
D: MERCEDES LOUGE, C: ALEJANDRO JARANDILLA, P: ALEJANDRO JARANDILLA
A: PUBLILAND, M: ALEJANDRO@PUBLILAND.COM.AR

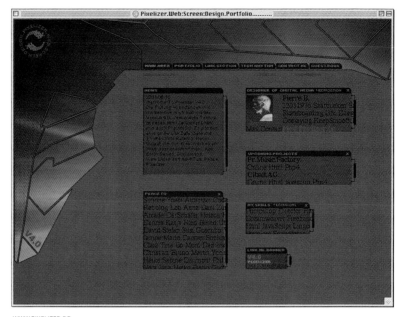

WWW.PIXELIZER.DE
D: PIERRE BROST, C: PIERRE BROST
M: ME@PIXELIZER.DE

WWW.HABBOHOTEL.COM
A: HABBO HOTEL, M: INFO@HABBOGROUP.COM

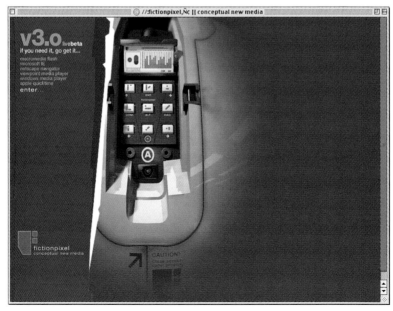

WWW.FICTIONPIXEL.COM
D: DADE ORGERON, C: DADE ORGERON
A: FICTIONPIXEL, M: DADE@FICTIONPIXEL.COM

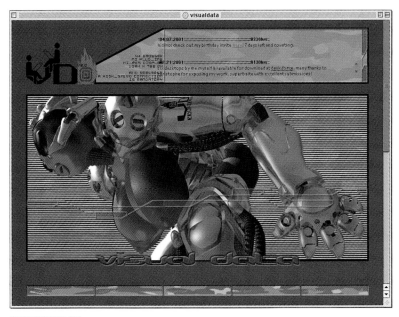

WWW.VISUALDATA.ORG
D: RONALD WISSE
A: VISUALDATA, **M:** VISUALDATA@CHELLO.NL

WWW.TERMINMASCHINE.DE/CALENDAR.HTML
D: ANDRÉ NITZE, **C:** ANDRÉ NITZE, **P:** ANDRÉ NITZE
A: NEW IMAGE CWS GMBH, **M:** NITZE@N-IMAGE.COM

WWW.77DESIGN.COM
D: JASON LERACE
M: JIERACE@HOTMAIL.COM

WWW.LIMMY.COM/PROJECTS/BIRDWATCHING/BIRDWATCHING_POPUP.HTM
M: LIMMY@LIMMY.COM

WWW.SOFTROOM.COM
D: SOPHIE CLINKARD
A: SOFTROOM LTD, **M:** SOFTROOM@SOFTROOM.CO

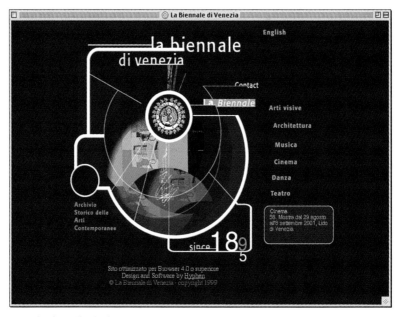

WWW.LABIENNALEDIVENEZIA.NET
D: GUERINO DELFINO
M: DELFINO@HYPHEN.IT

WWW.MAMALION.COM
D: SIOUXZAN PERRY, C: JIM BARROW, P: SIOUXZAN PERRY
A: MAKIN' WAVES, M: SIOUXZAN@MAKINWAVES.COM

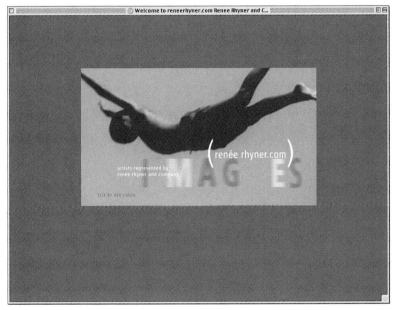

WWW.RENEERHYNER.COM
D: CAROLINE KAVANAGH, C: DEBORAH KOCH
A: RED CANOE

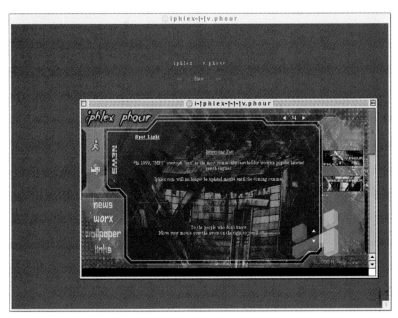

WWW.IPHLEX.COM
D: HOWARD, C: HOWARD
A: IPHLEX, M: IPHLEX@HOTMAIL,.COM

WWW.DONBARNETT.COM
D: DON BARNETT
M: INFO@DONBARNETT.COM

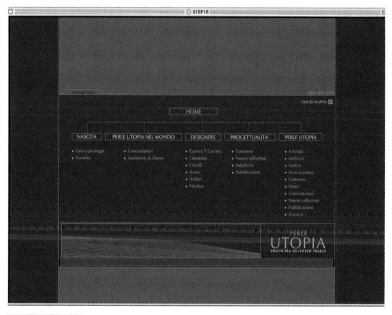

WWW.PERLEUTOPIA.COM
D: ALESSANDRO ORLANDI, **P:** SEVEN S.R.L.
M: SONIA.MARTINI@SEVEN.IT

WWW.EXPECTING.DE
D: MARCUS WACKER
M: MARCUS@EXPECTING.DE

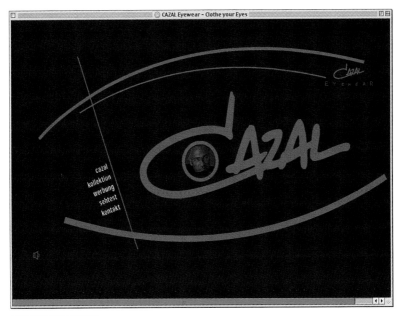

WWW.CAZAL.DE/CAZAL.HTML
D: COLLIN CROOME
M: COLLIN@COMA2.COM

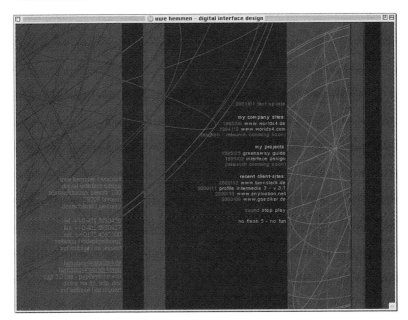

WWW.UWE-HEMMEN.DE
D: UWE HEMMEN, C: UWE HEMMEN
M: HEMMEN@WORLDS4.COM

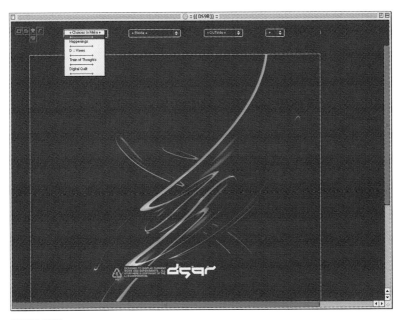

WWW.DS9R.COM
D: KEVIN VO, C: KEVIN VO
M: DS9R@DS9R.COM

WWW.GUERRESTELLARI.NET
D: ANGEL ATILAK
A: ATILAK CYBER-GOTHIC, M: ANGELO@ANGELICADUTI.ORG

WWW.BAIRESPIANOBAR.COM.AR
D: MERCEDES LOUGE, C: ALEJANDRO JARANDILLA, P: ALEJANDRO JARANDILLA
A: PUBLILAND, M: ALEJANDRO@PUBLILAND.COM.AR

WWW.007.COM
D: MICKEY STRETTON
A: DIGIT, M: DELYTH@DIGITLONDON.COM

WWW.SUCCESS-EZINE.COM
D: JERRY OVERTON, C: JERRY OVERTON
A: SUCCESS-EZINE, M: TRACY.OVERTON@HOME.COM

WWW.PRINTSONWEB.COM
D: MIRCO PASQUALINI, C: SIMONE MOREALI, P: SEVEN S.R.L.
A: SEVEN S.R.L., M: SONIA.MARTINI@SEVEN.IT

WWW.SYSTECHUSA.COM
D: VALERIO TEDESCO
M: INFO@OOTWORLD.CO

WWW.EDIBLEPLASTYC.COM
D: WARIK, C: WARIK
M: EDIBLEPLASTYC@IPRIMUS.COM.AU

WWW.V-I-P.NL
D: YACCO VYN, C: YACCO VYN, P: JURIAN VAN DER MEER
M: YACCO@YACCO.NET

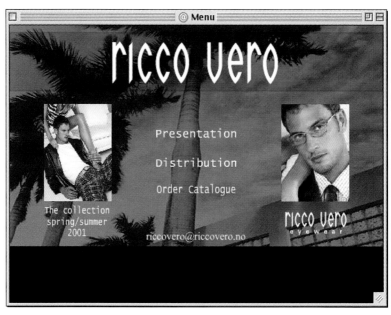

WWW.RICCOVERO.NO/MAINPAGE.HTML
A: SCREEN COMMUNICATION, M: RICCOVERO@RICCOVERO.NO

SUPERESC.COM/2001/POPUP.HTML
D: CALVIN SUN
M: CALVINS@CRITICALMASS.COM

WWW.TURNERCLASSICMOVIES.COM
D: ROB REED, C: CHANDLER MCWILLIAMS, P: KEITH PIZER
M: DARLEEN@CHOPPINGBLOCK.COM

WWW.SECONDSTORY.COM/?FEATURES
D: JULIE BEELER
M: JULIE@SECONDSTORY.COM

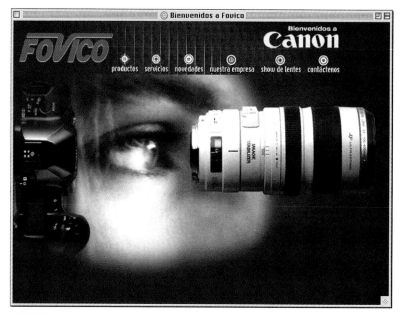

WWW.FOVICO.COM
D: MERCEDES LOUGE, **C:** ALEJANDRO JARANDILLA, **P:** ALEJANDRO JARANDILLA
A: PUBLILAND, **M:** ALEJANDRO@PUBLILAND.COM.AR

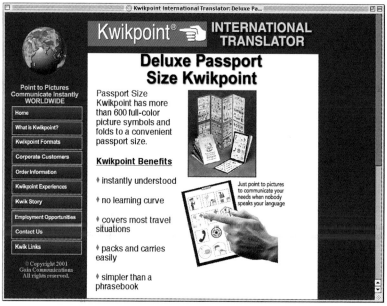

WWW.KWIKPOINT.COM/PASSPORT.HTML
D: ALAN STILLMAN
M: ASTILLMAN@KWIKPOINT.COM

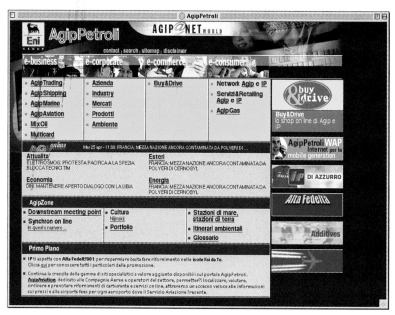

WWW.AGIPPETROLI.IT
D: GUERINO DELFINO
M: DELFINO@HYPHEN.IT

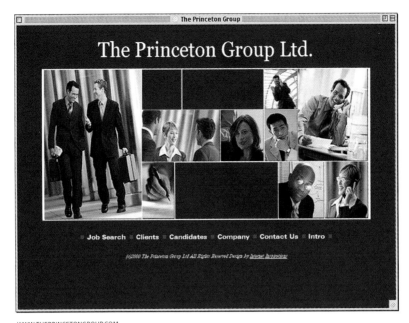

WWW.THEPRINCETONGROUP.COM
D: LUCAS LICZNERSKI, C: LUCAS LICZNERSKI, P: JAMIE JOHNSON
A: INTERNET INSPIRATIONS, M: LUCAS@INTERNETINSPIRATIONS.COM

WWW.ATMAG.DE
D: SÖREN PRÖPPER
A: WWW.81DESIGN.COM, M: SP@81DESIGN.COM

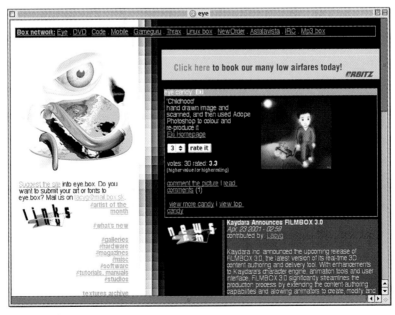

WWW.EYE.BOX.SK
D: LADISLAV CERNICKY
A: BOX NETWORK LTD., M: CERNICKY@NAPRI.SK

WWW.LUCCACO.COM
D: ALLYSSON LUCCA
M: LUCCA@LUCCACO.COM

WWW.MERANER.AT
D: MARKUS HÜBNER, C: LUKAS TUSCH, P: WORLD-DIRECT.COM
A: WORLD-DIRECT.COM, M: OFFICE@WORLD-DIRECT.COM

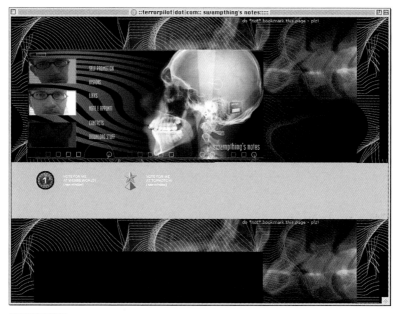

TERRORPILOT.COM
D: MAURO PISTOCCO
M: SWAMPTHING@TERRORPILOT.COM

WWW.SO-NET.NE.JP/CYBERJAPAN
A: CYBERJAPAN, M: CJINFO@RC4.SO-NET.NE.JP

WWW.CLUBSANDWICH.COM
D: BENOIT POULAIN
M: CONTACT@CLUBSANDWICH.COM

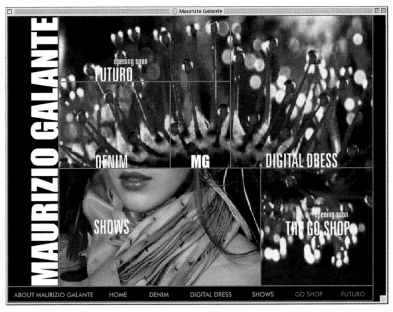

WWW.MAURIZIO-GALANTE.COM
A: SPILL INDUSTRIES, M: CONTACT@SPILL.NET

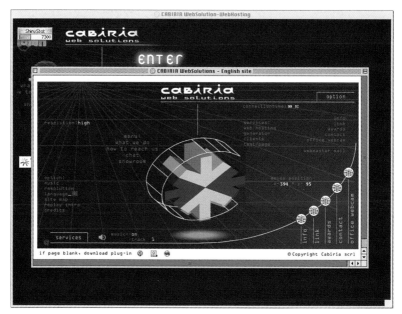

WWW.GENERATOR.LTT.IT
D: ALESSIO SARMELLI, **C:** CABIRIA WEB SOLUTIONS, **P:** CABIRIA WEB SOLUTIONS
A: CABIRIA WEB SOLUTIONS, **M:** ALESSIO@CABIRIA.NET

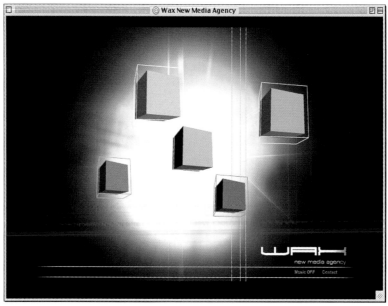

WWW.WAX.CO.UK/NOPENING.HTM
D: WAX
M: JAMES.GHANI@WAX.CO.UK

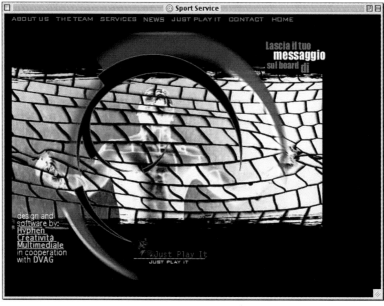

WWW.SPORTSERVICE.IT/HOMEIT.HTML
D: GUERINO DELFINO
M: DELFINO@HYPHEN.IT

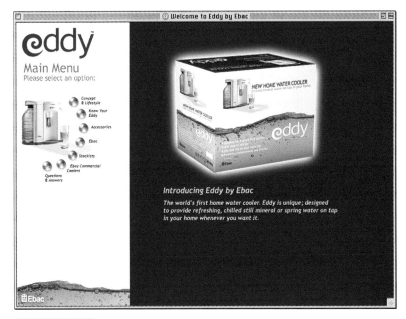

WWW.EDDY-BY-EBAC.COM
D: CHRIS JONES, C: CHRIS JONES
A: DIFFERENT ADVERTISING DESIGN & MARKETING LIMITED, M: CJONES@DIFFERENT-UK.COM

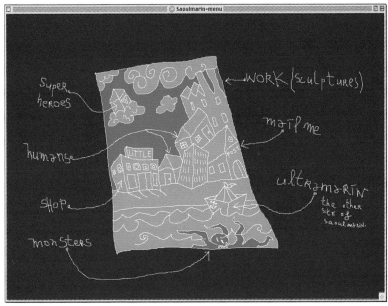

WWW.CHEZ.COM/SAOULMARIN/SOMMAIRE.HTM
D: ÉRIC CROES, C: PIERRE CROES
M: SAOULMARIN@HOTMAIL.COM

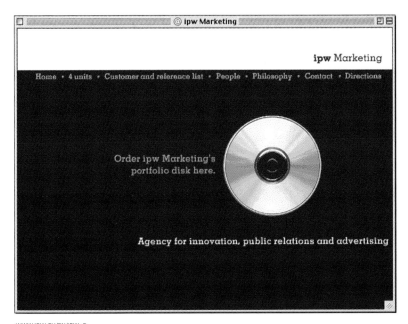

WWW.IPW.CH/EN/IPW4E
A: CUBUSÌMEDIA, M: CUBUS@CUBUSMEDIA.COM

WWW.DEUTSCHEGEGENRECHTEGEWALT.DE
D: P. L. OSTROWSKIJ, **C:** A. OYAN, **P:** P. L. OSTROWSKIJ
A: ART & GRAPHICS, **M:** MAIL@ART-GRAPHICS.COM

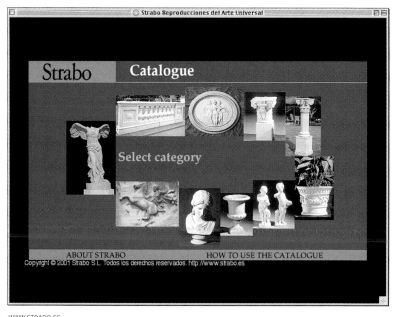

WWW.STRABO.ES
D: RAFAEL GUZMAN
M: RAFA.GUZMAN@NAVEGALIA.COM

WWW.URBAN75.COM
D: MIKE SLOCOMBE
M: MIKE@URBAN75.COM

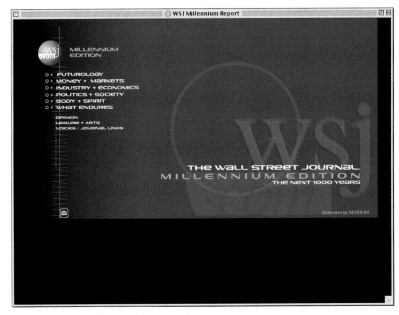

WWW.INTERACTIVE.WSJ.COM/MILLENNIUM/MILLENNIUM.HTML
D: MIRCO PASQUALINI
M: INFO@OOTWORLD.COM

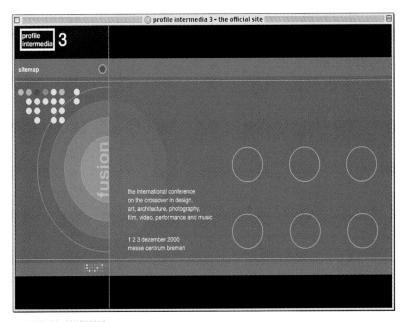

WWW.WORLDS4.COM/PROFILE3
D: UWE HEMMEN, C: UWE HEMMEN, P: UWE HEMMEN
M: HEMMEN@WORLDS4.COM

WWW.MUTE.CO.UK/SALE.HTM
M: INFO@MUTEHQ.CO.UK

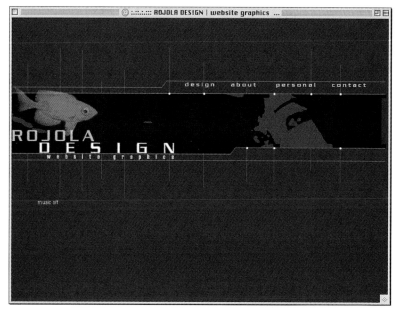

WWW.ROJOLA.NL
A: ROJOLA DESIGN, M: ROJOLA@PLANET.NL

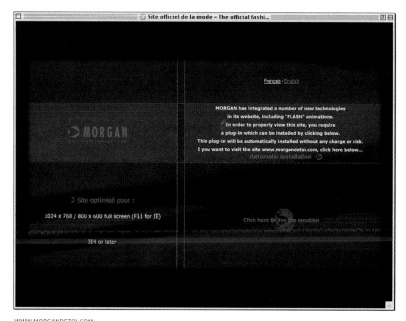

WWW.MORGANDETOI.COM
D: AZERAD GRÉGORY
A: MORGAN S.A., M: GAZERAD@MORGAN.FR

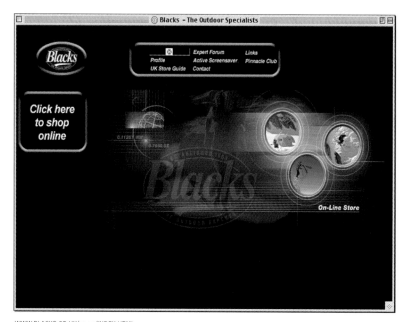

WWW.BLACKS.CO.UK/01_01/INDEX.HTML
A: WAX, M: JAMES.GHANI@WAX.CO.UK›

WWW.N9VE.COM/TOMORROW/INDEX_E.HTML
D: GEORGE SNOW AND CATHERINE DENVIR
A: 3D3 WORLD, M: GEORGE@3D3WORLD.COM

WWW.MIRAMAX-AHARDDAYSNIGHT.COM
D: TOM ROMER, C: TOBY BOUDREAUX, P: KEITH PIZER
A: THE CHOPPING BLOCK, M: DARLEEN@CHOPPINGBLOCK.COM

WWW.FATOE.COM
D: FATOE, C: FATOE
A: FATOE.COM, M: MORDUNA@SONYPICTURES.COM

WWW.SPACEINVADERS.RETROGAMES.COM/HTML/INDEX.HTML
D: DIRK BEHLAU
M: DIRK@PIXELEYE.DE

WWW.CRASHMEDIA.COM
D: CRAIG SWANN
A: CRASH!MEDIA, M: CRAIG@CRASHMEDIA.COM

WWW.FABIOTRENTINI.COM
D: ENRICO CAMPANER
A: FABIO TRENTINI, M: ECAMPANER@HOTMAIL.COM

WWW.LEMONBABIES.DE
D: KATHARINA MATTHIES
M: KATZY@T-ONLINE.DE

WWW.NOFEAR.COM/INDEX2.HTML
A: WAX, M: JAMES.GHANI@WAX.CO.UK

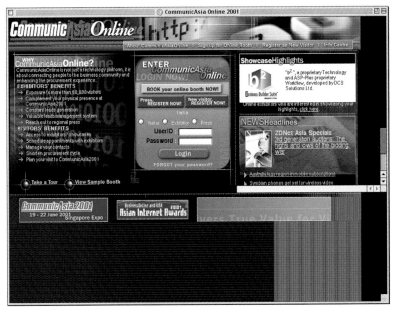

WWW.COMMUNICASIA-ONLINE.COM
D: GOH JULIANA, C: SIE LAYTIN, P: JAMES KHO
M: JOE@DCSSOLUTIONS.NET

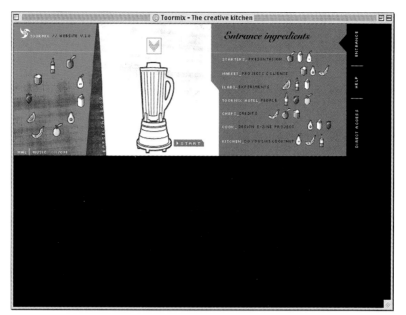

WWW.TOORMIX.COM
D: ORIOL ARMEGOU
A: TOORMIX, **M:** INFO@TOORMIX.COM

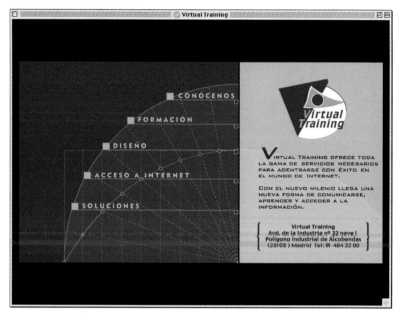

WWW.V-TRAINING.COM/INDEXo.HTM
A: VIRTUAL TRAINING, **M:** BUENROLLO@V-TRAINING.COM

WWW.BUDBELGIUM.COM
D: PETER VAN DEN WYNGAERT
M: PETER@NRG.BE

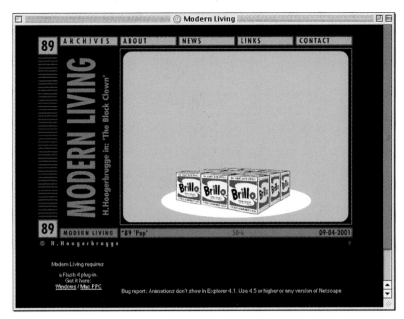

WWW.HOOGERBRUGGE.COM
D: HAN HOOGERBRUGGE
M: HAN@HOOGERBRUGGE.COM

WWW.SEESIDE.DE
A: CUBUS|MEDIA, **M:** CUBUS@CUBUSMEDIA.COM

WWW.ULTRASHOCK.COM
D: PATRICK MIKO, **P:** PETER VAN DEN WYNGAERT
M: INFO@ULTRASHOCK.COM

WWW.HIGH-ON-TECH.COM/WELCOME.HTM
D: BOBBY MELD
A: STOP, LOOK, LISTEN., **M**: I@SONOVAC.COM

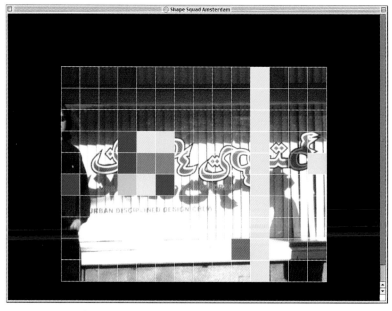

WWW.SHAPESQUAD.COM/START.HTML
A: SHAPE SQUAD, **M**: INFO@SHAPESQUAD.COM

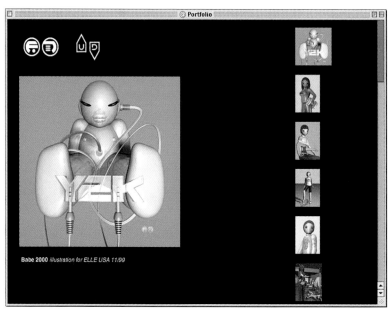

WWW.BAM-B.COM/PAGES/FOLIO.HTML
D: FAIYAZ JAFRI PEACE
M: FAIYAZ@BAM-B.COM

314

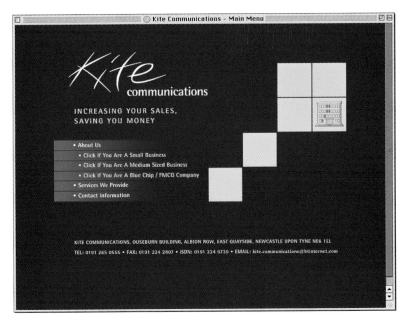

WWW.KITECOMMUNICATIONS.CO.UK
D: CHRIS JONES, C: CHRIS JONES
A: CLOCKWORK DESIGN, M: INFO@CLOCKWORK-DESIGN.CO.UK

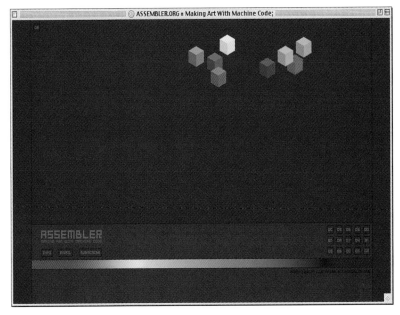

WWW.ASSEMBLER.ORG
D: BRENT GUSTAFSON
M: 2600@ASSEMBLER.ORG

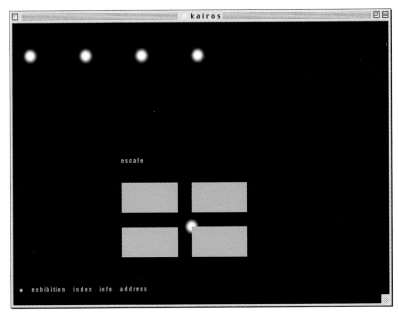

WWW.KAIROS.TO
D: GESINE GROTRIAN, C: VOLKER BERTELMANN, P: KAIROS, NONEX, ESCALE
A: FONS HICKMANN, M: HICKMANN@KAIROS.TO

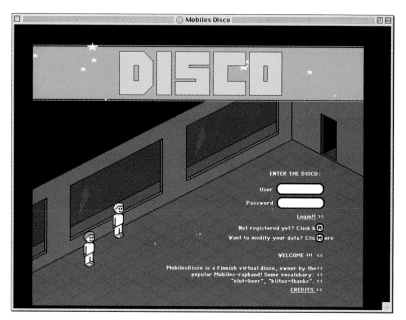

WWW.MOBILESDISCO.COM
D: APPARATUS, C: A. KYRPOV
M: APPARATUS@MOBILESDISCO.COM

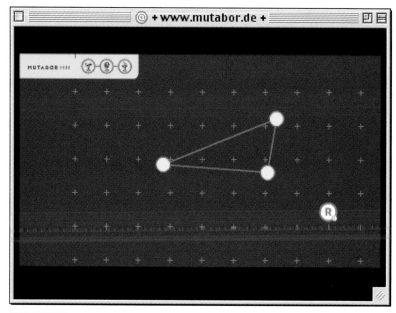

WWW.MUTABOR.DE
D: KLAAS KIELMANN
M: INFO@MUTABOR.DE

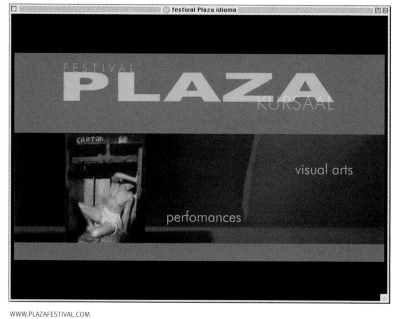

WWW.PLAZAFESTIVAL.COM
D: CONCHA BARRERA
M: CONCHABAR@TELEPOLIS.COM

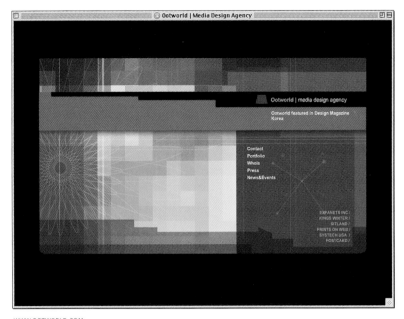

WWW.OOTWORLD.COM
D: MIRCO PASQUALINI
M: INFO@OOTWORLD.COM

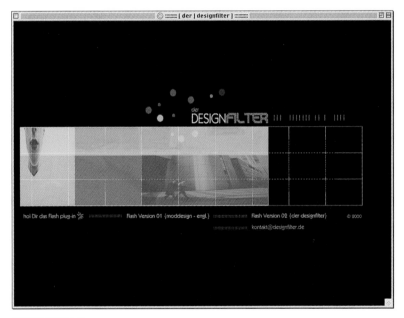

WWW.DESIGNFILTER.DE
D: MIKE JOHN OTTO, C: MIKE JOHN OTTO
A: DESIGNFILTER/MODDESIGN, M: JEKKU@T-ONLINE.DE

WWW.SPEEDYJ.COM/SITE.PHP3
A: BENG, M: HALLO@BENGBENG.NL

WWW.CONSTRUCTIONKID.NL
D: FRANK HAZEBROEK
A: CONSTRUCTIONKID, M: INFO@CONSTRUCTIONKID.NL

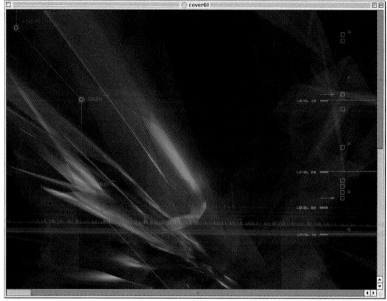

WWW.DCHOTOMY.COM
D: CHUA PATRIC
A: CHOTOMY, M: RIC@DCHOTOMY.COM

WWW.TYPOGRAPHIC.COM
D: JAMES CHEN, C: JAMES CHEN
A: TYPOGRAPHIC, M: MARC_NICHOLS_UK

WWW.WHIZZART.NL
D: ARNOUD VAN DELDEN, C: ARNOUD VAN DELDEN
M: ARNOUD@WHIZZART.NL

WWW.REBAZZAR.COM/IOPORT
D: REBAZZAR, C: REBAZZAR
A: REBAZZAR, INC., M: XEEROIIYA@HOTMAIL.COM

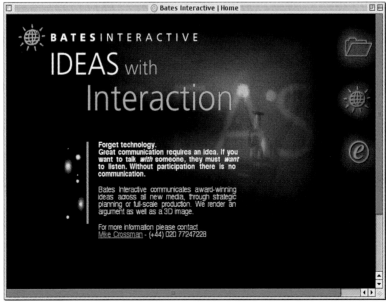

WWW.BATES-INTERACTIVE.CO.UK/MAIN.HTML
D: JOE DEAR
A: BATES INTERACTIVE, M: MCROSSMA@BATESUK.COM

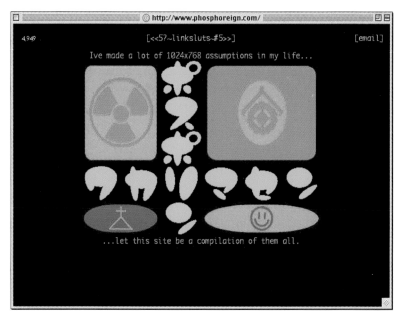

WWW.PHOSPHOREIGN.COM
A: PHOSPHOREIGN, M: PHOSPHOREIGN@HOTMAIL.COM

WWW.QUICKHONEY.COM/VECTOR/VECTOR.HTML
D: PETER STEMMLER
M: P@QUICKHONEY.COM

WWW.BLIW.NET
D: CHRISTEL LARSSON
M: INFO@ABELBAKER.COM

WWW.COUPLAND.COM/COUPLANDINDEX.HTML
D: DAVID JOHN WEIR
M: DJWEIR@ATTCANADA.CA

WWW.FRITZHANSEN.COM/DEFAULT_BIG.ASP
D: GEERT LARSEN
M: GL@FRITZHANSEN.COM

WWW.SCENA.ES.ORG
D: JUANJO LOPEZ ESPINOSA
M: JUANJOLORI@TELELINE.ES

WWW.LEILAMENDEZ.COM
A: VASAVA ARTWORKS, M: VASAVA@VASAVA.ES

WWW.SPEEDYJ.COM
A: BENG, M: HALLO@BENGBENG.NL

WWW.BASICORANGE.NL
D: JEROEN BRUIJN
M: ROBIN@BASICORANGE.NL

WWW.LOWDOWNANDIRTY.COM
D: NESSIM HIGSON, C: JARED LYVERS, P: LOWDOWNANDIRTY
A: LOWDOWNANDIRTY, M: NESSHIGSON@HOTMAIL.COM

WWW.CHAPTER3.NET
D: JENS KARLSSON
A: CHAPTER THREE, CHAPTER3.NET, M: JENS@CHAPTER3.NET

WWW.CUBADUST.GEARWORX.COM/CUBADUST.HTM
D: JONAS STRANDBERG-RINGH
M: CONTACT@CUBADUST.COM

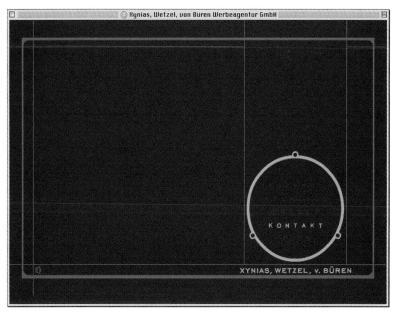

WWW.XWVB.DE
A: COMA2 - COLLECTIVE OF MEDIA ARTISTS, M: COLLIN@COMA2.COM

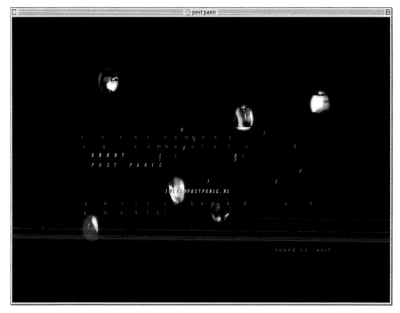

WWW.POSTPANIC.NL
D: JULES, C: JULES
A: POSTPANIC, M: JULES@POSTPANIC.NL

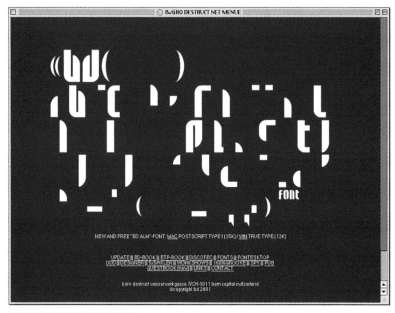

WWW.BERMUDA.CH/BD/HOME/INDEX.HTML
D: HEIWID
A: BURO DESTRUCT, M: BD@BERMUDA.CH

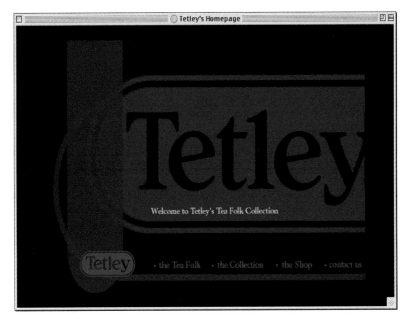

WWW.TEAFOLK.COM/INDEX_JS.HTML
A: WAX, M: JAMES.GHANI@WAX.CO.UK

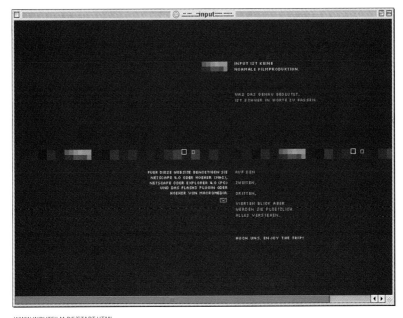

WWW.INPUTFILM.DE/START.HTML
A: INPUTFILM, M: NFO@INPUTFILM.DE

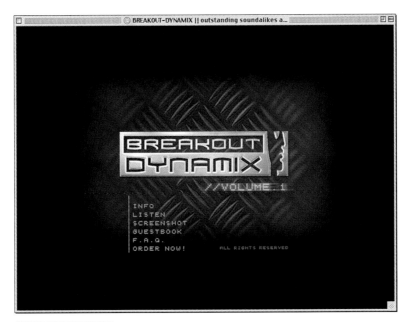

WWW.BREAKOUT-DYNAMIX.COM
D: PETER VAN DEN WYNGAERT
M: PETER@NRG.BE

WWW.LASTMINIT.HU/B-MONEY
D: LEHOCZKI ZOLTÁN
M: ZOLI@YOOHEY.HU

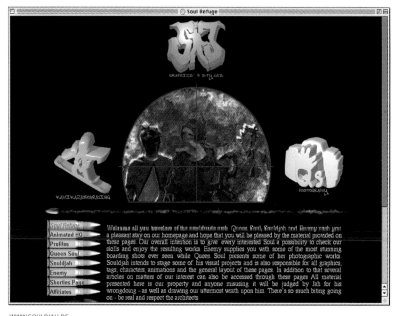

WWW.SOULDJAH.DE
D: SOULDJAH AKA SIMON DELL
M: SIMON.DELL@FREENET.DE

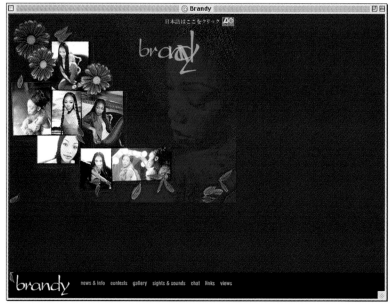

WWW.FOREVERBRANDY.COM
A: KIOKEN, INC., M: SKANG@KIOKEN.COM

WWW.ABNORMALBEHAVIORCHILD.COM/NUOVO/DEFAULT.HTML
D: NICOLA STUMPO
M: NIKO@QUAM.IT

WWW.HASSELBLAD.COM/PRODUCTS/INDEX.HTML
D: PATRIK MARK
M: PATRIK.MARK@HASSELBLAD.SE

WWW.GARDYDESIGN.RU/IDRAGON
C: ICE DRAGON, **P:** ICE DRAGON
M: IDRAGON@GARDYDESIGN.RU

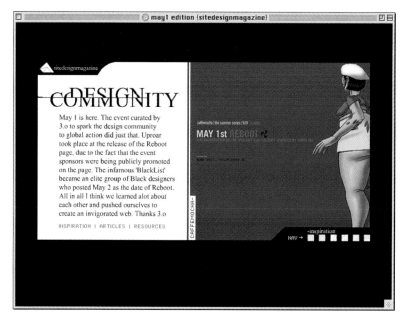

WWW.SITEDESIGNMAGAZINE.COM
D: PEDRO SOSTRE, C: PEDRO SOSTRE
A: PEDRO SOSTRE GRAPHIC DESIGN, M: WEBMASTER@SITEDESIGNMAGAZINE.COM

WWW.HYPNO.IT
D: MIRKO CACCARO, P: SEVEN S.R.L.
M: SONIA.MARTINI@SEVEN.IT

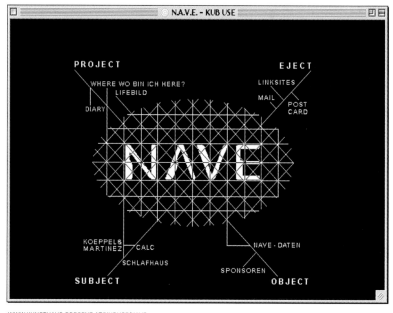

WWW.KUNSTHAUS-BREGENZ.AT/KUBUSE/NAVE
D: CALC, C: CALC, P: KUNSTHAUS BREGENZ
A: CALC, M: OMI@LAS.ES

WWW.SATIRA-ARTEFACT.PT/MINIMALANIMAL
D: PEDRO SOTTOMAYOR
A: ©2000 SÁTIRA, LDA, **M**: PEDROSOTTOMAYOR@DESIGN.CO.PT

WWW.JBSCOTCH.COM
A: BLACK ID, **M**: BLACK@BLACKID.COM

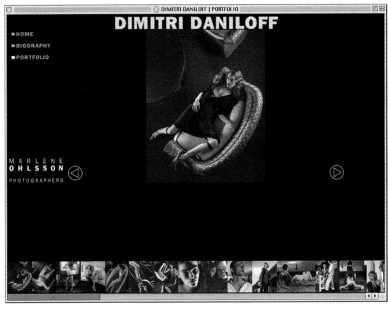

WWW.OHLSSON.DE
D: PETER WIESE, **C**: PETER WIESE
M: M@OHLSSON.DE

WWW.KOPF-ART.DE
D: WOLFGANG KOPF, C: MARC BRODT
M: INFO@KOPF-ART.DE

WWW.ENROUTE2.NET
D: KEN CHAN, C: DALE PILLARS, P: CLARENCE CHIEW
A: TEABAG, M: SKIN@PACIFIC.NET.SG

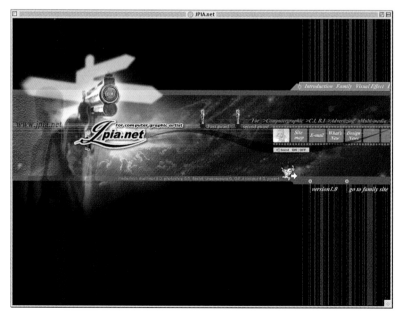

WWW.JPIA.NET
D: HOON JUNG
A: JPIA, M: 12PUPIL@HANMAIL.NET

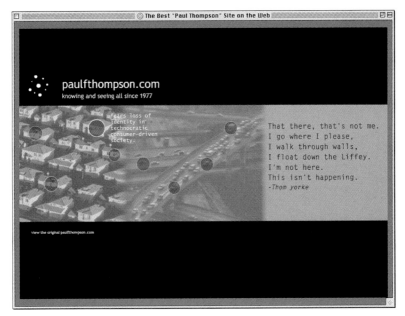

WWW.PAULFTHOMPSON.COM
D: PAUL THOMPSON, C: PAUL THOMPSON
M: RPUPKIN77@HOTMAIL.COM

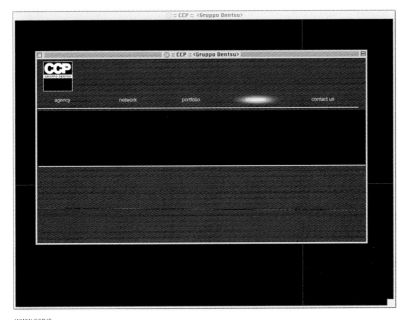

WWW.CCP.IT
C: JAY JAM, P: AIRY.IT
A: LEVEL11.NET, M: INFO@JAMFIVE.COM

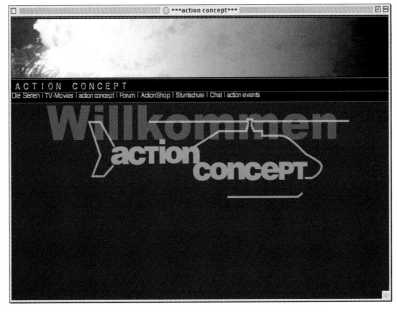

WWW.ACTIONCONCEPT.COM
D: MAIK ERNST, C: MAIK ERNST
A: ACTIONCONCEPT, M: MAIK.ERNST@ACTIONCONCEPT.COM

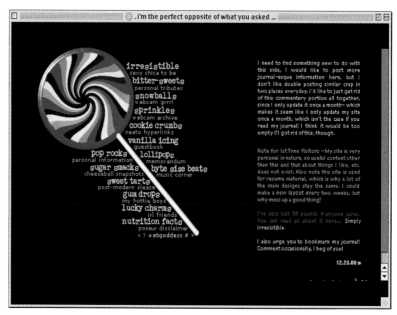

WWW.SUBURBANCHAOS.COM/MAIN.HTML
D: DAWN M. CROSS
M: DAWN@SUBURBANCHAOS.COM

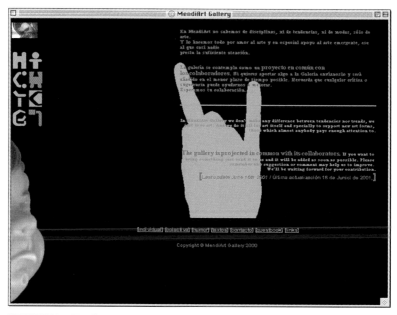

WWW.USUARIOS.TRIPOD.ES/MENDIART
D: DIEGO MENDIGUREN, C: DIEGO MENDIGUREN
M: MENDIART@HOTMAIL.COM

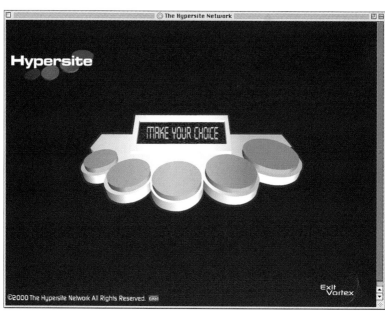

WWW.HYPERSITE.NET
P: HYPERSITE
A: HYPERSITE, M: SHANE@HYPERSITE.NET

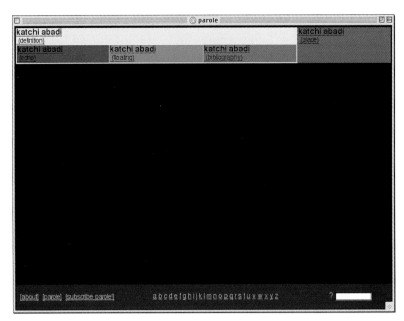

WWW.KING.DOM.DE
M: UNO@APOREE.ORG

WWW.LIGABUE.COM
D: MIRCO PASQUALINI
M: INFO@OOTWORLD.COM

WWW.DDWINC.COM
D: COLLEEN MILLER, C: COLLEEN MILLER
A: DIGITAL DESIGN WORKS, INC, M: TODD@DDWINC.COM

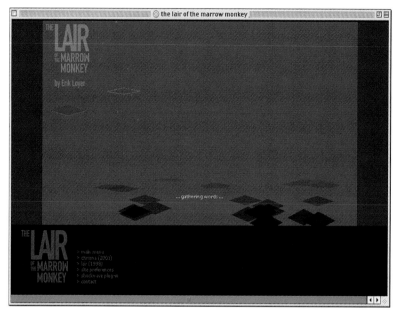

WWW.MARROWMONKEY.COM
D: ERIK LOYER
M: ERIK@MARROWMONKEY.COM

WWW.ANIMAL2000.ORG
D: BRIGITTA ERDÖDY
A: POWART-MULTIMEDIA , M: ERDOEDY@POWART.DE

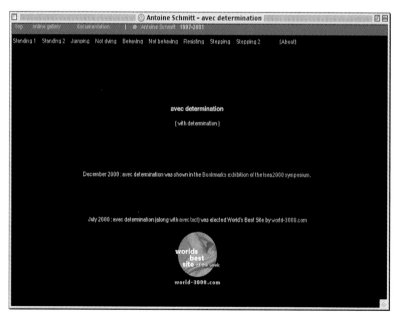

WWW.GRATIN.ORG/AS/AVECDETERMINATION
D: ANTOINE SCHMITT
M: AS@GRATIN.ORG

334

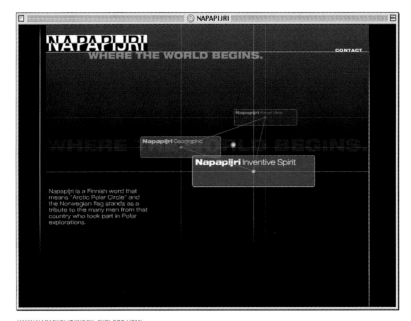

WWW.NAPAPIJRI.IT/INDEX_EXPLORE.HTML
D: GUERINO DELFINO
M: DELFINO@HYPHEN.IT

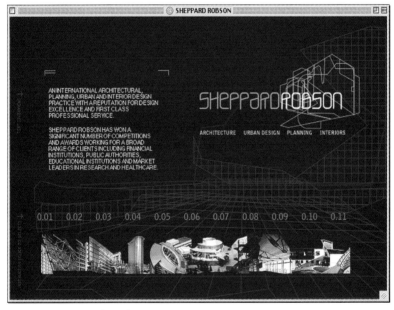

WWW.SHEPPARDROBSON.COM/ooMAIN/MAINMENU.HTML
A: ATTIK.COM, M: TRACEYT@ATTIK.COM

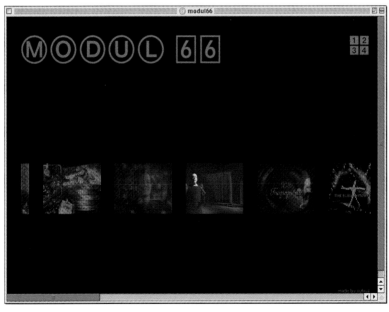

WWW.MODUL66.COM/MAIN.HTML
A: CUBUSIMEDIA, M: CUBUS@CUBUSMEDIA.COM

WWW.PROJEKTPETERSBERG.DE
D: PETRA GEBHARD
A: GEBHARDDESIGN, **M:** K1@T-ONLINE.DE

WWW.ART.CH/LINKS.HTML
D: MUELLER & HESS, **C:** BEATMAP.COM GMBH
M: LAURENCE@BEATMAP.COM

WWW.ATTIK.COM/PAGES/WORK01.HTML
A: ATTIK.COM, **M:** TRACEYT@ATTIK.COM

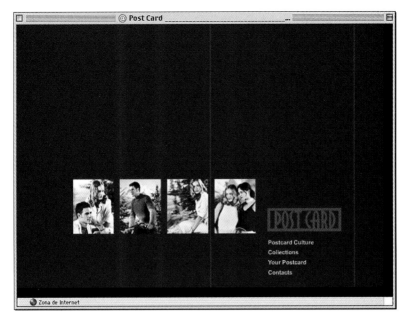

WWW.POSTCARD.IT/POPUP.HTM
D: MELISSA SALVARANI
M: INFO@OOTWORLD.COM

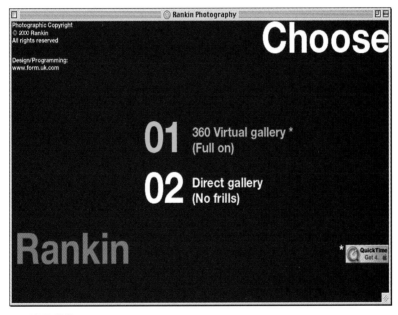

WWW.RANKIN.CO.UK
D: PAUL WEST
A: FORM®, M: FORM@DIRCON.CO.UK

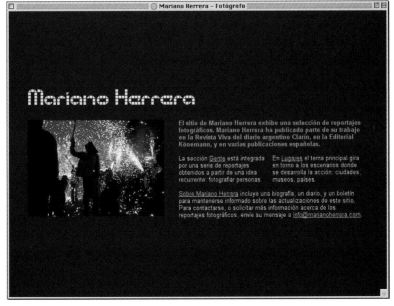

WWW.MARIANOHERRERA.COM
D: PEPINO
M: INFO@MARIANOHERRERA.COM

WWW.TCREC.COM
D: ALESSANDRO AMODIO, **C:** MANUEL INFANTI, **P:** ALESSANDRO AMODIO
M: AAMODIO@ALCHIMEDIA.COM

WWW.MARISCAL.COM/MARISCALWEB/FRAMEFLASH.HTM
D: JAVIER MARISCAL, **C:** SERGIO PORTER, **P:** ALBERT GARCIA VILA
A: ESTUDIO MARISCAL, **M:** ESTUDIO@MARISCAL.COM

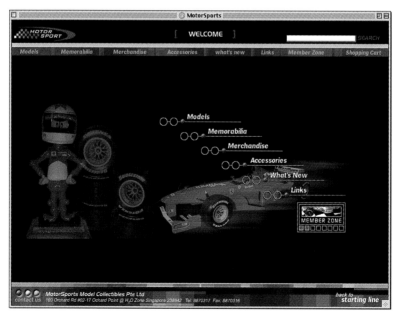

WWW.F1.COM.SG
D: KALINDA LOW, **C:** FOO YANLING, **P:** JOE CHUA
M: JOE@DCSSOLUTIONS.NET

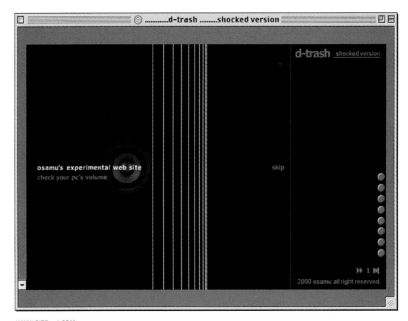

WWW.SITE036.COM
D: OSAMU TAKIKAWA
M: INFO@SITE036.COM

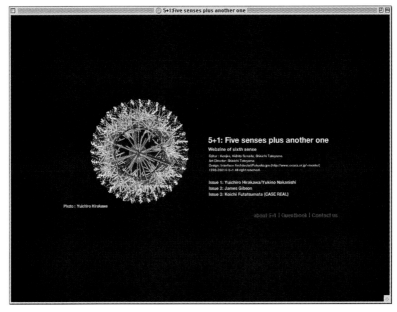

WWW.SOURCES.NE.JP/5+1
D: SHINICHI TATEYAMA
A: 5+1:FIVE SENSES PLUS ANOTHER ONE, M: 5PLUS1@SOURCES.NE.JP

WWW.RSRWEB.COM
D: SEAN GONSMAN, C: SEAN GONSMAN, P: SEAN GONSMAN
A: REALSOUND REMEDIES, M: SEAN@RSRWEB.COM

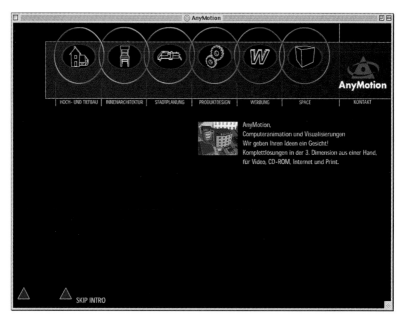

WWW.ANYMOTION.NET
D: UWE HEMMEN, C: UWE HEMMEN, P: UWE HEMMEN
M: HEMMEN@WORLDS4.COM

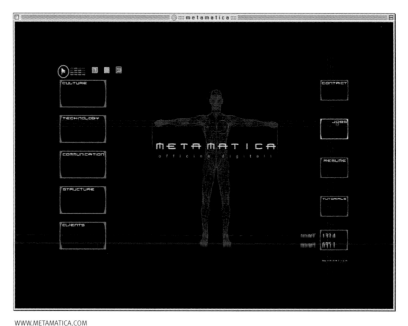

WWW.METAMATICA.COM
D: YONAH/INTERZONE
M: GALLUZZI@METAMATICA.COM

WWW.CREMATION.CH
D: FABIAN BIELER
M: INFO@CREMATION.CH

WWW.MOONLIGHT.PT
A: MOONLIGHT, M: INFO@MOONLIGHT.PT

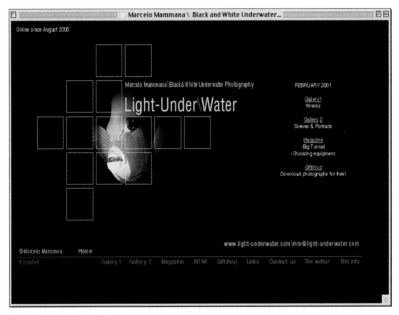

WWW.LIGHT-UNDERWATER.COM
D: MARCELO MAMMANA, C: MARCELO MAMMANA
A: MARCELO MAMMANA, M: MM@LIGHT-UNDERWATER.COM

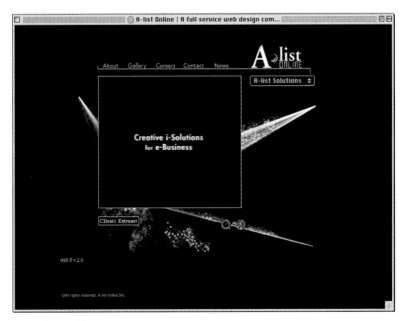

WWW.A-LISTONLINE.COM
A: A-LIST ONLINE, M: INFO@A-LISTONLINE.COM

WWW.MUSHI-MUSHI.ORG
C: LIGIA SANTOS, P: LIGIA SANTOS

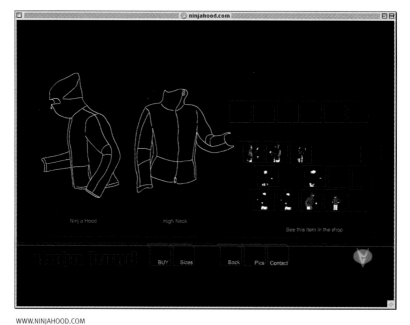

WWW.NINJAHOOD.COM
D: BRUNO MARTELLI
M: OFFICE@VEXED.CO.UK

WWW.FORM.UK.COM
D: PAUL WEST
A: FORM®, M: FORM@DIRCON.CO.UK

WWW.ANTSONLINE.ORG
D: ALEX Y.C. CHANG, C: ALEX Y.C. CHANG
M: ANTS_ONLINE@HOTMAIL.COM

WWW.ASYL.CO.JP
D: YOKO WASHIMINE
A: ASYL DESIGN, M: YOKO@ASYL.CO.JP

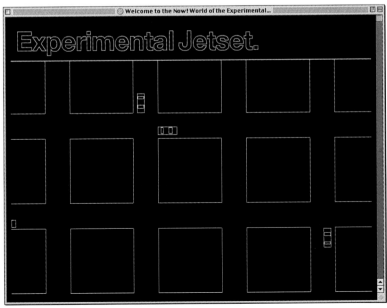

WWW.EXPERIMENTALJETSET.NL
A: EXPERIMENTALJETSET, M: EXPERIMENTAL@JETSET.NL

WWW.BAMBOO-PRODUCTIONS.COM
C: PACO LA LUCA
M: OFFICE.BCN@BAMBOO-PRODUCTIONS.COM

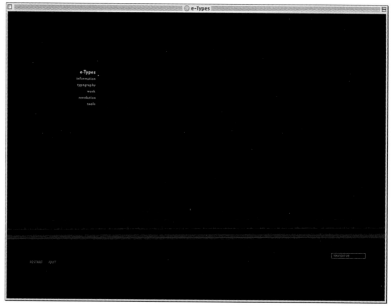

WWW.E-TYPES.COM
D: JONAS HECKSHER, C: JANNICK KNUDSEN
A: E-TYPES, M: INFO@E-TYPES.COM

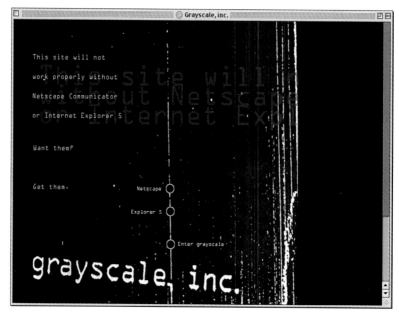

WWW.GRAYSCALE.NET
D: ERIK
M: TOKE@K10K.NET